Wolfer

A Memoir

Carter Niemeyer

Published by BottleFly Press

Published by BottleFly Press
Boise, Idaho

For inquiries, write to bottleflypress@gmail.com

Wolfer's website is www.carterniemeyer.com

Wolfer

Edited by Jenny Niemeyer
Contributing editor, Dee Lane
Cover design and interior layout by Beth Fischer
Cover photo by Joel Sartore/joelsartore.com
Maps by Jenny Niemeyer
Interior photos copyright © Carter Niemeyer,
except page 292 copyright © Isaac Babcock

This is a memoir. All of the events actually happened. Some names
and identifying details have been changed to protect the privacy
of individuals. Nothing is intended or should be interpreted
as expressing or representing the views of the United States
Government or other government departments or agencies.

Printed in the United States of America
Library of Congress Control Number (First Edition) 2010914921
ISBN-13 978-0-984-8113-0-4
ISBN-10 0984811303

Second paperback edition

10 9 8 7 6 5 4 3 2

For Jenny,
my guardian angel.

AUTHOR'S NOTE

I began keeping professional diaries in 1973. At first they were just the carbon-copied, federal forms that I was required to create and submit to my supervisors every week, but they eventually turned into daily narratives in bound books. I probably didn't need them; I remember almost everything. But in the wolf business they helped a lot. I was often the only person with a detailed, written account of exactly how things went down.

The only regret I have in putting together a narrative about my professional career is how much I've had to leave out. But I've gotten to know a few things about the editorial process and my editors assure me that I may well have a couple more books in me yet.

I first realized I had a story to tell at a class reunion in Iowa — Garner-Hayfield Class of 1965 — when, once the official party ended, a group of us decided to usher in the sunrise at a classmate's farm north of town. We eventually ended up in the farmhouse kitchen, where several friends went to work cooking up breakfast.

"Hey Slats," my friend Al Hawe said above all the voices. He always called me that – the same nickname my dad had. "Tell us about the wolves or whatever you're chasing these days."

So I did. The guys were intrigued. I thought the women were busy with their own conversations in the living room, but then Althea Shubert, the girl I used to rollerskate with in grade school, piped up.

"That's just a story. It isn't really true, is it?" she asked.

I didn't think my stories were that outlandish. But when I thought about it, I supposed my daily life was a little out of the ordinary. I explained my job – my career – and how it got that way. As I sat in that kitchen with the sun just starting to come through the curtains, and everyone still willing to listen to my tales, I realized that my life as a government predator trapper was really pretty unique.

"Well," I said after regaling them at length, "maybe I'll just put it all in a book someday."

They just laughed, then passed around the scrambled eggs.

INTRODUCTION

Sometimes people ask me which of my novels I most enjoyed writing. The answer is, of course, none of them. Writing is mostly just a hard slog up a mountain plus a lot of anguished staring at that little cursor blinking at the top of a blank page. However, if I ever get asked which was the novel I most enjoyed researching, there's no contest. It was *The Loop*, the story about wolves returning to a place where once they were hunted to extinction.

I had the idea for the book when I was researching *The Horse Whisperer*. I was in Missoula and had gone to meet a woman about a horse (as one does). Her husband was a professor at the University of Montana and specialized in wolves. His name was Bob Ream and over dinner wolves were all we talked about. It was the early nineties and there was a war going on between ranchers and environmentalists about a proposal to reintroduce wolves into Yellowstone National Park and Idaho. It was, I thought, the perfect background for a novel. When I contacted him again a couple of years later, Bob gave me a list of names, people in the wolf world who might help me with my research. Top of the list was a man called Carter Niemeyer.

He was working, at the time, for Animal Damage Control, part of the U.S. Department of Agriculture. This meant, as a wolf biologist and mutual friend explained at the time, that if a rancher had a problem with a *critter* – be it coyote, bear or bobcat – Carter would come in and dispose of it. I guess my misgivings must have shown, for he added: "Don't worry, he's not such a bad guy."

So I called Carter and introduced myself and he told me how to find his house in East Helena. He didn't really need to. I could have just opened the car window and followed my nose. When he opened the door two things struck me. First, he was a pretty imposing figure: about ten foot tall, it seemed, with a bone-crushing handshake. Even more intimidating was... well, the smell. Not him personally, I'm happy to say, but the waft that came out of that house was little short of evil. Nobody had mentioned that as well as being an ace trapper and marksman, Carter was also a keen and clever taxidermist. The foul smell came partly from a coyote skull that he was boiling on the kitchen stove and partly from a new brew of trap bait that he had been concocting, the key ingredient of which was a bobcat's anal gland. I can still turn green when I think about it.

Anyway, once I'd gotten over the smell, we got talking. I was interested in how he laid his traps and he took me out back and showed me. I took a lot of photographs and made a lot of notes. Carter was friendly and courteous. Funny too, in a dry kind of way. And as I got to know him in the months that followed, I realized that despite his job, despite all the *critters* he'd killed, he knew about and loved wild animals – especially wolves – with a quiet but genuine passion. The apparent contradiction in what he did for a living and where his heart truly lay fascinated me.

Nearly all the characters in my novels are purely fictional, but I have to admit that Bill Rimmer, the federal trapper in *The Loop*, is pretty shamelessly based on Carter Niemeyer. Tall, clever, funny, good-looking – I didn't think he'd mind too much.

That said, when I heard he was going to write a book about his life, I had some misgivings. People who have so many other talents (how many of us, after all, can dart a running wolf from a moving helicopter or carry out an autopsy on a shriveled steer carcass?), sometimes aren't so good at getting it all down on paper. How wrong I was. *Wolfer* turns out to be a fabulous book, written by a naturally gifted writer. Damn it, is there anything this man can't do? It's stuffed with funny and intriguing stories and at the same time throws new light on the politics of the pro- and anti- wolf lobbies. Carter stands between these warring groups, the furious ranchers and outraged environmentalists, mediating, doing what he has to do, often with a heavy heart. The decisions he has to make, the political pressures he has to withstand, the lives he has to take, all combine to make this book powerful, moving and full of insight. Carter Niemeyer is a big man in every sense. The wolf is lucky to have had such a strong and subtle supporter.

-Nicholas Evans, November 2010

"You can't just let nature run wild."

- Walter Hickel
  former Governor of Alaska
  and Secretary of the Interior

Wolfer / *WUL-fur*/*n.*
1. A hunter of wolves.
Merriam-Webster Dictionary

The chopper was already running when I got there. My pilot, Jack Fulton, gave me a long look as I handed him the shotgun and belted myself in. Soon we lifted into the cold, gray sky, making for the ridge along the East Fork of Idaho's Salmon River where the wolves had last been seen.

I had about 15 minutes to think.

It hardly seemed possible that seven years had passed since I'd helped reintroduce the first wolves into the Northern Rockies as part of a federal program to restore them to their ancient habitat in the mountain West. In total, 31 wolves went into Yellowstone National Park. Another 35 scampered out of metal cages and into the Frank Church-River of No Return Wilderness of central Idaho, a rugged and remote area some 60 miles from Dick and Betty Baker's ranch.

As our helicopter hummed its way over patches of April snow, I thought about the odd satisfaction I'd felt as wolves again put their paw prints on land that had been theirs long before it was ours. The irony of my role in it was something a lot of people enjoyed pointing out.

I'd spent most of my youth and adult life in an unusual profession – killing or trapping predators that preyed on livestock. I'd been employed for more than 26 years as a federal trapper for the U.S. Department of Agriculture. I was what you might call a hired gun of the livestock industry. I'd done it long enough to know where all the bodies were buried, you might say, and a lot of the predators I killed on behalf of ranchers were on public lands.

Public lands, especially those in the West, are just about all that's left for big carnivores like wolves, grizzlies and mountain lions. They are the only places that are wild enough and big enough – and in Idaho, steep enough – to keep people at bay. They are, for all practical purposes, tiny islands of habitat in an ocean of people.

A patchwork of federal government agencies manages – and sometimes mismanages – these lands and the wildlife living on them. The fate of such places lies in the hands of politicians and the government, usually the ones who wield the biggest club at the moment.

My relationship with the wildlife on these lands had been a bag of mixed signals from the beginning. I had worked for an agency whose mission was to make sure that ranchers weren't bothered by wild animals. To that end, some of my bosses and contemporaries would have been happy to see every predator in the West slung dead over a barbed-wire fence. So bringing back wolves wasn't just foolhardy, my agency said, it was un-American. Anything that went against sheep and cows and ranching was the moral equivalent to stomping on Old Glory.

It seemed to me, though, that returning wolves to even a slice of their historic range put something important back into an American West that had lost too much of what made it special. All of us owned the places where they were released, so why not? To see the West reversing, going back the other way, was a privilege, and I'd loved my role in it. It had changed me in ways I never could have anticipated. In a way, the wolves changed me far more than I changed them. It was a feeling that I hoped others would come to understand, in time, and maybe even share.

When the Clinton administration decided in the mid-1990s that the time was right to bring the wolves back, it was, to be honest, a job I could scarcely imagine myself doing. I'd spent my whole career killing predators or moving them when they got into trouble, and I'd known for sure, going in, that wolves were going to be controversial. They might not have been the biggest, meanest predator, or the final straw that put certain ranchers out of business, but I discovered up close that getting them back on the land was going to be an epic battle. Wolves are not all the things people want them to be, good or bad, but they've carried with them forever the most baggage. They are, without a doubt, one of the most feared, most persecuted animals in human history. Yet they also are among the most worshiped. Adding to imaginary problems that wolves cause people, there were the real issues: Reintroducing wolves meant that they would compete with hunters for elk and deer, and undeniably, with ranchers for dibs on their sheep and cattle.

The way we handled this was to try to keep track of the wolves and minimize the conflicts. The original wolves from Canada all were radio-collared before they were released. In Yellowstone, they were welcomed. In Idaho, not so much. They had multiplied and split off into other families and packs, and after a few years, we knew there was a group of them prowling the East Fork of the Salmon River drainage.

They were called the Whitehawk wolves, after a mountain range nearby, and were led by a big alpha female dubbed Alabaster because of her white fur. Her mate, the alpha male, was known only as B-47. The pair ruled a pack of 10, ranging in age down to yearlings.

At first, they did wolf things, preying on deer and elk. Then one day I got a call from Betty Baker saying wolves had started killing the family's cattle.

Most ranchers I know are decent folks who know and understand animals more than most people. They're not usually rabid anti-wolfers, generally getting as much of a thrill from a wolf's presence as any tourist. They just don't want wolves eating their livestock. So when Betty called, I knew it was serious.

"Let me see what I can do," I'd told her. I was in charge of this pack, and of the rest of the wolves in Idaho, having been recently deemed the only person suitable for this peculiar job with the U.S. Fish and Wildlife Service.

The Whitehawks had been in trouble since they first formed five years earlier – killing a sheep here, a calf there. But their habit had escalated. I don't know how many hours we burned on it or how many thousands of dollars we spent trying to drive the Whitehawks away from livestock. Nothing worked. I'd run out of ideas and I was faced with a decision, one I really didn't want to make: The wolves had to die.

Rick Williamson, the trapper I relied on most, already had killed five of the 10 a month earlier. His phone, like mine, was ringing three dozen times a day with people wanting to know what was happening with the Whitehawks. He didn't want to have to be the guy to finish them off.

"Bring your shotgun," he said over the phone.

Williamson had tried a few things himself. Leaning out the door of a helicopter, he had peppered the wolves with crackershells – fireworks, essentially – but they were back killing cattle the next day. Another time, he saw the pack retreating from the Baker's pasture, following each other single-file up a rock ridge. He pulled out his rifle and fired into the rocks all around them. The wolves stopped and looked at him. Just stood there. They weren't afraid at all.

It was spring. Alabaster would soon be giving birth and there would be another half-dozen or so mouths to feed. I had to do something now or Alabaster and the alpha-male would teach livestock killing to the young, and the cycle would go on. If I put it off any longer, I'd be killing a den full of puppies, with my bare hands or indirectly by starvation if their parents were dead. I didn't want that distinction. We could send them to a zoo, if we could find a taker, but what kind of sentence is that for a wild animal? I thought about the hundreds of people who had adopted Alabaster as their personal symbol of wilderness, of the way things should be. She was so unusual. Wolves seldom get old enough to turn white. People from as far away as Germany wrote to me about how Alabaster and her pack had given them hope that wild things could still exist.

As we flew, I kept my government-issue shotgun wedged between my knees. The doors were off the helicopter, the way they always were when I'd be leaning out to shoot. The ground rushed by underneath and the cold wind pelted me. I kept thinking hard: Was there any other way?

Rick Williamson's voice crackled in my headset. He and pilot Bob Danner were flying above us in Danner's fixed wing airplane and had spotted the Whitehawks. Alabaster, looking like a patch of snow, was on the move.

IOWA

My dad wasn't a trapper, but he knew enough to show me how to catch a pocket gopher. Every farmer in Iowa knew how to do that in 1956. He just didn't know it would change me forever.

He opened the door on our century old barn. It was dark inside and smelled of hay and horse manure. From a collection of junk hanging on the wall, he yanked loose a couple of small traps.

"Come on," he said, grabbing a spade. We crossed the railroad tracks and walked onto our 20 acres. I was nine years old.

"You go like this," Dad said, squatting and poking around the place where the gopher had pushed up the black Iowa dirt. He was looking for its tunnel. When he found it, he dug a hole through the little mound, revealing a small, mysterious tunnel. He put the trap there, turning it this way and that to get it just right. Then he staked it to the ground by its chain and covered the whole works with a piece of cardboard surrounded by dirt to keep it dark.

I kneeled in the damp earth, watching him and listening to his words so I would remember. I liked that I remembered everything my dad said. I was proud that he never had to tell me too many things twice.

"There," he said, brushing his tanned hands on his trousers. "Now first thing in the morning, we'll come look under that cardboard, okay?"

I nodded. It seemed simple enough, but I wondered if I could do it by myself. It seemed important to follow the steps just right.

The next day, sure enough, there was a gopher in the trap.

"Did you know that each of their front feet are worth a nickel at the courthouse?" Dad informed me as he knocked the gopher in the head. As he talked, he cut off the gopher's front feet and tossed them into the Folgers can, then buried the gopher in its own burrow.

He smiled and put his hand on my head.

"Why don't you see if you can get some?"

I practiced setting gopher traps, and then practiced some more. Once I was confident that I was doing it right, I looked for the telltale sign of gophers: freshly mounded dirt. It didn't take long – maybe a day or two – and I was hooked. I was so eager to look under that piece of cardboard that I couldn't sleep at night. Nothing seemed as exciting as catching gophers. No matter how much running around and playing I did that day, I couldn't sleep as long as I had traps set. I kept my clothes and shoes on the end of my bed so that I could feel for them in the dim light before sunrise. Then I'd grab my flashlight and rush down the narrow stairs and out the screen door, running to our field.

I grew up on the east edge of Garner, Iowa. It was, and still is, a small farm town with picket fences but no traffic lights, a place where everything was closed on Sundays. I thought of Garner as boundless and thrilling, with more possibilities for adventure than I could ever cram into one lifetime.

Garner wasn't, and still isn't, a place you'd ever hear about or even notice on a map unless you were lost. It sits at the upper end of tornado alley, but unlike neighboring towns, hasn't yet been flattened by one of those terrifying storms. Garner isn't famous for anything except a couple of brothers named Duesenberg who ran a bicycle shop, then invented a fancy car. By the time I came along in 1947, the town still hadn't changed a whole lot from when my dad was a kid and helped his father plow gardens with a mule team. In the years after I left, big agriculture companies came to town with their checkbooks and lured most small farmers out of business. Small was a thing of the past, they proclaimed, forcing the farmers who remained to plow every inch of land in pursuit of bigger yields of corn and soybeans, just so they could pay their bills. With that, Garner was sucked into the modern world, and with it, the fallow fields and tree groves and marshes that had supported so much wildlife.

A few years ago, a friend in Garner sent me a photo of my childhood home being burned for practice by the fire department. The place had fallen apart after my mother died, and the photo showed the merry faces of firefighters torching a ramshackle house – mine. I tore it up. After the house was gone, what was left of my mother's ferns and lilacs and honeysuckle was flattened with pavement and topped with a metal storage unit. No one would ever suspect that so much happened on that piece of land. I don't go back to Garner often, but when I do, I feel knotted up, like I just sat through a friend's funeral.

Our house was 100 years old by the time I was born. It sat on a double lot across from the Rock Island railroad tracks. In the summer, the wind blew the stink of the stockyards in our kitchen window. I could sometimes hear hogs screaming as they were being loaded into trucks. Every day on our gravel road, tractors and pickups came and went from the grain elevators three blocks away.

I called my grandmother Grams. She lived across the street. Though she died when I was only 10, I remember her coming over every day in her apron, her hair up in a bun, taking me by the hand to help her feed her chickens and gather eggs. She had a player piano in her parlor that I could look at but not touch, and a Christmas cactus inside her back door that was so big that I had to pin myself flat against the wall and slide along to get past it. Grams pumped water from a cistern, burned corncobs in a wood stove in her kitchen, and canned every bit of fruit her property produced.

I must have learned to work the latch on the screen door even as a toddler because I remember often going outside unattended. As a youngster, as long as I came home when my mother blew her whistle – or worse, screamed Car-ter in two drawn-out, embarrassing syllables, I was free to do as I pleased. I didn't have a curfew or a bunch of things I wasn't allowed to do. I had guns and sharp knives. I didn't wash my hands, didn't eat my vegetables (except corn), and my clothes didn't fit because I was too tall. My parents didn't spend a lot of time worrying about any of this. They had two expectations of me: that I go to church with them every Sunday and that I be good the rest of the week. This arrangement seemed to work, but later I realized that maybe they were just tired. They both were 35 when I was born – old to be having kids in those days – and my brother was seven years older than me, so when I really think about it, I was probably an accident. But I never missed a day of Sunday school and my grades were okay. In exchange, I had no discernable boundaries except for the one activated by the look on my dad's face when I overstepped myself.

Faced with being inside or out, I chose the outdoors. I could tell, even before I could talk, that it was the best place. I wasn't much more than 2 when I ventured to our 20 acres on my own, following our dogs while they hunted rabbits and sniffed around in the corn stubble. I waddled into the field in my diaper and rubber boots and was pretty far away when my mother, hysterical, finally found me. I loved wandering around out there. Along the railroad tracks, long grasses, some with tiny flowers, waved at me every summer. It was native prairie, and now that I know how rare that is, I realize it was waving goodbye.

I was always busy. I dug up ant colonies and put grasshoppers in screened boxes that Dad made for me. I loved bugs and it must have made an impression on the old folks because my aunt Mabel once wrote to Mom, "…is Carter still catching worms and hauling ants around in his red wagon?"

Everyone called my dad "Slats" even though his name was Clarence. He indulged my fixations on bugs by helping me bury an old refrigerator in our backyard where I raised earthworms. I fed them a diet of coffee grounds and old newspapers and sold them by the jar to fishermen on their way to catch bullheads at Clear Lake. Dad could see that my enterprise was a stunning success and had a professional painter make a blue and red sign:

CARTER'S WORMS
25 CENTS A DOZEN

I couldn't leave any bug untouched, including monarch butterfly larvae that I picked from the undersides of milkweeds that grew along the railroad tracks. I put the greenish worms in our covered porch and watched them do the same thing every year: climb to the top of the window screens, turn into a cocoon and wait. The morning finally came when my mom hollered up the stairs as she made my breakfast.

"Carter! Your butterflies have hatched!"

I couldn't get enough of those beautiful black and orange creatures. I coaxed the butterflies onto my fingers and carried them to the zinnias in the garden to sip their first nectar. I sat through a lot of church sermons and Sunday school lessons, but it was monarch butterflies that convinced me that there is a God and that He is very talented.

Our lives were not burdened by political correctness, which, thankfully, caused my parents to give me toy guns nearly every Christmas of my boyhood. My friends and I spent a considerable portion of our time playing cowboys and Indians. I had a pair of Fanner 50's with fake cartridges in a gun belt that I wore with my chaps and felt cowboy hat. We chose up sides and spent hours killing each other and arguing over who should be dead and who was just wounded.

Our acreage, next to the Rock Island railroad tracks, belonged to my grandpa, George Niemeyer, then my dad, who worked it more for amusement than money. The Niemeyers were no-nonsense folk from Ladbergen, Germany. On a trip there in 2006, I hoped to find that the Niemeyers were barons and lived in castles, but the former mayor of Ladbergen shook his head and corrected me in broken English, "No, no…Niemeyers very poor farmers." When a famine hit the German countryside, the Niemeyers moved to Ohio, then to Iowa, where the soil was rich. There they stayed.

Dad planned on being an ordinary farmer, but when my brother was born, Dad decided to get work that was more predictable and took a job as a lineman for the Hancock County Rural Electric Co-Op. For his paycheck, he climbed power poles and fixed electrical lines. The rest of his time was consumed doing good for others. He was Garner's volunteer fire chief, Hancock County's first-aid instructor, a deacon at the Zion Evangelical and Reformed Church, Garner's civil defense director, and a member of just about every club and organization within a 20-mile radius of our house. He even supervised German POWs during World War II.

Dad was a packrat and collected other people's junk, no matter the size. The garage in our yard where Dad parked his Chevy every night was once a service station. When Garner updated the county jail, Dad got his hands on the old cells and brought them home, setting them on slabs of concrete next to our driveway just so he could have them.

I went with him to farm auctions and estate sales, and at the end when there was a bunch of junk left over and everyone was starting to put on their coats and hats and leave, the auctioneer would call Dad by name and ask if he wanted to buy the whole lot for a dollar – picture frames, sewing machine parts, even a few Indian-head pennies. Of course he did. My job was to help him pile it into our station wagon.

The outside of our place was like a scene from a Ma and Pa Kettle movie, but the inside was squeaky-clean because of my mother. Her name was Opal and she spent all of her time at home, believing that working at a regular job would be an inappropriate distraction from her main devotion: Dad, my brother Craig, and me. We caused her a lot of cooking and cleaning and mending, but she seemed proud of it. Ma never learned to drive. Dad did the shopping and the errands and anything that involved a car. She was tall like my dad and spent a lot of time fussing with her hair. If her hair looked good, she said, she felt good. Her parents were from Norway and she had six siblings, all of whom helped run a combination hotel and grocery store in nearby Hayfield. Ma and Dad met on a blind date, and neither of them dated anyone else again.

We never threw anything away. It was all treasure to Dad, and because he loved it, so did Ma. She, on the other hand, kept more reasonable things like letters and photos and all of our schoolwork and report cards. When I feel nostalgic, I can pull from my bookshelf a ribbon-bound stack of yellowing letters that traces my parents' courtship when they lived in separate towns, Dad's curly handwriting, in pencil, outlining the day's events and wishing her a sweet goodnight.

My gopher trapping business was a great success, bringing me as much as 50 cents a week in bounty money. I blew it on comic books and cherry Cokes. I never ran out of gophers. In fact, there seemed to be more every year. I would have done it just for fun, but being able to earn money at something no one else was doing made me itch for it. My only regular job had been shoveling snow, and for that I was paid in cake and cookies. Trapping, therefore, was a great discovery, and I was determined to get good at it. I was getting a nickel from the county for every front foot, and the farmers were paying me an extra 50 cents as well. They wanted me trapping their fields thoroughly. Pocket gophers, with their relentless tunneling, made soft dirt mounds that screwed up the sickle bars during hay cutting. I added crows to my bounty-hunting repertoire, too, because they were considered a pest in Hancock County and their feet, like pocket gophers, were worth a nickel each.

A short bike ride from my house stood the Hancock County Courthouse with its wide lawn and leafy trees. I went there a couple of times a month. The routine was always the same: I dumped the feet onto the counter and a white-haired lady took a pencil from behind her ear and sorted them into groups. I was surprised how normal this seemed to the women in the office. Nobody was grossed out and nobody scrubbed off the counter when we were done. She made out a receipt and I walked down the hall to the treasury office where I was paid – in actual dollars. I discovered, quite by accident, that if I left the feet in the can too long, they rotted and sometimes stuck to the bottom. The first time this happened, the lady at the courthouse nearly puked and had me count them outside and report back. She paid me and told the janitor to throw everything in the incinerator. After that, I made a few extra nickels by letting the feet sit a good while before turning them in.

Of all the things that could have done it, guns were what brought the men in my family together. We may have been going every direction the rest of the year, but every fall we stopped to hunt pheasants, rabbits and squirrels. To repay him for all the favors he'd granted, farmers let Dad on their property before anyone else – and that meant me, too. Guns were tools and not to be feared as much as respected. There was a shotgun or rifle leaning in nearly every corner of our house, and before I was old enough to drive, I was allowed to use them with no restrictions other than an admonishment from Dad to be careful. He gave me a certain look that sealed the warning. He must have known that my biggest fear in life was disappointing him. Dad bought me a Savage single-shot .410 when I was nine and he decided I'd grown past my BB gun. He taught me to load it, sight in, and shoot it, and that no matter how the cowboys on TV shot their guns I was to keep both eyes open when aiming. I might kill my pets or worse, my friends and family, if I wasn't careful, he said. Those 15 or so minutes comprised the only gun safety lesson I've ever had. Beyond becoming a crack shot, I learned how to predict where varmints of all kinds hide and how to follow their tracks. My brother and I hunted rats in Gram's chicken house, lying in silence on our bellies in the dark, waiting for the fat, gray rats to emerge. No matter how many we killed, more took their place. Nature abhors a vacuum, even in a chicken house. We looked forward to rat-shooting trips at the city dump, too, where just after sunset, Dad would train the Chevy's headlights on one spot and we'd shoot until the rats wised up. I moped around for a week when the city began burying its garbage, ending the rat scourge and our special outings.

I heard somewhere that Audubon learned about birds by killing them. In that spirit, I did the same, carrying a field guide in my back pocket so I could keep track of what I shot. Rabbits, gophers and sparrows were my first victims. I examined each one carefully, counting feathers or teeth, looking at their feet. I sat motionless in the bushes and watched animals living their lives, making mental notes about their behaviors, which I understood must somehow go with their physical features. I kept it all in my head and felt no remorse for having killed the creatures that taught me so much. Similarly, I didn't feel sorry about putting a nightcrawler on a line or uprooting a plant in the garden, ending its life. Knowing what I know now about the decline of songbirds, however, I wish I'd left more in the sky.

"How could you kill a hummingbird?" my wife, Jenny, asked incredulously when I told her about my childhood hunting sprees.

"It's damn tough with a BB gun," I said. "The little guys are fast."

I thought it was pretty funny, but she just rolled her eyes.

In the 1950s, though, we weren't so concerned. Animals lived and then they died. We raised chickens and ducks, and I helped catch them when it was time to turn them into supper. Those same fowl were my pets sometimes, but their eventual deaths, whether on purpose or by accident, was a given. To have chicken for supper, you had to kill a chicken. There wasn't a lot to ponder.

Being around wild creatures, however, made me want to make them into pets. My pet crow, Crowy, would land near our kitchen door and squawk until somebody gave him a chunk of hamburger. When he ate all he could, he took off with the rest, hiding pieces between roof shakes, or ferrying the pink meat to the railroad tracks where he jammed it under the rails. He then checked his cache from all angles to see if any of it was visible. When I walked to school, Crowy followed me, flapping from one tree to the next. One day, as I passed the courthouse on my way home in the afternoon, I noticed that two groups of pigeons were strung along its tile roof, a lone crow dividing them. I stopped, suspicious.

"Crowy!"

He'd been waiting for me. He glided to a tree and followed me home.

Of all the animals I raised, I was most famous in Garner for pigeons. I even had a pigeon club, complete with a membership oath that ended in Amen. By the time I was a senior in high school, I had nearly 800 of them. Even I could admit that was too damn many and let most of them go, but at least I could brag that I had the biggest pigeon flock in the county.

Bing Greiman, an old trapper who sometimes shot at my pigeons, had a cylinder-head repair shop in his garage. My friends and I routinely stopped in and pretended to watch him work, but what we really wanted was for him to tell us hunting or trapping stories. Or maybe he'd show us where one of his fingers used to be before he got it cut off in a truck's fan belt at the fire station. My dad was there when it happened and he later showed me the hallowed finger, still in Bing's glove.

When our timing was good, Bing would sit and pick through the metal filings on the floor for a cigarette butt, then pinch it between two grimy fingers and tell us how to catch muskrats, or about the time he gassed fox pups in their den for a bounty of two dollars each.

Bing told us that he figured out which muskrat traps he'd be using in the coming season by snapping them on his nose; if they hurt, they were strong enough and he kept them. I saw him do this, but as I grew older, I realized Bing's finely honed tales were plain old bullshit, crafted by years of kids begging for stories. It didn't matter. I could see that Bing's competence as a trapper was what held his stories together and kept us coming back for more. Every time I heard one, I was more fired up than ever to be a trapper, too.

In my little world, I was making great headway, graduating from pocket gophers to skunks quite by accident when I caught one of the spotted varieties in one of my traps. I removed the cardboard cover and saw that the chain was pulled tight, disappearing down into the tunnel. I had something. I usually just tugged on it and my victim came struggling out with the trap clamped on its leg. This time, I tugged and a spray of yellow burst from the hole in the ground. I stumbled backward, sputtering and blinking, fairly sure I was going to die, or puke, or both. I outran the mist before I got much on me. I knew immediately what it was, but it never occurred to me that skunks came in a size small enough to crawl underground, much less through the narrow passageways made by rats or gophers.

I didn't think about what other trappers might be doing in other places until I saw something on a newsreel at the Avery Theater. Dad financed my trips to the Avery, flipping me a 50-cent piece. I sat next to Cherry Greiman, hoping that among her many suitors, I might somehow become her boyfriend. Before the movie started, a newsreel flickered on the screen, showing a wolf running in deep snow, then an airplane sliding up next to it. A man sitting with a shotgun leaned forward in the plane and fired. I leaned forward in my seat, watching the wolf tumble and die. Then the plane landed on its skis and the men stepped out. A photographer snapped pictures of them shaking hands and smiling as they posed with the dead wolf. I was transfixed. I think I dropped my popcorn, and maybe even forgot I was sitting next to Cherry. What would it be like to get a wolf? I occasionally saw red foxes run through a hayfield and I itched for the day that I could get my hands on one, but a wolf? Well, a wolf was the holy grail.

What I wanted more than anything when I was 14 was to catch a fox. I was obsessed with it. I subscribed to *Fur-Fish-Game* and flipped through its pages looking for stories about trapping predators. I absorbed them all and mixed their ideas with mine. Catching skunks and opossums was nothing compared to sneaking in on a fox. I had pretty good success trapping skunks in the grassy fencerows near my house, and a couple of close calls. Because of that, my teachers began informing me on a regular basis that I stank. My obsession with foxes, however, wasn't just about killing one, but about outsmarting it. I spent hours searching for their tracks in the hayfields and meadows around Garner, and when I found a fresh set, I followed it, only to see my target jump up a hundred yards ahead of me and run off. I was beginning to understand the fox's reputation. I learned to stalk foxes with a rifle and finally shot one on a hunting trip, but when it came to trapping them, they outfoxed me. Trapping a fox was going to take a whole new bag of tricks. I wasn't sure where to begin, even after reading everything I could get my hands on.

Before anything else though, I needed money. I had to finance my trapline and have enough left over for trips to Dairy Queen and the Avery Theater and a dozen other things. And there was no way I could earn enough on pocket gopher bounties to save for a car. At first, I cleaned hog pens and baled hay for local farmers, but I found a real job at the stinky, dirty North Iowa Turkey Hatchery, where I handled 90,000 turkeys five times each (or maybe more) – sorting them, loading them, moving them from one pen to another, feeding them, and building and tearing down miles of wire pens. By the time I was a senior in high school I'd saved enough to buy a car and almost enough to pay for college. I also ended up diagnosed with lumbar lardosis, or reverse curvature of the spine, from pitching shit with a shovel designed for a guy half my height.

I didn't get a car so I could go out on more dates; I got one so I could run a longer trapline. Having a car meant that I could cover more ground in my quest for foxes. I'd learned, mostly through failure, how to track them and stay downwind of them. I'd discovered that they habitually curled up next to their dens or slept on south-facing slopes in the winter. I'd learned that foxes liked high ground so they could see the approach of enemies like me. I often found foxes sleeping in the same spot year after year.

Charlie Brcka (*BRITCH-ka*) was a farmer like everyone else, but was much better at taxidermy. He wore wire glasses, striped bib overalls and lived with his mother. He was a middle-aged bachelor, though I'm not sure he planned it that way. I met him when I was 18, only because my pal, Tom Hartwig, bragged about him so much that I just had to meet this guy.

I didn't expect much as Brcka let us into his house, but in a few seconds, I was in awe. Hundreds of wildlife mounts that surely were of museum quality flew, rested or leapt forth in silence. Dozens of paintings, mostly New Testament scenes or animals in the woods, leaned or hung on walls. In other rooms, model airplanes and ships sat on tables and shelves. The man apparently wasn't satisfied with small-scale kits from stores, so he made his own replicas, only bigger, using wood, wire and plastic. They were flawless. His airplanes even had control sticks that moved the wing and tail flaps.

We were instant friends. I was captivated by Brcka's talent and suddenly, in addition to all my other plans, I wanted to be a taxidermist.

"Do you teach people how to do this?" I pointed to a pair of flying pheasants.

Brcka brayed and gasped. It was deafening and terrifying until I realized he wasn't choking, he was laughing.

"Oh yes, I can teach you," he said. "Go get yourself a crow or a pheasant and I'll help you."

As soon as I left, I went to one of my usual crow haunts and shot one, made a U-turn and was back on his front step.

"Oh, I don't have time to do it right now," Brcka chuckled, turning the warm, limp bird and looking it over. "I'll freeze it for you. It'll make a real nice mount."

I started hanging out there to watch him work, and as fall approached, he asked if I hunted pheasants. Of course I did. I was a fool for it. It was like asking if I breathed air. Brcka made me a proposition: he'd buy skinned-out pheasants for $1.25 a piece. He showed me how to skin a bird that was to be used for taxidermy. It was tedious compared to just ripping in to one that you planned to eat. I watched him while he described the cuts and later brought him many pheasant skins. He looked them over and told me I had natural talent, then offered me a job. I spent hundreds of hours working in his tiny basement where I was blasted by Bohemian polkas on the local radio station. He adored that music and hummed along and kept the beat by making trumpet noises.

Charlie Brcka's farm was a social center for sportsmen and the curious. When he went upstairs to entertain visitors, I tuned the radio to a rock 'n roll station. When he returned, he cheerfully switched it back. I ate lunch in his kitchen when hunters left a chunk of meat on the necks of the deer heads they brought in. Brcka cut the meat off, boiled it on the stove and plopped it onto two plates. It was bland and tough, but it was food. I decided not to complain.

Brcka taught me to think about animals in detail. His training was like taking advanced courses in mammalogy, ornithology and anatomy. I wanted to be just like him. He never let me forget that a grand creator was at work in nature, and he always closed his shop on Sundays.

Regular visitors to Brcka's place included state and federal biologists and game wardens. They sometimes brought specimens for mounting, but mostly they dropped by to keep up with hunting gossip. An important guy showed up one day and my life took what seemed like a surprising turn.

"Carter, here, is getting ready to graduate from high school and he wants to be a wildlife biologist," Brcka said to Dick Bishop, gesturing in my direction.

Bishop was the state waterfowl biologist for the Iowa Conservation Commission, which later became the Iowa Department of Natural Resources. He was a taxidermist, too, and liked to compare techniques with Brcka. Instead of saying something polite and meaningless, Bishop brightened and told me to stop by his office at Clear Lake; he might have some work for me. It was his wise counsel, or maybe something closer to a butt-kicking, that later kept me from making a dumb decision that would have prevented me from ever meeting a wolf.

I was an average kid in school and never really expected to do anything exciting, much less go to college. My brother was already getting on with life, landing a teaching job after making his way through college on a basketball scholarship. We couldn't have been more different. He was a jock and a perfectionist and so much older than me that he was more like a babysitter than a sibling. I liked trapping and hunting, but I never thought those skills would amount to anything. I sat in the back of class and tried to be invisible, even though I was the tallest kid in town. When it was time to write reports, mine were always about wildlife or becoming a biologist, although I once wrote one about manners and how people generally don't have any. I wasn't a joiner and stayed away from anything with a membership roster. Only when the principal pointed straight at me and pronounced me a member of the student council did I comply. At least then I had a say in where to have the class party. As for sports, I liked playing, but I couldn't get interested in letting it take over my life.

When the geese were migrating during football practice my junior year, I stood watching them, wondering if they might still be around on the weekend, so I could hunt a few. I spent the next half-hour running laps around the field, the coach yelling at me for not having my head in the practice. By the time I was headed toward my senior year, I'd had enough of the browbeating and went hunting instead, or helped my dad with chores. With all the piles of money I was making at the turkey farm, I bought a Texan brand shotgun shell reloader and an RCBS rifle press so that I could do my own reloading. My friends and I took turns driving to the Ventura Gun Club where we'd formed our own trapshooting team. It was better than holding the dummy for others at football practice.

Dick Bishop gave me a job as a biologist's aide, a fancy title for grunt, and I took it, not caring what it paid. I pulled into the parking lot a half-hour early on my first day. The doors were locked, so I sat in the grass and waited. I'd never had to wait to be put to work. Farms don't operate like this. A little after eight o'clock a few biologists showed up. Then Bishop wheeled in and I followed him inside. I stood in his doorway, waiting for an assignment. He hung up his jacket and reached for his billfold.

"Welcome to the ICC," Bishop said, handing me a few dollars. "Go to the bakery and get us some doughnuts, will ya?"

I did it, muttering about what I'd gotten into.

I worked on bird surveys and duck counts and putting up nest boxes. I didn't know it at the time, probably because Bishop seemed too friendly to be famous and more like a mischievous kid than anything, but he was a big player in the relatively small field of wildlife biology. One of his many accomplishments was restoring giant Canada geese to Iowa in 1964 – a species unknown yet native. Sixteen pair of geese grew into over 40,000 during his watch. From his early days, researching Mearns quail in Arizona for his master's thesis, to becoming the state waterfowl biologist for Iowa, Bishop rose through wildlife ranks, retiring a few years ago as the wildlife bureau chief for the state. Somehow he did all this without breaking his pick off with everyone along the way, and in the wildlife field, that's not easy. He never took himself too seriously. He was only about five years older than I was, but he'd already made his mark and I admired that.

I was pretty wound-up about getting to work for the state and I was eager as hell about everything. I just couldn't believe I was getting to work at a real wildlife job. What do you want me to do next? I was like a puppy jumping all over Bishop. He said I was intense, and called me Intensified Clyde because it rhymed. In time, the name caught on and everyone else called me Clyde, too.

About the same time, the state hired a furbearer biologist named Ron Andrews, who became known for a detailed study of Iowa foxes. Before that, Bishop, Andrews and I spent most of our time putting nest boxes in trees around the local marshes, hoping that wood ducks would use them. They didn't, but the fox squirrels loved them. So did starlings and deer mice. Climbing up and peering into the boxes became a personal test of nerves when a creature burst out of the hole and into my face, nearly knocking me off the ladder.

We also banded ducks at Ventura Marsh at night, and I smoked Swisher Sweets to keep the bugs out of my face. At night, every kind of bird and animal emerged. All of them were mesmerized by the sound of the generator that powered our headlamps and paid little attention to us motoring among them. But if anyone spoke, or if I accidentally banged the side of the boat, they scattered. Some nights, the water was so clear I could see everything – wiggling insect larvae and fish and plants.

Bishop, I discovered, had narcolepsy. Several times on our duck banding outings, his chin went suddenly to his chest, and each time someone had to wake him. Thankfully, most of these episodes occurred when he was doing something mundane like eating, though falling face-first into a pile of mashed potatoes must have made it hard to breathe.

All of our wildlife work was accomplished using a four-door sedan that had official-looking door emblems and tires that were almost bald. When I drove the back roads, I only vaguely noted that I was stuck with such a dumb car; I was busy disbelieving that I was getting paid for such work. I did a lot of surveying in that car, sometimes getting a quick glimpse of a whitetail deer; they were rare back then. Other times, I'd encounter a big snapping turtle crossing the road and I just had to stop and pester it for a while. This was the greatest job in the world and I planned on doing it forever.

In the fall of 1965, I did what I never thought I'd do: I went to college. It was only junior college in Mason City, but it was still more than I ever thought I'd venture. Bishop let me go part-time at my state job. He and Andrews were on me all the time about how important college was. They didn't want anything interfering with it – including my state job. I didn't really care for junior college. It seemed like high school all over again, and I found myself flunking tests and getting terrible grades in English and history, mostly because I was looking out the window thinking of all the other things I could be doing. I carpooled with friends every morning, but over the months, they stopped showing up and eventually dropped out, and I was soon making the trip alone. Though I wasn't thrilled with it, I decided I'd rather go to college than get drafted. I was practically in F territory when I had an epiphany: I'm paying for this? I'm paying to flunk a class? I earned that money breaking my back at a turkey farm

I panicked, wondering if Bishop and Andrews might find out about my grades. It took me a day to get my act together. I'd never heard of a "grade-point average," but I learned about it fast and I somehow salvaged mine.

By the following spring, I was feeling like an old hand at my wildlife job. Instead of banding ducks or doing nest surveys, I was squared up for a red fox tagging project that was meant to encompass the whole state. Everybody kept talking about how important this was going to be as part of a larger study going on throughout the Midwest. Foxes were just about the only native predator left in north Iowa, and they were popular with hunters and trappers. No one had ever studied them before and no one knew much about them. Ron Andrews was in charge of the project and the first thing he did was to hire a trapper: George Good.

Good was a self-taught legend in the small world of Iowa fox trapping. Ron Andrew's predecessor, Bob Phillips, discovered Good while perusing his morning paper over the years and seeing Good's photo appear again and again alongside beaming stories about the hundreds of foxes he'd caught within a 12-mile radius of his home. Good did most of his catching next to the big turkey farms in north-central Iowa and raked in a lot of money when bounties and fur markets were high.

That summer, I was paired with Good as his assistant. He never said a word, but I'm sure he grumbled at getting stuck with a 20 year-old greenhorn, even though he was only about 10 years older. Decades later, fellow trapper and Iowan Craig O'Gorman, who learned a thing or two from Good, laughed and shook his head while watching me set a trap.

"Watching you is like watching George," he said.

It's true that I learned almost everything I know about trapping from George Good, but it was tough going.

Good farmed 160 acres near Randall, Iowa. But as a former calf roper on the rodeo circuit, he was more inclined toward that – and fox trapping. While in the rodeo, he met and married a barrel racer named Faye and they raised two daughters. Good was lean, moved fast and often wore a Stetson, western-cut shirts and Wranglers. He looked like an Indian to me, but I never had the nerve to ask him about it. He was short-tempered, intense, and seemed pissed off about something all the time. His manner, combined with his amazing ability as a trapper, intimidated the hell out of me.

We hit the road in April 1967, and about a day into my new assignment, I felt like I was in boot camp. Our job was to find fox dens, capture the pups, ear tag them and record their locations. We worked off of public reports of fox dens that kept us going as long as there was daylight. We used a 60-foot, smooth steel cable known as a wire ferret that, when cranked down a fox den opening, would either snag pups by their fur or annoy them to the point that they ran out. Good guided the cable and I stood ready with a dip net. We caught dozens every week.

Good was a perfectionist. He barked orders at me and was intolerant of even the slightest screw-up. He exploded profanity when I did something wrong, like get out of the truck when he told me to stay put. I was leaving my scent all over, he yelled. This was apparently one of the biggest sins when trapping predators. We worked like madmen all day and covered as much ground as possible and sometimes a little more. Like varmints, we'd gulp down our supper every night and hole up in a motel room. Good sat cross-legged on the floor and cooked instant soup, putting it in his thermos for the next day's lunch. I presumed he liked soup because he could slurp it fast and get the business of eating over with. He didn't do breakfast and issued frequent warnings that if I did, I'd better get up early or he'd leave me behind. I crept off to whatever restaurant was open before dawn. When senior biologists traveled with us to see how the project was going, they slowed Good down and made him clench his jaw. The visits were only a couple of days long, but Good spent the next three days bitching about it. I never knew what was eating at him. He seemed to have been born that way.

I wasn't surprised to hear that Good had threatened to kill a few people around Randall for stealing his traps. He'd even asked the sheriff to ride along one morning and drove out to the place where the trap-stealers lived so Good could have a witness when he made the threat. He wasn't kidding. Shortly after that, he sold his farm and moved to Circle, Montana, where he took a job as a government trapper. There, coyote tracks troubled him, and he mumbled to himself about where they could have come from. Maybe the next county where lazy trappers let theirs get away. He was preoccupied with his job and blindly loyal to the sheep outfits in his area. Good was a great trapper, but he was wound so tight that he was his own worst enemy. He slumped over dead of a heart attack in 1990, while gunning coyotes out of the backseat of an airplane. He was only 54.

Before working with George Good, I'd never heard of a padded trap, but sometimes we couldn't get foxes out of their dens or entire fox families had to be relocated, and that's when Good set one. Each morning, two or three foxes hobbled, unhurt, in traps within feet of each other. I could see why this man had a reputation. He was obsessed – and the results were astonishing.

By mid-summer, I was exhausted in every way. Besides his relentless pursuit of foxes, Good liked to talk and expected me to listen – attentively. To him, a fox wasn't just a fox, but an individual. It was his habit to talk for hours on the subject and one of his favorite stories was about a fox with the big white tip on its tail that was missing two toes on its left hind foot that he caught in the same trap from which it escaped from death the year before.... He was talking about the fox the way a person might talk about an eccentric friend.

"...they don't all look alike," Good finished, as we flew down a dusty stretch of Iowa back road toward our next fox den.

The silence that followed his droning lecture snapped me out of the nap I was courting.

"They ain't all the same, is what I'm saying." He looked over to see if I was paying attention. "You got to really look at 'em. They're all a little bit different."

I wanted him to think I'd been listening, so I nodded. Then I thought about what he said. He'd tossed a valuable nugget my way. If I wanted to get good at trapping, I had to pay attention to the smallest detail. I wondered what else I'd missed.

Somehow, through the summer, Good and I developed mutual respect, but I wasn't ever sure if he liked me outright. I tolerated him when others might have walked away. He was critical of everyone and I wondered what he said about me when I wasn't around.

Because he didn't want me and my human scent polluting his trapline, I was stuck sitting in the truck cab, forced to watch Good from a distance as he set each trap in the dirt. Nobody gets near the trap except the trapper, he said. Canines can detect even the slightest thing with their noses. It was only out of necessity that the only human scent Good allowed on his trapline was his own. I could see what he was doing, but there seemed to be more to it than just the act of setting a trap. Lots more. How did he pick the location? How did he decide on the trap size? What was he using for lure? Why did he position the trap the way he did? If catching a fox was as simple as he made it look, everybody would be doing it, right? I had to know more, but I was intimidated. Some days, Good was fun to be around, but most days, he was impatient to the point that I thought he might kill me – with his bare hands. I wanted more than anything to know a few of his trapping secrets.

The summer was almost over and I'd spent days mustering the courage to ask him, trying to find the right time. One day, a lump rising in my throat, I just blurted it out.

"George, do you think there's any way I could learn to catch a fox like you do?" I thought I covered my head after speaking, but it was probably just my imagination. I braced for rejection, expecting him not just to say no, but *hell* no.

Instead, he praised my work ethic. I was so shocked that I don't remember what he said next, other than he'd be glad to show me so I would have no excuse for screwing it up.

We drove to Ventura Marsh and once he picked a spot and explained why he picked this place and not that one, he walked me through every detail he could think of, mostly about fox behavior.

"This goes for all predators, Carter," he told me. "Not just foxes. You learn this and you'll catch a fox, no problem."

"What about those guys who say all the fox are going to get all trapped up and there won't be any left?" I asked.

"Nah, that's bullshit," Good snorted. "It don't work that way. Those fellas think every fox out there belongs to them and they ain't gonna like a kid like you interfering with their take. But you have an edge now."

He finished setting the trap – making the "set." It was called a dirt-hole set because it appeared to be nothing more than a small hole dug by a squirrel. The area around the hole was just smooth, dry soil. It looked harmless. It was perfect. When a fox stepped on that spot, sniffing at the irresistibly stinky lure that he had placed in the hole, a trap would snap on the fox faster than it could blink. I'd tried to focus on every detail so I would remember because George Good didn't give his secrets to *anyone*.

He gave me another gem that day: Young foxes often disperse in the fall and in the spring, he said. It's when they travel long distances in search of new territories. If I could find their corridors of travel, I'd catch a hell of a lot of them. It was the reason he caught so many in such a small area around Randall, Iowa.

"You just go out there and do what I taught you," he said on our last day of work. "You'll do fine."

Once I was schooled under George Good in the art of fox trapping, I was thoroughly into it. Always ready for opportunities to run a trapline, I started keeping fox urine and bait in the back of my latest car, a red 1959 Chevy station wagon. Fox urine smells sort of like skunk, and the bait, made from ground up bobcat, horse or beaver can be plain raunchy. I made my own and I found out that it didn't take long for all that stink to travel from the jar where it seemed reasonably contained to the fabric of my car's seats. When I sold my station wagon to a friend and he tried to steam clean the interior, the hot water only made the smell worse. He ended up spending a good sum ripping out the seats and rugs entirely.

I had a run-in once with a skunk on my trapline and ended up with a load of stink in my hair. I jumped into the shower the second I got home and lathered up four or five times and hoped I'd squelched it because I was headed to a party that night. The thing about skunk odor is that when you're around it for a while you can't smell it anymore. I stopped to pick up beer on my way across town and I hadn't been in the grocery store two minutes when I overheard a discussion at the cash register about skunks. Customers ahead of me asked the cashier if one was perhaps stuck under the building. The cashier held her nose with one hand and rung up groceries with the other. I paid and left. I'm pretty sure no one knew it was me.

Sporting goods stores that deal in hunting sell something that claims to neutralize skunk odor, but I've never found anything that works except a sodium hydroxide mixture that I learned about in one of my chemistry books. If you put sodium hydroxide on skunk stink, a reaction occurs where the sulphur ion is replaced by an odorless sodium ion. Sulphur is what stinks about a skunk, the proper term for its foul essence being butyl mercaptan.

Trapping around Garner was fun and rewarding, but the things I'd learned in college opened a whole new world for me. I wouldn't really admit it at first because I didn't want my friends to think I was a nerd.

Life was falling together just as it should. I rolled down the window and thought about my rosy future one Sunday in October 1967 as I rode home from church with my parents. I'd be done with junior college in a year. I'd learned how to trap a fox and was getting good at it. I had a state job for the rest of my life. And in an hour or so, I'd be heading out for an afternoon duck hunt with my cousin. But another thing happened in those next few hours too: Dad died.

There wasn't a moment of any day, except when he was sleeping or in church, that Dad didn't have a cigarette in his mouth. Our whole house smelled like them and his car, especially. There were rows of burns on the edge of the oak dresser in his bedroom where he'd balanced a Lucky Strike and let it smolder just a little too long. Every morning, when I plodded into the bathroom, I peed on three or four butts already floating in the john. My mother frequently joined Dad in the frantic batting and flinging of couch cushions, looking for the hot tip of his cigarette that had suddenly dropped. After a meal, he used the floral edges of my mother's china as an ashtray. When he lacked another receptacle, he used the cuff of his pants, or his shirt pocket.

When I was 15, he asked me if he should quit. He'd had some heart palpitations that scared him.

"Yeah, I think that would be good," I said.

He died at the emergency room door of the Mason City General Hospital as he delivered an ambulance-load of kids who'd been in a bad car wreck. He'd had a heart attack at age 55. I believe that cigarettes killed him and I hated them for it. Still do. But I realized there were other less obvious reasons for his early death. At least when I was a kid, they seemed less obvious.

My dad was a perpetually tired man. He'd collected exhaustion over time the way he collected junk at estate sales. Over many years, he'd heaped it on himself until his body wouldn't take it anymore. He couldn't help it though, because he'd decided at some point that it was his job to make everyone in our town happy and comfortable. His desire, inexplicably, was to be everything to everyone and he'd pretty much achieved it by the time he died. He'd held nearly every office, volunteer or otherwise, except city government, and had managed to make himself completely indispensable to the farming community. Everybody knew and loved big Slats Niemeyer – and that's what killed him. I may have been oblivious to certain things when I was a kid, but I knew that my dad was stressed out. It was the only thing about him I didn't want to emulate.

Dad's death seemed like a freak, unthinkable event that could never be duplicated. But in 1994, my brother Craig also died of a heart attack. He, too, was 55, and a smoker. As I grew older, the sharp edges of these events wore down somewhat. Now they only grind on me a little. The day I turned 55, I pretended not to notice the hours passing, wondering where the hands on the clock would be when I dropped dead. When it didn't happen, I vowed to try and love each day, not knowing how many I might have left.

My new function in life in the fall of 1967 was to try to keep my mother's spirits up. Mine were shot, but hers were completely destroyed. I had another year of junior college to go. Though I refused to drop out, I couldn't make my brain do anything. My brother was away, teaching in another part of the state, which left me as the man of the house. I realized that if I didn't take over, my mother would be content to close the drapes and rot away. The transition from boyhood to manhood took about a day. I didn't have the luxury of thinking about it. I bought the groceries, paid the bills and kept up the house and farm. Every day, I drove to and from Mason City for my classes. My mother rarely left the house except to get her hair done once a week at Rose Klemm's beauty parlor. I drove her, waited, and brought her home, just as Dad had done.

That winter, I hunted and trapped for no other reason than to feel the cold on my face and try to keep a grip on my sanity. I felt my dad's absence like it was hunger. I walked miles every day as though I could walk out of grief the same way I walk the soles off my shoes. I thought up something during those walks that I believed might bring a smile to my mother's face. I began trapping muskrats and kept 31 of the best chocolate-brown pelts, then sent them away to be made into a fur cape – one with a satin lining that would drape over her shoulders and fasten in front. It worked. She wore the cape often, especially when she went to supper with her friends. I could tell she was proud of it, and that it might have even made her friends a little jealous. There weren't many women in farm towns wearing fur.

Most farmers in Garner in the 1960s liked having pheasants – and pheasant hunters – around. To maintain a steady supply of birds, they left substantial hedgerows between farms as well as stands of corn in winter. Farmers only rarely used pesticides, which meant that hatchling pheasants had plenty to eat. Where pheasants did well, so did foxes, making a fat living in miles of wild if narrow habitat. I had a fox in nearly every trap every morning of Christmas vacation in 1968, and in time, I had 18, which I skinned, stretched on tapered boards, and hung in a neat row. If I bountied them at the courthouse, I could have collected two dollars apiece, but their fur, properly prepared, was worth a lot more – maybe three times as much.

Two brothers, Dean and Claire Tompkins, were Garner's primary fox hunters. They also went after wild mink and muskrats, and had traps in every creek bottom. They never told me to leave in so many words, but I heard through others that they were annoyed at me for horning in on their turf. Their habit was to set dozens of traps and kill every furbearer for miles, then move on. I was young and I should have been no competition, but George Good had taught me well and my trapline was prolific. I got permission from about a dozen farmers to set traps in their fields. My dad's good standing with the farmers lived on long after he was gone and it was the key to my success as a fledgling trapper.

"You're Slats Niemeyer's boy, aren't you?" a farmer would say when I knocked at his door. I'd nod and he'd tell me to have the run of the place. I was allowed in when others were turned away.

Talk of my trapline traveled fast and it wasn't long before the Tompkins brothers paid me a visit. They were nice enough at first, standing in the driveway with their hands in their pockets, making small talk.

"Been catching a lot of foxes?" One of them finally got to the point.

"Thirty-six this month," I said. "You wanna see 'em?"

They followed me around the corner of the garage. There, nailed up in the shade, were my pelts, cleaned of every trace of flesh, stretched and dried. Beautiful, cherry red, prime-condition furs. It was my first big catch. The men examined the pelts in silence. For years, the Tompkins brothers hunted foxes and hung them unskinned on their barns, facing the road, for all to see. It wasn't long before the carcasses rotted and the men hauled the stinking varmints to the courthouse for the two-dollar bounty.

"You know, Carter, these are real nice," Claire nodded at my catch, then abruptly changed his tone. "But if everybody did this, there wouldn't be any fox left, now would there?"

We stood there looking at each other, but none of us said anything more. I knew they wanted me to back off. They could tell I wouldn't. Things had turned out just like George Good warned me. I kept trapping and so did they, but they'd been outdone by a kid and they knew it.

I graduated from junior college, but didn't go to the ceremony. Mom didn't feel like attending, so I celebrated in my head and waited for my diploma in the mail. It was the same for the next two degrees I earned. It seemed dispiriting to be handed a diploma and put my tassel on the other side when my mom was too depressed to be there. She hadn't felt like doing much of anything after Dad died. She hardly left the house. Even my getting married the next year to Pam Ruppert, our down-the-street neighbor, didn't buoy her much.

A college deferment, Dad's death and my bad back, courtesy of the turkey farm, saved me from a military hitch even though the Army bused me to Des Moines to take the requisite physical. When I walked into the doctor's office there wearing a back brace – and once he took a look at my medical records that showed all my trips to the chiropractor – I was dismissed.

I still had my part-time job as a biologist's aide, but Bishop and Andrews encouraged me to keep on with school and go get my bachelor's degree. Maybe there would be a job waiting when I got out, they said.

I thought about attending Utah State University at Logan because a few high school classmates went to forestry school there. But I didn't know anything about the school except what propaganda it put out. Utah seemed too far from Garner. I was still feeling compelled to look after my mother, so I enrolled at Iowa State University. At least I could come home to visit Pam and Mom most weekends.

I made the 65-mile drive south to Ames, where I found a place off campus – an upstairs apartment in the home of 86-year old Nellie Lande. Another student, Dale Mullin, was my across-the-hall roommate. Mrs. Lande cooked rib-sticking meals for us sometimes, and baked a pie once in awhile, which she left on the landing next to the stairs for us to notice. She also warned me about water bugs that I might encounter in the bathtub. I saw a few inch-long cockroaches; maybe that's what she meant. I found them entertaining when they got into my food in the basement kitchen. I came down one night and in the shadows saw a lettuce leaf creeping across the floor. I picked up a broom, flipped on the light and slammed the broom down on the lettuce. I expected a stunned mouse but instead there were six giant cockroaches in various stages of death.

I was pleased to find that students in wildlife studies at Iowa State had one common thread: Most of us hunted and fished and trapped, and most of us grew up in rural areas. We killed and consumed wild game. My friends at home considered me an egghead for going to college, but I tried not to let their opinions hijack my ambitions. After all, I was just doing what Bishop and Andrews told me to do.

Iowa State was grueling. I studied with pre-vet and pre-med students in courses like vertebrate zoology, embryology, comparative anatomy and other intimidating courses. I had to learn complicated words and know their meanings and spellings. I also had to learn a huge number of creatures and plants by their scientific names.

I had dreams of being a veterinarian once, but realized I'd not only hate getting there, I'd also hate being in an exam room or a barn all day. And being on call around the clock sounded like something only a fool would do. I guess I became a fool later, but at least I succeeded in not becoming a vet.

Certain courses, like ornithology, sounded fun and easy and students signed up for them in hoards because what could be better than looking at birds all day? Then they took their first tests and flunked out. The dropout rate was high and the competition ferocious. I learned seemingly irrelevant things – like public speaking – because I had to. In junior college, I tried to give a speech, but stood in front of the class dumbstruck with fear. I couldn't remember my name or what I was supposed to talk about. Humiliated, I slinked back to my seat. My buddies snickered.

At Iowa State, I stared out the window during lectures and pondered my future, wondering if I'd ever see the end of all this schooling. I walked back to my apartment each afternoon with a dull headache. To keep my sanity, I drove the country roads, walked along the Skunk River and hunted squirrels in the oak forests that surrounded town. I busted with pride the summer day in 1970 when I graduated with a bachelor's degree in wildlife biology, with minors in chemistry and botany. I was officially a biologist. I never wanted to see the inside of a lecture hall again.

A team of professors at Iowa State, including my mammalogy professor, Dr. Michael Peterson, had been busy all year hatching a plan. They'd even formed a committee around their idea, which was to create the university's first interdisciplinary research project between the veterinary and wildlife schools. They had it all figured out, including the subject of the study: to discover the incidence of rabies in striped skunks, one of the main vectors of the disease in Iowa. If only they could find a student to turn it into a graduate project.

I knew Dr. Peterson pretty well. He'd asked me to take care of his pet turtle once when he went to Mexico. I fattened it up by feeding it every cockroach I could catch in Mrs. Lande's basement. When Dr. Peterson asked me to stop by his office, I thought maybe the turtle was sick.

"I hear you've been putting up furs to pay your way through school," he said.

It was true. Fox prices were good and I was getting between one and 12 dollars a nose from my old fur-buyer friend, Ludy Sheda, for cleaning and sewing them up and getting them in presentable condition for resale. Sheda bought shot-up foxes from hunters for next to nothing. Whenever he had a bunch ready, I'd make the hour and a half drive to his place in Chelsea, Iowa, and pick them up. I kept them frozen until I could work on them. Once I had the flesh off the hides, I gave the pelts a good sudsing in the washing machine at my rental house. A washing machine is a fur preparer's best friend. I used cold water and mild soap and I never plugged it up. At least I didn't do like fellow trapper, Wayne Morgan, and skin a couple of hundred fox a year and wash them at the local Laundromat, horrifying the patrons. The real work began once the pelts were clean and dry. Most hunters weren't after the fur, so they shot delicate foxes using high-powered rifles. Salvaging such blown-apart pelts required a lot of sewing. Sometimes I'd sew the front half of one to the back half of another so that when they were on the stretching board they looked like a perfect, whole fox. I matched the subtle color of one fox with another and often fit several pieces together to make an entire pelt. I did the best I could with each one, and in return, Sheda trusted my judgment and let me tell him what he owed me. He paid me well because the better the pelts looked, the more he earned from furriers up the line.

Dr. Peterson somehow knew about my moonlighting, and went on to describe me to me, going on about all of the hunting and trapping I'd done. It was like he was talking about someone else – even I was impressed. Then he asked me if I'd ever thought about graduate school.

I wanted to laugh hysterically, but his demeanor and the situation didn't allow it. He had hundreds of student candidates at his disposal, but he picked me – the guy who not only was sick of college but also flat-out hated school. I couldn't see myself as a researcher or a teacher, having to wear cardigan sweaters and smoke a pipe.

"Uh no, Dr. Peterson, I have other plans," I heard myself say. I felt like a jerk after all his praise.

He paused, but didn't waver.

"Well, think about it, will you?

In Vietnam, in less than a year's time, my friend, turkey farm co-worker and best hunting partner, Monty Schlawin, earned three purple hearts. Injured by explosions twice and shot once, he only told his parents about two of the incidents. By the time the third one rolled around, he said he didn't see the point in worrying them. He earned his sergeant stripes leading infantry patrols through the jungles looking for the VC. Once when one of his soldiers heard the *click* of having stepped on a land mine, Schlawin coached the terrified kid to keep steady pressure on that foot because it's the release, not the compression that causes the detonation. Schlawin kept on him while others worked to disable the mine. But the kid started shaking, first a little, and then a lot. Then came the explosion.

Schlawin came home, and though he wrote to me about a few harrowing experiences, he never talked about his time over there and I never saw him in uniform. None of my friends who went to Vietnam ever wore their uniforms. They left in civilian clothes and came home in them. I was completely naive about Vietnam and didn't understand the seriousness or futility of it. I never even noticed the war protesters that demonstrated at Iowa State, but I did watch young men hobble with one leg to their seats in class, having just returned from a tour of duty. I was too busy to read newspapers and it never occurred to me to watch the news at night. I always wondered if my friends held it against me because I didn't go over there.

I returned to my summer job with the Iowa Conservation Commission, degree in hand, and told my role models, Bishop and Andrews, about the graduate school opportunity. I interjected the story with comments like, "Have you ever heard of anything so stupid?"

Bishop looked exasperated.

"You get your butt back down to Ames and tell them yes. Do you know how hard it is to get into graduate school? Universities don't ask *you* to go to graduate school, you ask *them*." Bishop rolled his eyes and slapped his forehead and added that he wouldn't give me a permanent job now that he knew I'd use it to avoid graduate school. Andrews stood behind him, nodding.

I decided to get a second opinion.

My brother, Craig was a professional – a teacher. He had lots of experience with academics. He'd give me the right answer.

"You'd be a fool to turn it down, Carter," he said. He didn't have a graduate degree and wished he did.

I couldn't find a single person who agreed with me. I expanded my survey, asking some real lowlifes what they thought. Sounds like a hell of an opportunity, they muttered over their beers.

Guilt morphed into anxiety. What should I do? Maybe, if I procrastinated long enough, Dr. Peterson would forget about me and the offer would slip away. Then I panicked, thinking that might really happen.

Graduate school turned out to be a breeze. The cutthroat competition for grades disappeared and the professor's expectations were different. I was graded on initiative rather than how I ranked among others. Because of this slight shift in attitude, my grade point average shot up. To help me with expenses, the university gave me a part-time job as a lab instructor, which was plain fun. I taught undergraduates how to trap small mammals and make study skins. We took field trips to look at habitat features, identify birds and animals in the wild, and recognize their presence from tracks, scats and vocalizations. Sometimes we got sidetracked and went mushroom hunting.

It appeared the university needed my trapping skills more than I needed their degree, or so I told myself. After several meetings with academic advisors, my mission was established: I was to look for rabies by way of serum antibody titers in striped skunks, raccoons and opossums in a 26,200-acre study area, or a two-mile radius, roughly, of Ames. The study had all kinds of requirements and procedures that involved blood sampling and tagging and examining relationships between all the species and their habitats. To me, though, it sounded like a giant trapline and I couldn't wait to get started.

I took a series of rabies shots to raise my immunity in case I was exposed to the virus. If I really got it, I'd need more shots, but these were good for now. My professors gave me a set of metal live-traps so I could get started immediately, but the traps were inadequate. Maybe they'd never seen an Iowa raccoon. The mesh wire traps might hold a large skunk or a docile opossum, but raccoons in Iowa were fat, clever hogs and they would soon learn to reach through and take the bait. Not only that, their big butts would keep the door from shutting. I described this in great detail to my advisors. They shook their heads. I had to build my own.

I bought one-inch welded wire, split two-by-four boards lengthwise, cut out sheet metal for the doors and treadles. Once assembled, these parts formed a two-foot-long trap with a guillotine-style door and a safety catch. I got Dean Stromer involved, a farm kid five years my junior who could fix anything or make it himself. We cranked out more than 30 traps in his dad's machine shed.

Farmers and homeowners around Ames enthusiastically let me onto their properties. They were eager to find out exactly how many of the varmints were eating their pet food or shitting on the hay in their barns. My daily trap checks were cheap entertainment as folks watched me handle the animals. Sometimes my Garner buddies came down and helped me.

A German farmer, Otto Reinholz, told me about Theodore, a colossal raccoon he named after Teddy Roosevelt. The mysterious behemoth had been raiding Reinholz' sweet corn patch every year for the past 20 years. It was bigger, meaner and more elusive than any other raccoon that walked the earth. Its feet were the size of a child's, he said, and it killed nearly every dog that went after it.

"You can try to catch him," Reinholz, in his bib overalls, wagged his finger at me, "but those traps are too small and he is ver-ry smart."

I caught 10 raccoons but none was Theodore, Reinholz said. That raccoon is probably still out there somewhere.

I had no idea how to immobilize an animal and keep it alive at the same time. I'd always done all my immobilizing with my rifle. A vet student in one of my classes offered to help. After some testing, we determined that Ketamine was the drug of choice – in fact, it was a miracle. It was simple, safe and of short duration for what I needed, and I never had one animal die of complications. Whenever I needed more, I simply opened the drawer at the veterinary school and grabbed a handful of the little vials, stuffing them into my field kit. When I was through with them, I tossed the vials in the garbage. Now Ketamine is a Schedule 3 drug, known on the street as Special K, or the date-rape drug. Agencies that use it for animal immobilization must keep the drug under lock and key, and every drop must be accounted for with a pile of paperwork.

Once injected, an animal's eyes began to twitch, saliva oozed from its mouth, and in about five minutes, it was helpless. An hour after I tagged it and measured it and took a blood sample, the animal was ready to walk away, with only a little wobbling. All of my research animals were released alive so I could study their population size, home range, territory, dispersal, habitat preference, and the relationships between individuals. All of it was to find out more about how rabies, a usually fatal virus that attacks the brain, was transmitted in the wild. Rabies prevalence isn't the problem it used to be, although the Centers for Disease Control and Prevention estimate that the cost of rabies prevention in the United States currently exceeds $300 million a year.

My study, *An Ecological and Serological Survey of Rabies in Some Central Iowa Mammals*, took place because the number of rabid wild animals was increasing in the United States in the 1960s. Striped skunks, several species of bats, raccoons and gray foxes were emerging as hosts of the disease in various parts of the country. Striped skunks in Iowa had the highest occurrence. Rabies wasn't being transmitted to dogs much because of strictly enforced vaccine programs, but its prevalence in wild animal populations left researchers scratching their heads about how it was spreading.

In June 1971, I set live traps throughout the Ames city limits, but concentrated them near streams in the city's parks. My first capture was a large, male raccoon. It chewed up my trap, snarling and blowing snot, but it didn't escape. For the first time in my life, I departed from what I knew: Instead of killing it, I poked the raccoon with a loaded syringe and waited about 10 minutes before I dared stick my hand in the trap. Then I pulled the limp animal onto a tarp and began my data-gathering routine, one I would repeat more than 550 times in the next two years.

Veterinary instructors taught me to collect blood directly from an animal's heart using a syringe. A cardiac puncture seemed bizarre, but it worked. I clipped two ear tags on my victims with information about my project and a set of consecutive numbers, took various measurements, and estimated the raccoon's age based on tooth wear, body size and weight. Then I sat back and waited again while the raccoon regained its senses. It made me smile to think I could do all this without having to shoot the poor old bugger. The raccoon became rigid, then slowly lifted his head. His eyes were twitching and he looked drunk. After nearly an hour, he gathered his feet under him and staggered into the brush. I decided to change my protocol and leave all drugged animals in their traps until they recovered. They were too vulnerable rambling around town in such a state.

Once word of my project got around, I started getting tips on places to trap. By late summer, I'd caught 27 striped skunks, four spotted skunks, 90 raccoons, 30 opossums, and a lot of house cats. The skunks were the toughest customers. My traps were concealed in the weeds and I could usually tell by looking from afar if I'd caught something, because the guillotine door would be down. Identifying exactly what was in the trap was difficult though. Skunks had a habit of hiding once they were caught, pulling grass and leaves through the wire and huddling in the wad of greenery.

I was questioned daily by students and faculty: "Have you been sprayed yet?" Their faces were annoyingly eager. I'd made a six-foot long syringe pole out of electrical conduit pipe so I could keep far away from the business end of the skunk, but I still had to figure a way to get the trap away from the capture site and out in the open with the skunk still in it so I could use my new invention. My solution was to gently lay a towel over the trap. Deprived of visual stimulus, the skunk calmed down. I moved in, sticking the syringe pole under the towel just enough to see what I was doing. I let it sniff the needle, then moved slowly toward its rear – and doink! A drugged skunk.

My daily challenge wasn't handling the animals; it was finding bait for my traps. I bought canned sardines and tuna at first, but that got too expensive. Then I started using scraps from home, but keeping bait in 30 traps required volume.

I was checking out a skunk report at Charco's Kentucky Fried Chicken when it came to me: the dumpster. I explained my plight to the manager and he gave me permission to pick through the garbage. Soon I was coming up with piles of old chicken scraps. I went there daily and conducted my searches in full view of the restaurant. It didn't take long before the manager came out and asked that I not do this during business hours; I was grossing out the customers. I protested, standing waist-deep in greasy boxes and rubbery wads of the Colonel's secret recipe.

"The garbage truck will haul it all away!" I whined.

He thought for a moment. "Come back after we close tonight."

I returned at 10 o'clock and followed the manager to the kitchen, where he opened the oven and emptied a tray of leftovers into a cardboard box.

"It's all going into the trash anyway," he said. "If you come at closing time, I can give you the day's leftovers. Just stay out of my garbage bin, okay?"

I liked this arrangement, and to celebrate my ingenuity, ate a couple of drumsticks on the way home.

In spring 1972, my study got even more complicated. I needed to put live, pregnant skunks in captivity so that I could examine blood titers that were passed from mother to offspring to see if rabies could be passed that way. I knew that skunks would be breeding in March and I planned to capture them by surprise attack. I rigged my car with spotlighting gear, plugging an airplane landing light into the dashboard. I'd rounded up a couple of undergraduates from my labs to drive my station wagon slowly down the road while I rode on the hood, shining the spotlight into the weeds. When we got hungry, we ate whatever fried chicken I didn't use for bait.

When I found a skunk, I handed the spotlight to my partners, jumped off the hood and ran it down with my dip net. I pinned it to the ground, put my foot on its tail so it couldn't spray me, and injected it with Ketamine. I put the females in traps and released the males after I took a blood sample and outfitted them with ear tags.

It wasn't hard to entice undergrads to help me. Besides the day-old fried chicken, they liked the adventure, and presumably, the learning. We extracted raccoons from the walls and attics of expensive homes. I even caught an albino raccoon once. All of the students had a story to tell when I was done with them.

A couple of veterinarians at the university showed me how to remove the scent glands from the skunks. They performed the delicate procedure on the tailgate of a truck. I watched, ready to move fast, marveling as one of them made an incision and slowly extracted a miniature balloon filled with yellow stink. It was like watching a bomb expert dismantling a dangerous device. But halfway through the next extraction, the bomb went off.

We stumbled away from the tailgate, rubbing our eyes and coughing. But like any dignified doctor, the veterinarians choked less than the rest of us. They walked around in circles a few times, wiped themselves off and proceeded without further incident. I was glad I hadn't done it; I could have accomplished the same thing by hitting a skunk with a stick. I later modified the technique by partially extracting each anal gland, using a needle and syringe to remove the liquid. I never had one of the little yellow bombs go off. Skunk stink makes excellent attractant for fox trapping.

The university's veterinary school owned a farm south of Ames where students raised mice for certain experiments. Aptly, they named it the mouse house. I got permission to keep my pregnant skunks in the basement and built plywood pens for them. Each pen contained a water bowl, a nest box, straw bedding, and one mother skunk. I fed them dry dog food.

In a span of 12 days that May, 45 skunks were born. I periodically drew blood from their little veins. The rest of the time, they frolicked and were accustomed to my visits. I regularly brought them eggs, purely for the entertainment of seeing how a skunk opens one: It pulls the egg under its chest with its front feet, then hikes it like a football against a hard surface – like the side of a plywood pen – whereupon the egg shatters and is eagerly consumed.

My work in the basement resulted in the mouse house being renamed the skunk house. The mouse people were being driven away, holding their noses, as my nearly adult skunks began playing rougher, eventually discovering their talent for producing a horrible smell. But there was another reason for the stench: I'd been keeping a plastic bottle of extracted skunk essence on a south-facing, sunny windowsill outside; the bottle had some kind of photochemical meltdown, oozing its contents down the siding. I may have unwittingly discovered a natural way to break down plastic.

I became so notorious for my unconventional rabies study that *The Des Moines Register* sent a reporter with me on my trapline. A few days later, a picture and story appeared in the paper's outdoor section, showing me setting a trap in a river bottom.

In the spring of 1973, I got up in front of the Iowa Academy of Science at Grinnell College and presented my thesis. It was the last thing I had to do before I was given the fancy sheet of paper that said I had a master's degree. I was excited as hell about everything I'd been doing the past two years, so much so that presenting what I'd discovered through my studies seemed like no effort at all. Bob Phillips, the former Iowa Conservation Commission furbearer biologist, came to hear my presentation. I eyed him in the audience and was already thinking about the conversation I wanted to have with him afterward.

Phillips had taken a job with the Bureau of Sport Fisheries and Wildlife, now the U.S. Fish and Wildlife Service, in Missoula, Montana. I remembered reading once about government trappers, but I didn't think there were such jobs in modern times. George Good had quit farming in Iowa practically overnight to take a government trapper job in Montana. He'd had enough. But folks at the Department of the Interior's predator control branch in Montana were looking for a man like Good, so he went there.

"George is setting some pretty good fox records in his district," Phillips told me. I was so envious I'd forgotten that I was done with my graduate studies and should be celebrating my accomplishment. I wanted to be a government trapper. I didn't know if the job was prestigious or if it would even pay the bills. I was just in love with the idea.

"You couldn't find me a job like that, could you?" I said.

I'd done what they wanted, and now I had my job back, working for Dick Bishop counting ducks and doing bird surveys. But I'd noticed that since I'd moved back to Garner with all my degrees, I'd been stuck in a back room at the Iowa Conservation Commission, digging through volumes of waterfowl harvest data in fat, bound books. I was trying to cross-reference the bands on dead ducks with migration corridors in the Mississippi Flyway.

Bishop stopped and leaned in with his coffee cup.

"Isn't this fun? This is what you degree-toting biologists get to do," he smiled.

No, I hated it. But I did it anyway. I was sure there were some duck studies or another fox project coming down the line. I kept reminding myself that I'd gotten my ticket punched like I was supposed to. Now I would sit back and let the rest of my life at the Iowa Conservation Commission unfold as it should.

It had been four days since I defended my thesis when Bob Phillips called.

"I've got something I think you might find interesting."

The Montana Department of Livestock, he explained, was looking for somebody to do a rabies project in the northeast part of the state; there was an outbreak of the disease in striped skunks.

I thought he was kidding.

"Who do I talk to?" I waited for him to bust out laughing, telling me it was just a joke.

I'd never been to Montana and wasn't even sure where it was on a map. We talked some more. He wasn't kidding. I sat down and fired off an application letter to Montana, telling the livestock department that I was their man. I dropped George Good and Bob Phillips into the letter – just for good measure.

Only after I mailed it did I consider what I'd do if I got the job. My wife, Pam, was four months pregnant and having difficulty. She'd already had one miscarriage. There was no way she could leave her doctor's care.

But we could worry about that later.

It took less than a week for my letter to make its way from Iowa to Montana, and for Ken Seyler at the Department of Livestock to read it, think about it, and call to offer me the job.

Montana. It was like considering Mars or Bangladesh. My head swam with all the magazine ads I'd seen as a kid – government hunters wearing hats and badges and sleeping under the stars. The job description was for a state trapper, but they really needed a professional biologist.

"I'm gonna need an answer. We've gotta get this thing going on June 4."

Seyler was one of several managers at the state's brands-enforcement division. He had my letter in front of him, he said. I could hear it crinkle as he talked. June 4 was four days away.

I wanted to blurt out *yes*, but held back. It was Thursday. I should think about it for a day, I told him.

On Friday, I thought about it. It was only a temporary job, but maybe it would turn into something else. On Saturday, I moved my pregnant wife in with her parents, and on Sunday morning, I was on a train headed west. In my pocket, was a piece of paper with the name of the Montana town where I was supposed to get off – Wolf Point. It sounded ominous. I wondered what it meant.

MONTANA

I was 23, and had never been on a train. I'd never really been anywhere, except to the Black Hills with my parents when I was 10. Several old ladies wondered why they couldn't see any animals from their seats in the upper deck. I sat between them and pointed out deer and antelope all the way across the Dakotas. When daylight ran out, I crawled into my tiny cabin and slept. Soon, it was getting light again. The green countryside had turned dust-colored. The sky was as open and as bright as I'd ever seen it. I had no idea where I was because I hadn't taken time to look at a map.

The train slowed and everyone grabbed their bags. When it stopped, they scattered across the sunny platform at Wolf Point. I blinked and shaded my eyes. I was distressed that there weren't horses tied up and cowboys wearing six-shooters. A sign nearby said something about the town's name coming from the number of wolves in the area back in the 1870s. Wolf hunters, or "wolfers" killed so many one winter that the carcasses were piled high next to the river, awaiting spring and the fur trade boats, it claimed. I didn't know there were still places like this. I read it again, then picked up my bag and moved on.

I'd described myself as probably the tallest guy on the train so Seyler could spot me. I must have done a good job because a man approached me and shook my hand.

"Well, the first thing you get is a long ride to Plentywood to get yourself settled," Seyler said as we walked to his truck.

I wanted to talk and get acquainted while we drove, but I was distracted by the landscape. It was agriculture country, but not the way I knew it. Wheat and barley strips, vast hay fields and rolling grassland met an intense blue sky. Green license plates claimed Montana was Big Sky Country, and I could see why. Wetlands and prairie potholes were everywhere, and in my head, I fast-forwarded to the weekend and perhaps some duck hunting. Everything was stretched out horizontally. There were few cars and fewer roads.

My job, Seyler summarized, would be trapping and poisoning skunks according to a certain protocol. His plan was to draw a three-mile radius on a map and have me kill every skunk inside of it. He thought using eggs injected with strychnine would be easiest, but I could trap or shoot them if I wanted.

We drove on and I couldn't believe the tremendous distances between farms. It was even farther between towns. In Iowa, I could count on seeing a town every six miles. I wondered how I would keep my gas tank full and how I would ever find a skunk in all this vastness.

Plentywood was small and stark and mean looking. It was practically in Canada. I wondered about its name. Maybe it was an instruction rather than a description: Bring plenty of wood; there are few trees.

Our first stop was the Sheridan County Courthouse, which I was told would be my office when I needed it. I wasn't sure what that meant. Seyler walked me around and introduced me to the sheriff and other guys with badges. The people seemed friendly, not crazy as I half-expected, though I saw a teenage girl stuff a pinch of Copenhagen in her lip.

"Some of 'em start pretty young around here," Seyler said.

Downstairs, living in a jail cell, was Jim Stevens. He was to be my trapping partner for the summer. He had a beard twice the size of his head and a skunk-skin hat.

"Hey, a fellow Iowegian!" Stevens shoved his hand into mine.

Stevens came to Helena in the early 1960s because the trapping was good, but never got around to leaving. He baled hay and did other odd jobs on farms, drove a Wells Fargo truck and did a little firefighting, but his love was trapping.

"Uh, Jim, you really need to move out of the jail. Maybe you guys can find a place in town to live," Seyler said. The sheriff nodded his agreement. But the jail was so cheap, Stevens argued.

The motel room we rented was small quarters, which meant I got to know Stevens real fast. In the evenings, he'd pluck on a guitar and sing to himself, trailing off because he didn't know all the words. He had a couple of small watercolors in progress, but never quite finished them. When we went out for supper in his red Datsun pickup with its broken bench seat, we had to give it a jump because the battery was always dead.

On our first official workday, Stevens and I sat at a table in a Sheridan café with Seyler, who scribbled skunk eradication plans on a napkin, wadded it up and started again. Stevens and I ate our hamburgers and glanced at each other. After lunch, Seyler marched us to the drugstore where he announced in a loud voice his plan to commandeer the pharmacy scales to measure strychnine powder for toxic eggs. The pharmacist cleared his throat and motioned for Seyler to lean in a little closer, away from customers who were eyeing us uneasily. The pharmacist declined to cooperate with this idea. Seyler reminded the pharmacist that this was state business. The pharmacist reminded Seyler where the door was. Stevens and I followed Seyler out.

Instead, we measured the poison ourselves, working in a small room in the courthouse. Over the next few days, we injected 100 eggs. Then, we stamped them with red ink: POISON.

The county dug around and found an old Willys Jeep for me to use. It had a frayed canvas top and no doors. Stevens drove his dead Datsun. We moved out of the motel and into a huge house owned by the local furniture store. It had 13 beds.

We needed one last thing before we could finally get started on our skunk-killing mission; Stevens was squirming about it before we got to the doctor's office.

"I heard about this guy who got rabies shots and they had to shove really long needles three different times right into his gut," I said, opening the waiting room door for Stevens. His color drained and he sank into a chair. The nurses behind their sliding window looked over their glasses at us.

"I'm not doing it! I get light-headed around needles!" Stevens hid his face in his hands.

I was enjoying this, and added a few more horrible details about blood and screaming and that some people need to be held down for the shots. A nurse called his name and he sprang out of the chair. Then he gathered his senses and shuffled behind her into a white room where she got right to it with a needle no bigger than a bee's stinger. It made nothing more than a little red spot on his belly.

A normal day went like this: I awoke at dawn, ate breakfast and was ready to leave the house. Jim awoke, panicked and yelled for me not to leave yet. Then he stumbled downstairs and out to his Datsun. I pushed him down the street, where he popped the clutch and made a circle back to the house. He parked it, still running, and went back inside.

"How can you keep doing this?" I asked. I was sick of pushing the thing.

"I just leave it on an incline or leave it running," he said, slurping his cereal out of the bowl.

He hadn't gotten around to buying a battery yet.

By following Seyler's map, I met farmers and ranchers whose property rolled along for miles. It was June, and the air was mild. Though I was far from anything familiar, I loved this new place. It was wide and open and seemed slightly dangerous.

I knocked on doors and explained my quest. Most folks wanted skunks dead regardless of the reason and signed on with glee. Try not to kill our pets, they said. I put poison eggs inside of road culverts, under abandoned buildings and in rock piles. Nearby I posted a sign: *Strychnine Poison. Stay Away.* Many of the culverts had porcupines and fox pups living in them. I didn't want to kill those. I avoided putting eggs where I might kill non-target species easily. My attitude wasn't common; a good government trapper kills every predator he can.

Once a skunk eats a poisoned egg, it only lives a few minutes. In fact, most of the skunks I found died within inches or feet of their final meals. I could smell them before I ever found them because as they died they emptied their stink in one massive spasm. Some eggs disappeared, and I suspected raccoons and foxes were eating them or carrying them off. The culprit sometimes left yolky footprints.

Stevens and I spread hundreds of eggs around the county. We cut the heads off of dead skunks, put them in plastic bags and stuck them in the freezer at Dr. Robert Kane's vet clinic to await shipping to the state lab. Tests showed there was more rabies lurking in the skunk population than we thought. We drew more circles on maps and expanded our operation into neighboring counties, becoming accidental celebrities in the process.

On Friday nights, when Stevens and I went for a beer at the Golden Wheel, the band stopped and struck up "Dead Skunk in the Middle of the Road." We also drew the affections of several young ladies who were always in the bar. They just wanted to dance. But soon the girls were regularly dropping by our house with the 13 beds, and this, of course, got back to Ken Seyler. He paid us a visit one afternoon, and in our absence, the girls greeted him and told him to make himself at home.

It was barely light one morning when the dishes rattled in the sink. Stevens could never be up that early, but I sank back into my pillow believing my roommate had finally quit being a lazy-ass and was up doing the dishes. Then I heard the stairs creak; a third person was in the house. I bolted upright, and at the same time, my bedroom door flew open. Stevens leapt in.

"Why didn't you tell me Debbie was here?" he whispered.

"I didn't know she was out there," I whispered back. "I thought it was you!"

Debbie was a gal from the bar who had a terrible crush on Jim.

"I come down the goddamn steps with my pee-pee half hanging outta my shorts and find out she's down in the kitchen," Stevens muttered.

He hid until Debbie left.

I was so sick of helping him push-start his truck that when I ran across a way to get back at Stevens I couldn't pass it up. I was going out the door one morning as two Jehovah's Witnesses were about to knock. Would I like to talk about Jesus? I'd love to, I told the ladies, but I was late for work.

"You go on in and make yourselves comfortable and wait for my roommate." I held the door open for them and hollered up the stairs for Stevens. "I think he'd be very interested."

I left, and some moments later, Stevens ambled downstairs, unawares, again in his undies. He was mad at me for a week.

There was a period of time when we were finding people in our house – women especially – at all hours. One night, I was awakened at 3 a.m. when my bedroom light came on. Sitting up and reaching for my glasses, I saw the barmaid from the Golden Wheel, standing in the doorway in a lavender mini-skirt.

"What are you doing out at this hour?" I croaked, pulling the covers around me.

"Well, I just got off work and I was on my way home," she started. "I wanted to stop by and tell you what a nice guy you are."

I wondered why we never thought of locking the front door. I brought out my hand and showed her my wedding ring. She shrugged and sat on the end of the bed. I had talked to her many times at the Golden Wheel. She showed me the cigarette burns on her arms – administered by an old boyfriend. She was a tall, blond, lovely girl and I offered her some advice that seemed obvious: Stay away from that asshole. Now she was in my bedroom. I wasn't sure what the plan was, but at least I was awake now. We talked and soon it was light. I bought her breakfast in town and she went home. I wasn't sure what it was all about, but she seemed happier when she said goodbye.

By summer's end, Stevens and I had put out 4,000 strychnine eggs and killed 264 skunks, 17 foxes, seven badgers, two raccoons, three dogs, one cat and a weasel. I was given the task of writing a final report, and Stevens was sent back to Helena to work as a state trapper killing coyotes.

I was invited to present our findings at the Sixth Vertebrate Pest Conference the following year. The Department of Livestock bought me a plane ticket to Anaheim, California, where my name appeared on the program. I was scheduled to give a 20-minute talk.

I sat through every presentation on the first day, but didn't understand a damn thing. Scientists used big words and showed pie charts and statistics on a big screen. Half the people who stepped to the microphone had unintelligible accents. I nodded off. The next day, I slipped out of a boring session and discovered that most of the attendees were yucking it up in the lobby.

My presentation had no pie charts, only photos of the Montana countryside, close-ups of poison eggs and dead skunks, a picture of Jim Stevens and me, and a couple of slides summarizing our results. My palms were sweaty when I stepped away and I wasn't sure I had made any sense, but the audience applauded so I must have done something right. Later in the lobby, I was surprised to have so many people say they found my presentation interesting. Don Balser, chief of predator damage for the U.S. Bureau of Sport Fisheries and Wildlife's research center in Denver, and whose name I recognized from my studies at Iowa State, shook my hand and went on at length about my study. He was a legend. I couldn't believe he was talking to me.

I circulated through the crowd reading name tags. I was relieved to find that going to conferences seemed to be more about getting together to talk than sitting in dim rooms looking at pie charts. Problems were solved over drinks in the bar, and young, aspiring biologists were offered job possibilities.

The evening before I flew home, I took a walk. Hundreds of teenagers were out on the street, most of them hurrying past me. Dozens of motorcycle cops moved in the same direction. There must be a riot, I thought, and followed them around the corner to the Anaheim Convention Center. There

I paused, and two young men asked if I was a cop. I was wearing blue jeans and a button-down shirt, which must have screamed nerd. The guys and gals around me wore psychedelic clothes, including some that were see-through. When the boys were convinced that I wasn't a cop, they offered to sell me a ticket to the Joni Mitchell concert that was about to start. They wanted five dollars. I couldn't go wrong for that price. I was swept along to the entrance where cops were frisking everybody and pulling beer cans and other contraband from strange places on the teenagers.

Once inside, I was overwhelmed by chaos and incense. I couldn't find my assigned seat and asked an usher to show me. Pushing and shoving our way through thousands of stoned teenagers, the usher pointed to a lonely seat dwarfed by the smelly throngs. Pop cans and beer bottles littered the floor, and I stepped on each one as I worked my way over and sat. I was trying to recall if I'd ever felt more out of place. A heavy metal band screeched and thumped on the stage, presumably the opener. Then I felt a tap on my shoulder and a guy with a headband took a drag from a joint and handed it to me. Holy crap. I didn't smoke, but it would be my luck to get caught holding this thing. I tried to be cool and took it, handing it to the guy on my right. He took a drag and down the row it went. Finally, Joni Mitchell strutted onstage and things improved. Between Joni and the beer, whiskey, and half-naked girls, I got a lot for my five bucks.

I was finally headed back to Montana, which the California experience had made me miss more than ever. I waited in the airport, reading a newspaper and occasionally looking up to check the progress of a bunch of Hare Krishnas, who were playing drums and bugging people for money. They eventually spotted me and gyrated their way over. A female disciple in orange drapes wondered if I wanted to buy a book about The Beatles.

"No thank you," I said, and kept reading.

She didn't leave. Instead she sat down next to me.

"What do you do, if I might ask?" She leaned well into my personal space. The rest of them surrounded us, banging their bongos. I sighed, folded the newspaper in half and looked at her.

"I'm a skunk trapper from Montana."

Her mouth opened a little, then snapped shut. Then she stood and walked away, her drapes fluttering. Her accomplices had a hard time keeping up with her as she disappeared down the terminal.

When I got home, Ken Seyler broke the news that by fall I would be out of a job. I'd almost forgotten that my skunk-trapping gig was a temporary arrangement. He believed the Montana Department of Livestock would continue with the rabies program, but he couldn't say for sure. It all had to do with money.

Based on the number of foxes I saw that summer, I knew I could make a good wad of money fur trapping once I was out of a regular job with the state. But if I was going to trap in the winter, I needed a four-wheel drive. A pickup would be ideal, but was out of my financial bracket, which hovered somewhere around broke. I scoured the paper and found an ad for a 1951 Willys Jeep for $500. I'd have to borrow that kind of money. The Jeep was similar to the one I'd been driving all summer for the skunk project, but this one was aqua green and had mostly original parts, including a four-cylinder engine and a tiny gas tank. The gas gauge was busted, as was most of the instrument panel. The front wheels shimmied until I could barely hang on to the steering wheel, and it wouldn't quit until I brought it to a complete stop. Also, the heater didn't work. I loved it. I got as much fixed as I could, but nobody could replace my little gas tank, which was always empty or close to it. All I could do was carry an extra jerrycan. I took the doors off because I liked it that way, then I bought a case of spray paint, making it metallic blue with bright red rims.

Before I was off the state payroll, Seyler wanted me to get some experience working with a federal predator trapper. I knew one person who worked for that outfit and he wasn't that far from me: George Good.

Montana's Garfield and McCone counties are tough places to drive. Dotted throughout their sagebrush badlands are sinkholes and nasty roads that are impassible when wet. Clay sticks to tires the way snow picks up more snow until the wheels simply seize up, unable to turn inside their fenders. It's hot in the summer, cold in the winter, and muddy a lot of the time. A man can go for hours or most of a day without meeting another soul. Now that I know better, I realize that area could have killed me, or at least gotten me good and stuck for days on end. It was also where Good lived, west of Circle, with his family. I was sent there to reunite with my old trapping instructor after he'd put in a good word for me with the higher-ups. As a federal trapper, Good was getting to be a legend, catching hundreds of foxes and coyotes to the delight of ranchers, but the dismay of other trappers.

Good was interested in what Ken Seyler said and did because of an ongoing pissing match between the agencies. The state had the statutory authority over predator control within its borders, but usually contracted the work to the federal Animal Damage Control. My trip to see Good ruffled Seyler's feathers, even though he wanted me to spend time with a federal trapper. I found out afterward that the two men very nearly hated each other. Still, it was a chance to hang out with my old mentor while I was still on the state payroll.

We were out early each morning. Good shaded his eyes with his hat and squinted toward the hills, watching for any coyote that dared move through his district.

Since it was all about how many traps he could run in a day, Good had developed a routine. He skidded to a stop, shot any fox or coyote in his traps from the truck window, flew out of the truck like he was roping a calf, and finished resetting the trap in a cloud of dust. I got out, too, because I wanted to take his picture and lollygag, maybe talk a little trapping.

"Let's go, let's go!" he admonished me for getting out of the truck. I'd only been with my old mentor a day and he was starting to piss me off.

Coyotes killed a lot of sheep in Montana, but somehow I couldn't muster Good's wild enthusiasm for killing the little canines. I could see that ranchers not only welcomed and encouraged Good, but also considered him a hero. It was this kind of alliance that started the war between the state and the feds.

The next day was more of the same, and thinking that it might continue this way, I steered our conversations away from coyotes, asking whether he had something in mind besides me watching him trap. He did: a couple of 30-mile long scent post surveys he'd been avoiding. He smiled. It was just the thing for a college boy, he said.

The feds had coyote surveys going all over the west in the 1970s. The information gleaned from them went into a huge database that tracked coyote population trends. The locations were the same every year: 3/10 of a mile apart for 30 miles. The protocol called for laying a three-foot diameter ring on the ground and filling the center of it with fine-sifted dirt. In the center a plastic capsule was placed on a tiny peg and filled with a standard predator lure. My job was to build the survey line and check it for predator tracks every morning for three consecutive days. I couldn't kill anything that visited the posts and I had to write down all my observations on an official form.

My first observation, which I didn't write down, was that my Jeep was not made for this kind of country. I almost ran my tank dry daily. I got a flat tire, too. Good chastised me the first day he saw my Jeep.

"Get rid of that goddamn thing," he snorted. "It's gonna get you killed." He ordered me to get a pickup, but with what? I nodded and thought about my empty bank account.

I finished the survey, a quick diversion in my trip to get experience with a fed, and was ready to head back to Plentywood as a now unemployed state trapper. Before I left though, I finally met Paul Bunke when he stopped by Good's place. Bunke was Good's boss. He was a stocky, easy-going guy and Good seemed to really like him, which was odd for Good, who still seemed like he didn't like anybody. Bunke was an Animal Damage Control supervisor and pilot, flying many of his trappers when they gunned down coyotes.

Everything seemed to have calmed down with Ken Seyler, Bunke reassured me, apologizing. I squirmed. He didn't need to try and excuse my boss. Then he gave me a quick primer on the bad blood between the feds and the Montana Department of Livestock. I thought I'd better be careful of Seyler if I was going to score a permanent job – and keep it. From what I could tell, the two agencies were committed to the same purpose, but refused to get along with each other.

I thought about the agencies and their stupid turf war until I hit the outskirts of Plentywood, where the countryside changed, then I involuntarily started thinking about fox trapping. It was a frame of mind that had worn a permanent, comfortable groove in me. I'd picked up on a few things during the summer, primarily that in Montana, foxes and coyotes could be killed year round. I didn't even need a hunting license. They were classified as predators, which is to say the state considered them vermin. Therefore, these animals had no protection under state law and no restrictions on bag limits. I knocked on doors of farmers and ranchers all over the county and soon had permission to run traplines. The pelts would be getting prime soon. My timing was perfect because temperatures were falling daily, which meant thicker fur.

I had to decide: Go back to Iowa when my job ended, or continue on in Montana? Once I had this to contemplate, I realized that Pam, my mother and everything in Iowa had crossed my mind few times that summer. It was like thinking about someone else's life. I wished that I didn't have anything tying me there. Then I felt guilty. But I'd fallen in love with Montana in just a few months, and with its people, too. Some of them, I discovered, had first cousins in my hometown. They'd fed me, showed me pictures of their pioneer parents and their grandchildren, and insisted that I stay on. This place had grit. It was where Sitting Bull surrendered to the Army, and where Butch Cassidy spent a lot of time. Rustling was still a problem here. Plus, I'd never seen so many red foxes in my life. They played in fields and huddled in road culverts and ran across the road like rabbits. Farmers liked the idea of me trapping foxes. Few government guys were doing it. People I'd never met called and asked me to trap at their places. It seemed stupid, but I was going to stay in Plentywood and see if I could make some money going solo. I had no idea if the state would re-hire me later and wasn't sure I cared. I didn't have anything to lose except time; the weather was turning cold.

I was set, and sure I could make some good money on the fur market.

Then a phone call from Iowa changed everything.

The first time I held my daughter, Shadron, was Christmas 1973 – three months after she was born. She was too tiny and frail before that. She had been born prematurely, weighing only three pounds, with a birth defect of the esophagus. Her condition was compounded by pneumonia, which almost killed her. As if that weren't enough, I'd missed her birth, too. I couldn't get there fast enough.

I called my friend Ray Wang, a farmer and cattleman living outside Plentywood, and asked him to take over my trapline. I drew him a rough map and asked him to check the traps, kill the foxes, and hang them in the barn until I came home. Ray had become a good friend over the summer and he was intrigued with my trapping adventures. He'd gone with me a few times on the skunk project and now I needed this favor.

I locked up the house, jumped in my car, and began the thousand-mile drive to Iowa. I got as far as western Minnesota before I started nodding off. I found a farm lane between two cornfields and turned off the engine. I just needed a couple of hours of sleep. Sometime later, I woke with a spotlight shining in my face and a deputy tapping on my window. I told him my story and he must have thought it sounded pretty good because he said I could go back to sleep. But by then I was awake and off again. Still, I arrived after Shadron's birth. She required immediate surgery.

I prayed a lot that day while doctors and nurses whisked my daughter away and frantically searched for a surgeon. The little girl made it through the operation to reattach her esophagus, stabilized and started to gain weight, but her condition meant special care, and that meant money. The bill rang up at $10,000 and was growing daily. I had no insurance.

It would have been great to stay in Garner, but we needed money. I could make a lot of it trapping foxes in Plentywood, I told Pam. They were 30 bucks apiece on the fur market. We had long talks about it, but I'd already decided: I was going back.

I had two good weeks of trapping before the weather turned foul, raining at first, then an early snowstorm. But I'd caught 60 foxes and two coyotes. Despite blowing and drifting snow, Montana's arid climate and porous dirt made my vocation easy, although a long-line fox trapper like me should have owned hundreds of traps. I could only afford 40. I made dirt-hole sets the way George Good taught me and worked the edges of farm roads and trails where I could check my traps fast in my Jeep.

I had images in my head of hundreds of pelts hanging in my fur shed, or rather the basement of my rental house with the thirteen beds where I remained after Jim Stevens left. But I couldn't take a pelt off of an animal without my snoopy neighbor complaining to the sheriff that dead animals littered the yard.

"It's not the same pile of carcasses every day," I told the deputies who showed up to check things out.

I explained that each night I skinned my catch and threw the carcasses out in the yard, but I always hauled them away in the morning.

Clean up your act or your neighbor might press charges, the deputies told me.

My trapline wasn't without problems, either. I approached one of my sets and saw that the trap was missing but a pronounced circle in the dirt indicated I'd caught a fox. Then I saw clotted blood on the ground. Somebody killed the fox and took my trap. I looked around to see if whoever did it was dumb enough to stick around. A couple of kids were playing around the landfill. They seemed innocent, but I quizzed them until they told me about a bald guy in a yellow truck. That afternoon I found out all about the cueball. The sheriff even gave me the guy's address.

"You've got something that belongs to me and I want it back," I said when the door opened. The bald man glared at me. A crappy yellow pickup sat in the driveway.

"You took my fox trap *and* the fox that was in it. I have witnesses," I went on.

At first he said nothing. Then he got mad.

"I know who you are!" he spewed. "You're that out-of-state guy."

We argued about my presence in Plentywood and I said I had permission to be on the farms where I was trapping.

"So it's really none of your business, is it?" I said.

He reluctantly led me to a chest freezer and opened it up.

"You know which one is yours?" he asked, expecting that I didn't. There were several stiff contorted animals but only one had a dent across its foot.

"This one," I pointed. "Unless you're running a trapline, too."

He grabbed the fox, flung it at me and slammed the freezer. Then he shoved the trap at me.

In town, a few days later, a young fellow who ranched with his father near the Canadian border and helped me for a bit on the skunk project, approached me on the sidewalk.

"You better stay out of the country north of here," he said, getting a few inches from my face. "The least I'll do is kick your ass and I'll bust every one of your traps. Skunks are one thing, but foxes are somethin' else."

I figured he was crazy enough to do exactly what he said. I didn't have any reason to be up there, anyway. I reported my run-in to the sheriff who informed me that the cueball trap thief was this fellow's good buddy.

Snow kept falling and soon my trapping operation was paralyzed anyway. Roads filled with drifts and my little Jeep got stuck more often. The ground was soaked and beginning to freeze. I went to Plan B: George Good's trademark dry-manure set, which he'd taught me back in Iowa. I bought burlap sacks and scouted out abandoned barns for the old, powdery manure inside long-abandoned stalls. The snow was too deep to keep trapping on the roads so I moved my sets to windblown ridges where it wasn't accumulating. I slung the sacks of dry manure over my shoulders and walked. By now, my Jeep was almost useless.

I caught foxes on the ridges, but I earned every one. Fleas crawled into my gloves and migrated into my clothing. Worse yet, I was perpetually cold and wet. My Jeep had no heater so I was forced to put its doors back on and wear all the clothing I owned. The only good part was that my windshield never froze because it was as cold inside as outside.

I kept warm, I suppose, on adrenaline and digging and hauling sacks of manure every day. I shot pheasants and ducks for supper and made cold sandwiches out of the leftovers. A couple of weeks before Christmas, the Jeep got away from me, going sideways down a steep slope. I tried to regain control, but couldn't. Going downhill was fine, but below me was a cut bank that dropped straight off to an iced-over farm pond. I put all my weight on the brake pedal and threw it in reverse. All four wheels were turning backward, but I kept sliding forward. I had less than 40 feet to think about how thick that pond ice might be. I put it in second gear and floored it. The Jeep went airborne over the bank and landed well toward the middle of the pond, then bounced off the ice, but didn't break it. I kept it floored and went like hell toward land. I waited to hear a big crack and feel the icy water as it drowned me. But I made it across and peeled up onto the road. I didn't look back, not even in my mirror.

Not a week later, I almost killed myself again while enjoying the weather and daydreaming as I jostled across a shallow stream at Bucky Darvis's ranch. Somehow, I rolled. My Jeep was half underwater and quickly being devoured by the stream bank. I pushed the driver's door straight up and pulled myself into a standing position. Brightly wrapped Christmas presents, my rifle, my binoculars and other things that had been in the back seat were on their way down the stream. I flailed, climbing over the top of the Jeep, and started grabbing. After I'd piled my possessions on the streambank, I plodded, dripping and freezing, toward the ranch house. I met Darvis on the road in his truck. He rolled down his window, grinning and shaking his head. I guessed I didn't have to explain too much. He returned home and grabbed a tow rope from his shed.

I realized, looking closer, that the right front wheel had dropped into a natural spring where the current had undercut the bank. I was already soaked, so I waded in and hooked the rope to my bumper. Darvis hooked the other end to his pickup. His wheels churned the ground, but the Jeep didn't move.

"I don't think my truck's big enough to get 'er out, Carter."

We stood there surveying the disaster, Darvis's truck idling. He figured if he kept it up, he'd ruin my Jeep.

"Can you just make a helluva run at it?" I asked, shivering. I really didn't care what happened. I had traps to check, a rifle to clean and an engine that was going to cost a bundle.

He backed up, cranked it into low gear and took off like he was at a car race, flinging mud. The rope snapped taut, and with a violent jerk the Jeep sprang into the air, bounced once, and landed on all four wheels. As I looked it over, a grinning Bucky Darvis emerged from his truck, his chest puffed. The Jeep fired right up. All the commercials and hype about Jeeps and water were true, I marveled. All it needed was its fluids changed.

By Christmas, I had 144 foxes and 17 coyotes pelted and ready for sale. I mailed a couple of samples to Ludy Sheda, in Chelsea, Iowa, the fur buyer I'd worked for during college. Now I was on the other end of the business. Sheda moved fast and talked fast, almost stumbling over his Czech accent.

"What do you think of 'em?" I asked him over the phone.

"Ya ya ya I got them Carter," Sheda started. His sentences had no pauses or audible punctuation. He went at a conversation like a fat man gulping down dessert.

"I never seen such nice heavy fox pelts goddamn they're so pale almost yellow I'm telling you if them fox had that cherry red color like in Iowa with that heavy fur you got in Montana it'd be the best goddamn combination you could want in a fox pelt . ..."

He went on for a bit about the coyotes I'd sent him, too.

"Them are top quality Carter how many you got? I want them all."

Most buyers tell you all the things wrong with your furs: dirty, greasy, trapped too early, trapped too late, rubbed, poor color, stretched too wide, stretched too short, should have used wood stretchers instead of wire, or vice versa. Ludy Sheda was different. He was honest and fair and best of all he liked my work. Now I wanted to hear what all this exceptional fur was worth.

"I put a lot of work into these and you know I take good care of fur," I pitched. "I got a lot of bills to pay and a sick little girl so I need a good price...."

"I'll give you $32.50 per nose count for everything sight unseen straight across with no grading," Ludy cut me off. "If the furs look like the ones you sent me in the mail then that's my offer."

I was dumbfounded. That was a damn good price. Most fur buyers look at every pelt, shake it, stroke it, blow into it and look for flaws so that they can tell you it's a grade lower than you expected, which wipes the proud smile from your face. Sheda's offer was based on trust.

"You own them," I said.

"Ya ya ya, I'll see you when you get here," he said. "And get some more of them coyotes; I want a whole bunch more before spring."

It was kind of fun talking to Sheda. He was totally preoccupied with fur. When he was done on the phone, he simply hung up, not even saying goodbye.

I had a lot of work to do before I left for Iowa that Christmas, and I was still catching foxes despite the deep snow. I hadn't had any run-ins with the locals since September, but just thinking about it reminded me there was something important I needed to do.

I called the border patrol agents I'd met at the courthouse. We'd hit it off when I traded them trapping stories for ones about illegal immigrants avoiding arrest by jumping out of second-story windows. They'd checked traps with me a few times and experienced the thrill of the catch. I wanted someone to take a photo of me with all my furs and the Montana countryside as a backdrop. It was for posterity but also for insurance – in case they were stolen. I had a small fortune on my hands. A hundred and fifty fur pelts hanging in a row was a sight the men said they couldn't imagine. I picked an abandoned ranch with weathered boards and drove nails along a fence every six inches until I had one for every pelt. When I was done, I stepped back to take it all in. It was with mixed feelings that I was selling them. So much work. I stepped up and rested my arm on the fence and one of the men snapped a photo.

Iowa was technically my home because that's where my family was, but I had no intention of ever living there again. I took my furs on the train in several cardboard boxes and headed back for what I hoped would be my last Christmas in the Midwest. I was restless the second I left Montana. The West had captured my heart and I wanted my family to share it with me. Shadron would be fine, according to her doctor, and since the baby was the center of attention, Pam's mother announced that she and Pam's youngest sister, Joannie, were going to Montana, too.

But first I had some business to take care of at Ludy Sheda's.

The place was a mixture of stink that only a trapper could love: skunk essence, fox piss, muskrat and beaver glands hung in the air. The steps to Sheda's basement were greased with animal fat and hairballs. Racks of raw furs crowded each other.

Sheda was like a kid at Christmas as he slit open the cardboard box and pulled out a fox pelt by the nose. He shook it until it was fluffy and smiled.

"You got some nice fox out in Montana," Ludy said. He moved toward pencil and paper that lay on the desk, stepping over a dead opossum and kicking a skunk out of the way to get to his swivel chair. He started figuring, muttering to himself.

"How many you got?" He paused long enough to look at me.

"This load, 144 foxes and 17 coyotes. I got a few more drying out in Montana, but we'll have to deal with them later."

He kept figuring, and finally, at the bottom of the paper was a number over $5,200. We shook on it and he wrote me a check. Before I left, he gave me a quick tour of his fur sheds. Muskrat and raccoon pelts were stacked like pancakes from floor to ceiling. There were thousands of them, and hundreds more dried on racks. Skinners that he employed toiled over fleshing beams, scraping the fat from recent catches. It was familiar, Sheda's place, a tantalizing stench of sweetness and decay.

After New Years 1974, while I was visiting in Garner, I bought Monty Schlawin's Chevy Blazer. It was only two years old – the newest vehicle I'd ever owned. Schlawin had a thing about buying a new truck every couple of years. We packed the Blazer, attached a small trailer for everything else we owned, and moved for good to Montana. We arrived, tired and bleary-eyed, and I unlocked the door to the house with the 13 beds. But there was a weird noise in the basement. I flipped on the light and started down the steps. The sound became a roar. The basement was filled with three feet of water and it was still pouring in. I stared at furniture floating by, some of it upside down. To find the source, I waded in. After I was up to my waist, I realized how stupid I was. I could have been electrocuted. Around the corner, water sprayed ceiling-high from the broken water main. I didn't know whether to get mad, cuss, call the fire department, or turn around and go back to Iowa. I just stood there in the cold water. I remembered my fox pelts and hoped they weren't ruined. I sloshed toward a dark corner and saw they were still hanging, but the tips of their tails were touching the water. A fox carcass that I'd left unfinished on the basement steps bobbed past me and floated into the shadows.

I got my wits back and slogged upstairs to call my landlord, who didn't seem too worried and told me to check the basement drain. Maybe it was plugged with one of those rubber balls that keep sewer gas out of the house. I poked and jabbed at the floor with a broom handle. The water was getting deeper. I kept at it and suddenly a blue ball popped to the surface. Only in Plentywood could water pipes freeze because the furnace oil froze.

By spring, I'd doubled my catch and shipped 160 more pelts to Ludy. In turn, I got another fat check. Fur prices held steady and I'd averaged about $2,000 a month. I'd made substantial payments to the hospital and the bank, and only nearly killed myself on my trapline one more time.

Bob Phillips had kept in touch all winter. He'd been hounding his agency, the U.S. Fish and Wildlife Service, to create a temporary biologist job in Miles City, in east central Montana, and apparently had me in mind. But Ken Seyler wanted me for a pencil-pusher job with the state. He'd decided that my college degrees would make me the perfect guy to research and write predator control documents.

Sitting around an office and writing sounded like almost as much fun as being stabbed. I wanted a trapping job, but I decided to take whichever came up first. I still had a lot of bills – and now a family.

Seyler got to me first and had me staying in Helena for days at a time to review the state's predator control practices. Read everything, then write an environmental impact statement about the entire program, he said.

I didn't want to sound dumb, but what the hell was that? Before I could ask, he led me down the hall of the livestock building near the Helena capitol to a room jammed with documents and pointed at the bound volumes sagging on their shelves.

"Start here and do a lot of reading," he said. "You can worry about the writing later."

He left and I approached the reports, picking out a few that looked interesting. Then someone knocked.

"Hi there! Would you like to join us for coffee and doughnuts?" A woman from across the hall leaned in. I figured I better not turn down a doughnut and put down the report about predator-killing and state budgets. I joined the group and shook hands with a few people. The party didn't seem like it would end, so I dismissed myself.

I found the spot where I left off, flipped the pages back and settled into a chair. I'd gotten through a few paragraphs when Seyler poked his head in the door.

"You wanna go shoot some hoops at the Y? We have a team."

I went and I played, then we ate lunch, and finally I was back at my reading.

The reports were intriguing. They showed that the more predators the federal trappers killed, the more money the state program received to keep doing the same thing. I was beginning to understand how the system worked when I heard a voice.

"We're having a coffee break, do you want to come over?" It was yet another woman from an office somewhere.

I didn't want to be rude, so I said yes and joined another group of office workers, shaking more hands. This coffee break also seemed endless, so I excused myself and went back to the reports. An hour later, Seyler stuck his head in and said he was going home. It was four o'clock, and since he was my ride, I had to leave, too.

This went on daily for weeks. I had to get out of there. I called Bob Phillips to see if something could possibly work out in Miles City.

While I waited for Phillips to wade through federal red tape and get me that trapping job, I kept commuting to Helena, staying at Seyler's house during the week. I read hundreds of reports and letters that outlined clearly the relationships between the state's executive offices, the federal Animal Damage Control and the Montana Department of Livestock. I discovered, only because it was in black-and-white in front of me, that predator control was an entirely cultural and political activity, and was such an integral part of life in the state that it almost warranted its own branch of government. The latest documents indicated that Seyler was a recent employee with aspirations of amassing his own crew of biologists. I thought about the warnings from George Good and his boss, Paul Bunke. I wondered if it was like this at all the agencies.

As far as I could see, my college training was a curse. Because of it, I'd been pegged as some kind of administrator. Jim Stevens, in the meantime, was put on the rabies project again and other federal trappers stayed busy with their number one task: killing coyotes. I absorbed a few more reports, then resigned without having written a single word of the state's environmental impact statement. Bob Phillips had come through just in time.

As a federal "bio-tech" for the U.S. Fish and Wildlife Service, I'd make $8,000 a year. It was a little less than the state paid, but was a lot more promising. Pam and I loaded up a trailer again and I said goodbye to all the farmers and ranchers and other characters I'd met. I was going to miss Plentywood. A season of potentially fantastic fur trapping went down the tubes, too, but I reckoned it was time to move on.

In contrast to the rental in Plentywood, Phillips found us a modern house that sat between two others at the Miles City National Fish Hatchery on the south edge of town. Our neighbors worked at the hatchery.

I liked Phillips, not just because he was a fellow Iowan, but for his mild manner. He never got excited about anything. I was eager to do a first-rate job for him. Once Pam and I got settled, Phillips drove over from Missoula to start me on the species survey. The project extended from the Tongue River to Colstrip, and we drove the area looking things over. Federal and state agencies were jockeying to generate the most data with studies that measured the potential effects of coal mining on nature in that area. My job was to find out what kind of non-game species were around, including raptors, coyotes, foxes, bobcats and other smaller carnivores like badgers, skunks and raccoons. He also wanted me to do bird and rabbit surveys. It was an ambitious order.

We formed a plan. Phillips took me to Forsyth to meet with other feds at the Bureau of Land Management. A bunch of biologists had set up a command post in a motel and I was astonished that so many of them could be working on basically the same thing. We wandered the hallways and Phillips ran in to a few people that he knew, but when he asked what they were studying, they were suddenly like school kids during a test, covering their papers so no one could peek at their answers.

Along with everything else on my list, Phillips wanted me to focus on prairie falcons, so I drove the countryside looking for sandstone pillars and outcroppings. I introduced myself to ranchers around Colstrip and asked if I could survey their properties where they mingled with federal and state lands. In this way, I ran across a cowboy named Wally McCrae who owned a 30,000-acre ranch along Rosebud Creek. He asked me in for a cup of coffee and talked under his giant mustache about his days on the range and how horse wrecks had broken nearly all of his bones. He was held together with metal pins.

"So what critter are *you* studying?" He sipped his coffee.

I was focusing on prairie falcons, but tossed out a list of other critters I expected to find.

"Seems like every time we kick over a cow pie there's another biologist under there." His wife appeared and refilled my cup.

McCrae had had a gutful of biologists knocking on his door asking for permission to study this or that on his ranch. He'd been visited by bug-ologists, grass-ologists, bird-ologists, and a host of other -ologists looking for whatever crawled, flew or stood still.

"Do you have a business card?" He asked, opening a small box on the kitchen table. It was crammed with the names and phone numbers of -ologists.

"No I don't. Look, I'm sorry for bothering you. I'm sure I can get my survey done without having to put you through any more of this," I said. On behalf of all the biologists that had knocked on his door, I was embarrassed.

"Aw, you can look around if you want," he said. "You know, you're not like the others. You don't treat me like I'm some illiterate rancher."

We talked more about the alphabet soup of agencies who wanted access to his land.

"They don't know that I have a degree in zoology or that I studied chemistry. I still know a few big words from my college days," he chuckled. "I like to throw out one or two just to see the looks on their faces."

I didn't see much of McCrae after that. He ended up being pretty busy as a famous cowboy poet. Maybe he made up some good ones about biologists.

My next stop was the Diamond Ranch on Rosebud Creek. It was a place that still had a road carved by George Custer and the 7th Cavalry. I spotted a buckaroo leaning on a post in front of the house. He was unshaven, wore a filthy Stetson and had a huge wad of tobacco in his lip. He launched a string of brown juice from his mouth, then started toward me as I pulled in.

"Carter Niemeyer," I said, putting my hand out the window. We talked for a bit about the roads and the weather. I gave him a couple of details about why I was there, careful not to sound like I was expecting something. I'd learned that this was the approach to take in these parts, as well as taking care not to get to the point too quickly, or talk too much or too fast.

His name was Bob Scalese and he looked like one of Custer's troops. He talked with the reserved drawl that a man gets from living far enough out that he doesn't often meet a stranger. Scalese looked me up and down. I figured Montanans got a kick out of sizing me up, especially when they learned I was an Iowa flatlander, and a greenhorn, too. He listened to me explain myself, spitting a couple more times. Scalese said he was just the ranch foreman, so he couldn't give me permission to be there. I got the feeling he was personally interested in what I was doing though, and hadn't been approached by a dozen others about the same thing.

"Come back next week and I'll show you around," he promised. I took it to mean I had a good chance of getting to do my study.

When I returned, Scalese looked like he was still wearing the same clothes. He said he'd done the asking for me and I could be on the ranch anytime. Then he climbed in my truck and took me on a detailed tour of the place. It took the better part of the day.

Scalese was born and raised in the Sweet Grass hills near the Canadian border. His family raised cattle, sheep and horses, but he'd learned roping and trick riding, too. Over the course of the summer, we became great friends.

On one of my many visits, he was on his horse, sorting cattle between two pastures. He saw me and trotted over. Would I stand guard at the corral gate while he chased in an escaped range cow? Sure, why not. Scalese went after the cow, which was wild and refused to be driven, so he threw a lariat around the cow's neck and wrapped his end around the saddle horn. There was apparently more than one way to get a cow to go where you wanted. Scalese and his smart horse towed the slobbering, bellowing cow toward the corral. When he got her through the gate, I pulled it shut and stepped up on a rail.

"Niemeyer, slip that rope off her neck for me." Scalese hollered. He and his horse faced the crabby cow. I looked at this situation and swallowed.

"Go on, get in there," he ordered.

I stepped into the corral and gingerly walked between the two animals. I took hold of the slack in the rope and cautiously moved toward the drooling cow. I'd completed maybe three steps when she lowered her head and charged. I ran like hell, with the cow grunting and blowing snot right behind me. I dodged to the side, but she made the turn and kept coming. Around the corral I ran. I figured if the cow didn't get me, the rope would.

"Goddammit, Niemeyer, quit running in circles and get outta there!" Scalese yelled as I leaped onto a fence rail.

He chuckled and shook some slack into the rope. With a few maneuvers, it was off the cow's neck.

"You know, Bob," I said, catching my breath, "you and me ought to team up as wranglers."

He leaned forward in his saddle. "Niemeyer, you wouldn't make a pimple on the ass of a cowboy."

I convinced Bob Phillips that if I did wildlife surveys around Colstrip we'd just be duplicating what everyone else was doing. I talked him into looking at other areas slated for coal development along the Tongue River directly south of Miles City. As a result, Bob changed his research goals to include a bobcat home-range study. A wealthy banker in Miles City who owned a tremendous amount of land along the Tongue River let me conduct my surveys on his property. His place was a natural, checkerboarded as it was with federal and state lands. By late summer, I had a reason to be setting traps.

Catching bobcats was different from catching fox and coyotes. I made sets using a hanging attractant for eye-appeal – like a bird feather or tin foil that flashed in the sun. I used bobcat urine, feces and catnip to lead them in by their noses to the traps that I'd concealed in the dirt. Like George Good taught me, it was the same principle for all predators. This style of set made fox and coyotes cautious about approaching and prevented non-target species from getting snapped in the traps.

I caught my first bobcat that summer, a big male that weighed 25 pounds and growled like a lion. It sat quietly in the trap until I approached, then ran in circles trying to climb anything it could sink its claws into.

I'd used Ketamine to knock down raccoons at Iowa State, but bobcats were another story. When I injected the animal using a homemade syringe pole, I was nervous. Cats are more sensitive to everything. Its eyes began to twitch and dilate immediately, then its face went blank. I fitted it with a radio collar and checked the signal, then checked it again. It was the first time I'd placed a radio collar on an animal and I was anxious about doing things right. I liked the way the cat's foot conformed to the trap jaws. Its paw flattened out and there were no obvious injuries. I was checking my traps every 24 hours, which minimized the amount of time for serious injuries to occur. I was sure it hadn't fought hard until it saw me. Not fighting, I'd learned, was good for the health of an animal's foot.

I wasn't comfortable leaving the bobcat in the brush to recover. Something could kill it when it was in that drugged state. I gathered it up and hauled it home in a portable cage and put it in my basement for the night. Before sunrise the next morning, I loaded the recovered and now growling cat into my truck and released it where I'd caught it. In three huge bounds, the spotted cat was gone. I turned on my receiver and smiled at the regular ping of a collar that works like it's supposed to.

I often sneaked up on the bobcats I'd collared to see what they were doing, walking within a few yards of them as they slept, curled up in a dry wash and hidden by dense stands of sagebrush. When snow began to fall, I tracked the cats and saw them hunting and choosing shelter. They unwittingly showed me everything I needed to know in order to trap them.

By early winter, I had captured a dozen bobcats, but needed a better way to follow all of them. Paul Bunke got hired to fly my study area, with me wedged into the backseat of his Super Cub, my head rubbing on its ceiling. Bunke showed me how airplanes made it easy to kill coyotes, flying down next to one as it ran wildly. I wasn't sure about all this airplane business. I didn't see the point in killing from the air and leaving carcasses lying around. It was a waste of beautiful fur. I decided to keep my ideas to myself; I was still new. I'd keep on getting varmints my way, even if it took longer and meant more work.

If it weren't for Don Helms, my neighbor who worked at the hatchery in Miles City, I would have never met and fallen in love with a huge meat grinder.

Helms spent the winters guiding deer hunters, but he was intrigued – maybe obsessed – with the idea of trapping. He'd never done it and asked a million questions one day while he gave me a tour of the hatchery. We moseyed around and that's when I saw it: a giant electric meat grinder shoved in a corner. It had five fan belts. Helms said they used it make food for the fish. I had used an axe to chop up meat for my lure recipes, but had graduated to a hand grinder clamped to a workbench.

"Man, could I make some mean coyote bait with that thing," I said. Helms looked at me.

"What do you mean?"

I didn't hear him. I was staring longingly at the grinder.

"So what would you grind in it?" Helms tried again.

"Prairie dogs," I said. They were all over the place and made great bait. Coyotes loved them. "Or beaver or horse or cat, maybe."

I went on for a while on the topic of predator bait. I'd become an expert on it and found the whole topic fascinating. I assumed that other people did, too. Government trappers usually make their own lures and baits not just because they're cheaper (and trappers are cheapskates), but because they want to find out what exactly draws a certain predator. When predators learn that certain smells mean they might get their toes pinched in a trap, that bait is no longer effective. Therefore it's common for trappers to try new ingredients or combinations of them – and to share few of their recipes.

Helms was excited that I was excited and suggested we leave immediately and go find some prairie dogs to grind. Within a couple of days, we'd shot a freezer-full of the little rodents.

We picked a weekend when employees – and his boss – were sure to be gone and pulled the grinder away from the wall. I'd been thawing the prairie dogs in anticipation of the occasion and we spent awhile gutting the little guys so that the meat didn't get tainted. Helms plugged in the grinder and pushed a big red button. The ominous machine whirred to life, flywheels and gears spinning.

I peered into the gaping mouth at the top of the grinder where a human arm or maybe a leg could fit. Helms nodded. The roar of the grinder made it impossible to communicate any other way. I put a five-gallon bucket under the spout, picked a prairie dog out of the pile and, hesitating for a moment, let it hover over the hungry grinder's mouth. Then, I let go and the machine gulped it out of my hand. In less than a second, red paste shot 20 feet across the room and splatted on the door. Curls of meat and hair paused before dropping to the floor.

"Oops," I said. "I think we forgot the deflector."

M y surveys were getting close to ending and so were my paychecks. Bob Phillips was doing everything he could to get me a full-time job. I had a high Civil Service score, but couldn't get to the top of the list because I wasn't a veteran. While I waited, winter arrived. Snow followed by clear skies made the government-sponsored business of coyote-killing easier. I'd studied predator control some in college. In the west, coyotes killed sheep more than any other predator. The government came to the rescue, killing as many coyotes as possible to ensure ranchers had an easier time of things.

I saw the Animal Damage Control airplane flying from time to time. The gunners had started picking up all of their kills because a winter coyote pelt was bringing good money on the fur market. I wanted in on this. I really wanted to be a government trapper, even though I wasn't sure about hunting from an airplane. It seemed like unfair chase. Still, I stopped by their warehouse intent on getting better acquainted – and seeing what kind of tally the gunners had.

Two or three guys worked inside the tiny building peeling coyotes. They'd hung the animals by one back leg from the rafters, and the roof shook and wobbled with every yank of the carcass. We talked a little, but that only got me so far. I didn't know them, but they were about to know me a little better. I rolled up my sleeves, took out my knife, and began skinning.

Waiting on a full-time government position was a waste of time, I started thinking. Maybe I should go into the fur business, where prices kept climbing and the money would be easy. Ludy Sheda was willing to front me some start-up money and I daydreamed about moving back to Plentywood. It was an exciting idea, but a counterproductive one after the misery I'd put myself through to get two wildlife degrees.

By taking a job with the feds, I'd burned my bridge with the state Department of Livestock. The relationship between the two agencies was akin to two brats in a sandbox. Still, the feds weren't helping much, hiring me and laying me off and making decisions about my future employment at the speed of frozen molasses. I had had enough right about the time Paul Bunke and George Good got wind of a problem near Dillon, where golden eagles were killing lambs. They put my name in the ear of Norton Miner, the federal Animal Damage Control director in Montana. Not long after that, I was moving my family to Dillon.

Ranchers Joe Helle, his father-in-law, Pete Rebish, and Pete's brother, George, had been losing lambs to golden eagles for several years on their private ranches as well as on land they leased yearly from the Bureau of Land Management. In 1974 alone, the eagles killed and ate $38,000 worth of lambs. Helle and the Rebishes had finally had enough. They couldn't just shoot the giant predatory birds, even though private property was involved. Several federal laws protected eagles; if Helle and his family were caught, the fines would be staggering.

But something had to give. Law enforcement agents from the U.S. Fish and Wildlife Service visited the ranch and confirmed that the dead, picked-over lambs had indeed been killed by golden eagles. In response, Helle demanded a permit from the Service to kill the birds, but the agency and the powerful wildlife laws it wielded stood in the way. Helle agreed to stop pressing for a kill-permit if the agency agreed to move the eagles. Animal Damage Control trappers made a run at catching the birds to move them, but only got three. Their business was killing, not capturing, they said. This was where I came in.

It took a high-powered meeting of 12 U.S. Fish and Wildlife Service officials one week to come up with a plan and the paperwork that went with it. The eagles would be trapped and moved, starting in April 1975. It had been a year since lambs were killed, but everyone involved expected the birds to be back.

For the most part, this was new ground. I was picked as the trapper. I thought it sounded like a dream job, even though I was probably going to wreck my Blazer doing it. The feds said they couldn't spring for a truck.

I'd hardly moved to Dillon when Norton Miner called and told me to keep my mouth shut about the project.

"I don't want a bunch of people out here protesting and screwing everything up," he said. "I'm hiring somebody to help you, but that's it. Keep it quiet."

But everyone in the wildlife business already knew about it. John Craighead, Bart O'Gara, Vince Yannone and Erwin Boeker – all raptor or wildlife experts – traveled to Dillon to talk to me – and to Helle and the Rebishes – about how historic this was going to be.

Meanwhile, Miner wondered if I might know the guy he just hired as my assistant: Red Schlichting. Yeah, I knew him. He'd volunteered to help with my rabies project in Iowa.

April, as it turned out, was the perfect time to start the project. We'd be ready when lambing started and eagles would be drawn to the birthing grounds. Eagles didn't usually bother adult sheep.

I got a crash-course on how to trap an eagle, using jackrabbits we'd been shooting expressly for this purpose. Two rubber padded coyote traps connected with six feet of chain were set so that, if an eagle was caught in one trap, the other trap served as a weighted drag and the eagle couldn't become airborne. I set a total of four coyote traps on each side of a rabbit or lamb carcass, which was staked and wired to the ground so the giant bird couldn't take off with it. I concealed the traps with sifted dirt and dried grass, and tried to make it more appealing to an eagle by plucking a bit of the rabbit's fur and scattering it.

It looked convincing, but in case there was any doubt, I perched real eagles nearby as decoys. The birds were unreleasable cripples – grounded by a shot-off wing or other injury. They were permanent residents at rehabilitation centers throughout the country, but on this project they'd been put to work convincing lamb-eating eagles to land at the trap sites.

Schlichting and I had a final lesson before we were turned loose on the project: caring for the handicapped eagles. Mike Lockhart, a trapper from Texas, was our teacher. We met in Dillon, where he pulled into the parking lot of the Royal Inn motel with a huge eagle sitting in the passenger's seat. Lockhart explained that the bird was his pet and that they'd been everywhere together doing exhibitions. The eagle climbed on his hand without much coaxing and hopped onto his arm. He carried it up to one of the rooms and we followed. Once in the door, Lockhart laid the eagle on its back on the floor and covered its head with a cloth. It stayed put, its legs folded up and feet in the air. He went on talking, as though this was a normal situation. I tried to pay attention but kept eyeing the bird.

"How long will it lay there like that?" I asked.

"Oh, it won't move unless you make a sudden noise or move real fast."

He continued with whatever he'd been talking about, but I was focused on the eagle. The fluffy feathers around its rear-end were unfurling like a blooming flower.

"Why is it doing that?" I pointed.

"Oh shit!" Lockhart yelled, and the eagle did just that. A two-foot long streak of white crap shot out of the reclining bird, settling into the green shag carpet.

Lockhart sighed and bent down with a motel towel to scrub the rug. I learned some new wildlife lingo that day: Eagles don't shit. They "slice."

A few days later, we were ready to give trapping a try, so Lockhart put his eagle near the spot we'd set up. We drove about a mile away where we could sit and watch through binoculars. After an hour or two, I doubted whether this decoy thing would work. I scoured the skies for eagles. Nothing. Lockhart was full of stories about his life around eagles and I got distracted to the point where I wasn't even watching the trap site anymore. I could feel discouragement building and wondered if this project was going to be more hype than action.

Another hour passed, and we were still leaning over the hood of Lockhart's pickup, talking and occasionally looking through our binoculars. The decoy was a tiny dot on the snow, but I also saw a bigger dot next to it. I commented on it.

"Then we've got an eagle in a trap!" Lockhart announced.

We drove closer and I was sure that the blob on the snow wasn't an eagle. But then I could see that the eagle didn't look right from a distance because it was lying on its breast with both wings open, the trap chain stretched behind it. It had one foot caught in a trap. The trap at the other end was just heavy enough to keep the bird from flying away. We followed Lockhart through the snow. I was eager to see how he'd handle a trapped eagle, but it lay helpless and didn't offer a struggle. Lockhart reached first for the eagle's free leg, then its trapped one. It was caught by its rear toe, or hallux. Once he had control of its legs, he stepped on the trap's springs and released the huge bird. In one motion, he lifted it and it closed its wings. He kept control of its legs, mindful of an eagle's primary weapon: its powerful feet and sharp talons. He was careful not to crimp its elegant tail feathers. I was curious whether the padded trap had hurt it, but other than a slight depression on its toe, the eagle appeared unscathed. It was a sub-adult male – less than fully mature. We put a permanent, riveted aluminum band on it with the number 599-11501. All of the band information was archived at the North American Bird Banding Laboratory in Patuxent, Maryland, so that its place of initial capture was recorded.

The decoy eagle was oblivious to all this activity. Lockhart explained that decoys were effective because they attracted food thieves – other eagles. The incoming eagle wouldn't attack the one already on the ground, just try and intimidate it to give up a meal. I also was surprised to learn that even the biggest golden eagle weighs no more than 15 pounds.

Lockhart stayed a few days, then Schlichting and I were on our own. We worked independently to cover more ground, setting trap lines on ridge tops of the Rock Creek drainage and eventually in the Sweetwater Basin. I set out from my house every morning before dawn because some of the best trapping was at sunrise. Soon, weather was our biggest challenge. Snow drifted and blocked roads, preventing us from getting to our traplines at times. A grader operator tried to keep roads open, but even he wasn't immune to the weather and rolled his machine down an embankment when he got too close to the road's edge. We were worried about keeping our decoy eagles and captive birds from dying. They could succumb quickly to dehydration or starvation, or both, even though we tried to get to them to make sure they were watered and fed, and kept them in old log cabins that dotted the ranches. The calendar proclaimed it was spring and the ranchers turned their sheep out to graze like they always did, but the late snows made it risky. The storms, which had lasted into May, killed dozens of calves at the nearby Matador Cattle Company as well as hundreds of lambs belonging to Helle and Rebish.

We set eagle traps on the perimeter of the middle of nowhere, where two thousand sheep grazed. We checked the traps hourly from dawn until dusk, and looked in on the herders before heading back to town on 30 miles of bad dirt roads.

As we passed by, Rebish's herder stood in the doorway of the sheepwagon in his insulated coveralls, his floppy hat pulled down over his ears. He'd towed up a trailer of hay and was getting ready to feed the sheep before they bedded down for the night. His dog ran out to greet us.

"Just checking to see if you need anything," I hollered out the window.

He offered us coffee, but we declined.

"I'm gonna throw some hay out, then fix some supper and go to bed," he called back.

I waved, rolled up the window and drove on. It was spitting snow again and the failing light had a blue cast to it. Wouldn't being a sheepherder be just wonderful, I thought – freezing your ass, stoking a tiny woodstove all night, having no one to talk to. Everybody gets the idea that this kind of living would be fun.

The next morning, the road was blanketed with huge snowdrifts. We came into the open and drove toward the sheepwagon, but the usual column of smoke wasn't rising from its chimney. The herder's truck was 50 yards away, nose-first into a barbed wire fence, a drift of snow growing around it. The trailer it was pulling still had hay on it. I waited for the herder to open his door. Then the dog popped out of a snowbank near the truck. We sped up, jumped out and approached the truck.

I looked into the driver's side window, then opened the door. The herder was slumped over in the seat. Schlichting went to the passenger's side and put his hand on the man's neck, checking for a pulse. Schlichting shook his head. The herder was dressed exactly as he'd been the night before. He apparently got in his truck and died at the wheel. His feet were still on the pedals.

"He's frozen," Schlichting said.

I thought about our footprints. They might look suspicious, being the only ones.

"We oughtta just back away," I said.

We headed back to Dillon and I called the sheriff and Pete Rebish. Everyone assembled and followed us back to the sheep camp.

After a brief investigation, the herder's body was lifted out of the truck and taken to Dillon. As the Beaverhead County authorities maneuvered down the road, a mountain lion ran in front of their truck and one of the men stepped out fast enough to shoot it. They loaded the big cat under the same tarp as the herder. Joe Helle told me later that when the group reached town to unload the unfortunate cargo, he saw a pair of boots and a pair of paws sticking out.

"That old herder didn't like lions, but I bet he would've been damn proud to know that he got to ride into town like that," Helle said.

A few days after the herder's death, Rebish stopped me in town.

"I was wondering why you didn't check that herder's pockets?" he said.

"Well, Pete," I hesitated. "I don't normally search a dead man for valuables."

Rebish shook his head.

"Hmmm. It's too bad," he said, pushing back his hat. "He didn't have any family, so everything he owned went to the county. You know, he had $10,000 rolled up in his shirt pocket? I sure wish you boys could've had it instead."

The abandoned log cabins near our trapline could hold about 15 eagles before they were too crowded. I called Norton Miner about once a week and he hauled them to their new homes. The Fish and Wildlife Service wanted the birds turned loose at one of three spots: the Pawnee Grasslands in Colorado, the Seeley-Swan Valley in northwestern Montana, or near Soda Butte in Yellowstone National Park.

Winter storms finally yielded to spring, and suddenly, though snow persisted on the ground, the air temperature was more than warm. We worked early in the morning so the eagles wouldn't overheat, drawing blood from the big veins in their wings to screen for pesticides and other environmental contaminants that the birds were known to get into. Then we loaded them into individual plywood boxes and onto Miner's flatbed trailer for the long ride.

Miner usually liked to take a break before the big drive. He tipped the rear seat forward in his government truck, revealing a sparkling array of booze and mixers resting in a box.

"What'll you have, Carter?" Miner jangled the bottles and mixed himself a Bloody Mary. I hesitated, then took a beer. He slapped a hunk of elk salami on bread, smothered it with homemade hot mustard, chilies and jalapenos, then handed it to me.

The log cabins were dark inside, so I had to use a flashlight and big net to catch the birds. It was intimidating to have them flapping around in the dark. I crouched as I approached them to keep from hitting my head on the low ceiling, and I kept my arm near my face in case one tried to land on me. I waved the net evenly, trying not to injure their wings, but I needed to pin them to the floor quickly so I could get hold of their dangerous feet. One morning, I was reaching toward an eagle resting on the ground when, out of the dark, on my right, a foot closed around my hand. Its dagger-like talons sunk in. I yelled and tried to knock it away, but it wouldn't let go. Miner and Schlichting stumbled in to find me. It took both of them to pry the eagle's foot open. After the birds were loaded, I headed to town for a tetanus shot.

By mid-May, we'd caught 68 golden eagles and shipped them away from the sheep. Lambing was underway and I thought we'd done a great job. The timing couldn't have been better and my reports were confident and enthusiastic: the lambs were finally safe.

But Joe Helle disagreed. More eagles were coming, he said.

On Memorial Day weekend, Roy Carpenter, the federal trapper in Dillon, called me.

"Lodgepole, have you been up to Rock Creek lately?"

I'm six-foot-six, and the first time I met this man, he looked me up and down and pronounced me the tallest sonofabitch he'd ever seen.

"I'm gonna call you Lodgepole, because you're like a damn lodgepole pine," he said. And he did from then on. Whereas Clyde had been my nickname in Iowa, Lodgepole was what a lot of people in Montana called me. Everybody who knew Carpenter called him Carp. He had a nickname for everyone and everything. He also knew Beaverhead County intimately because he spent a good portion of each day hunting coyotes from the rear seat of a Super Cub airplane. We got along because I knew better than to cross him. Carp didn't trust supervisors. They were just out to get him, he said.

I later became his boss, but was never really able to give him an order. He tried to warn me about the higher-ups once: "Carter, you're young and you mean well, but you'll learn."

Carp had hands like Easter hams and a temper as big as his barrel chest. As a young man, he'd boxed barehanded in logging camp prizefights. He had a cauliflower nose, big brows and a deep, slow voice. Carp smoked all the time. If he didn't understand what I was telling him, or just plain didn't like it, he smoked faster, punctuating the drags with an abrupt "uh-huh" or "oooo-kay," or "so what are you saying there, Lodgepole?"

When Carp called about Rock Creek, I admitted I'd neglected the area in favor of other parts of Helle's ranch and areas where he had grazing leases.

"Well, you better get up there because there are Helle buzzards all over the goddamn place."

I went to see for myself. Carp called them Helle buzzards, but I knew what he meant. I scanned the sky and saw no eagles, but went on. Ahead, I saw what I thought were vultures circling, but as I got closer my stomach knotted: golden eagles – lots of them. More of the birds loafed on boulders and lifted into the breeze when I got closer. There was something dead nearby, judging from their behavior. I knew that when I walked over the hill to find out what it was, I was going to see newborn lambs strewn everywhere. The eagles soared no more than 50 feet over my head. I could hear the air rushing through their stiff wings.

I counted the eagles as I walked, and by the time I saw what was attracting them, I'd come up with 27. Over the rise lay a mule deer carcass. Even more eagles loafed nearby. I muttered to myself because I'd forgotten my camera. We'd already moved 70 of them and now we had this many more.

I looked at the tracks coming and going from the carcass. The deer died that morning and I concluded that no ground predators had fed on it yet, only eagles, magpies and ravens. I backtracked the deer to see what had happened. It had been bounding down the ridge when a golden eagle struck it from the side. I could see where the eagle's wings brushed the fresh snow, marking each wing beat before the two collided. The deer dropped instantly and the hungry eagles were making short work of it.

Only five miles east, were Pete Rebish's sheep, and the eagles could easily be swarming the lambing operation that was in full swing. I dreaded what I'd find, but jumped in my truck and peeled out. I should have listened to Helle.

Golden eagles sailed in tight circles over the Rock Creek lambing grounds and I was forced to slow to a crawl to keep from alarming the sleeping newborn lambs. They are known for becoming startled at movement even when only an hour or two old. The lambs tend to jump to their wobbly legs and follow the first thing they see. This is good if what they see is their mother, but many times they follow trucks and, if the driver doesn't notice, the lamb becomes lost and may die. I was in a huge hurry to see about the eagles, but had to stop frequently and let the lambs bleat to find their mothers.

I found several dead lambs. Some had died natural deaths, but eagles had killed a few. I gathered up the carcasses, giving them a cursory look to see if I could tell what exactly did them in. Dr. Bart O'Gara at the University of Montana was on deck to do the necropsies during this study and be the final word. Carp arrived and offered to help set eagle traps. I accepted, hoping Schlichting would show up soon, too. Things were going to be a lot trickier with all the sheep and lambs around. I talked to the herder and asked him to keep the sheep south of the traps. I felt panic rising in my throat. Trapping these birds was a slow process and trapping a lot of them during this kind of emergency was going to make it seem even slower. Then there was finding food for the eagles once they were captured….

Some scientific literature about golden eagles says they're solitary and seldom migrate, but my experience near Dillon, Montana, proved that it was just the opposite. Both juvenile and subadult golden eagles showed up in large numbers, obviously migrating from somewhere. It's of course easier for them to kill small animals like lambs, as well as marmots, rabbits, ground squirrels and other birds, but I have seen them kill full-grown antelope and, on the capture project, that mule deer.

Beginning that Labor Day until the end of the following June, we caught 80 more golden eagles. Food for the captives was becoming critical, as was their general welfare. It made me nervous having so many federally protected birds confined in such a small space. At one time, we had 57 in the log cabins waiting to be hauled away. Some of them refused to eat and we had trouble keeping up with the appetites of others.

Our project had other problems, too. Norton Miner wanted the Bureau of Land Management's state director to muzzle one of the agency's biologists who was vehemently opposed to eagles being trapped on public land. Meanwhile, Schlichting had been bragging up the project in town, leading local newspapers to demand a story while Miner was trying to keep things quiet.

When our project ended that summer, we'd caught and moved 149 golden eagles. It was an expensive experiment. Some of the birds died from stress before they could be moved. Others died before Miner got them to their release site. I wrote it all up, but by the time the paper reached meetings and conferences where the project's significance could be touted, only one name appeared on it: Norton Miner.

I got a promotion and was put in charge of the eagle project, which continued through 1982. One of the biggest pains was finding the right people for it. Every year, Animal Damage Control advertised its need for temporary trappers. Miner hired some of them sight unseen, and the University of Montana furnished a few students once in awhile. Every year, when eagle-trapping season came around, I was resigned that the entire summer would be one endless pain in the ass. The project became the training ground for greenhorns looking to wedge a foot in the door with the government. If nothing else, it taught me patience.

In 1976, I hired my childhood friend, Tom Hartwig, the guy who could climb any tree in town. He was still living in Garner. Hartwig's trapping partner was to be Dave Mindell, whom Miner hired over the phone. All of us agreed to meet and go over things at the Royal Inn in Dillon.

Miner and I drove together, passing a guy standing near the highway who was wearing boots so worn out that he'd fastened their soles with hog rings. "Hey, maybe that's your guy," I said as we pulled into the parking lot.

"Jesus Christ! It better not be," Miner snorted.

Miner liked his clothes pressed and even put a crease in his Wranglers. His dress-up gear included a sportcoat, a Stetson and western boots. A war veteran of the South Pacific, he was old-school in principle and behavior, and he made everyone around him believe they were an inch away from being fired – or slugged.

Hartwig waited in the lobby wearing a Stetson, his hair spilling out from under it like Wild Bill Hickok. Miner wore his Stetson, too. He stared at Hartwig's hair, then suggested we take our meeting to the motel's café. If Mindell didn't show, we'd eat without him, he said.

When the waitress brought our burgers, Miner took a bite and spit it out, telling her he wouldn't feed it to his dog and to bring him something else. Right then, the tattered guy from the highway walked in. It was Mindell. I stifled a snicker.

Miner did some stern indoctrinating, telling his new recruits that by tomorrow he wanted them looking clean-cut. We met the next morning, Hartwig and Mindell walking into the restaurant together. Hartwig's hair was barely an inch shorter. Mindell's was chopped unevenly, his bare scalp showing here and there.

Miner looked at the two and blew coffee through his nose.

"I cut it myself," Mindell announced proudly.

Miner pulled me aside after breakfast.

"Make sure they get their fuckin' hair fixed – the both of 'em!" he spewed.

Both of the trainees did their jobs adequately, but neither returned.

The next year, I was informed that our eagle trappers had been hired through the University of Montana. One of them, Al Harmata, was a Vietnam vet who lost an arm and a leg in the war. He made it clear without actually saying so that he didn't want any preferential treatment. I watched him put jesses on eagles – a sort of leather foot leash for raptors – tying knots with his teeth while he held the bird with his good hand. I also watched him replace the entire exhaust system on his truck. That was all the convincing I needed. Harmata eventually went on to earn a doctorate and become a world authority on eagles.

I arranged to let Harmata and his trapping partner, Dave Stahlecker, stay at the old Brown ranch near Blacktail Creek, about 20 miles outside Dillon. I have a picture of Harmata sitting proudly on its deck in a rocking chair, wearing a hillbilly hat and holding a shotgun.

Normally these two didn't need a lot of supervision, but one night they decided to go to town for supper. They weren't supposed to be driving the government truck when they were off the clock and they would have gotten away with it if a drunken herder hadn't t-boned them. The herder jumped out of his truck and started to run, but Harmata went after him, hobbling down the street as fast as his prosthetic leg would let him. He jumped on the herder and held him down until the cops arrived. It was this kind of thing that kept me driving back and forth between Helena and Dillon a couple of times a week, answering for my men more than I should have had to.

I always hoped, but 1978 wasn't much better. I hired tall, skinny Lon Shipe, a self-made mountain man who trapped beaver and made his own clothes from leather. He had a scruffy black beard, a sweet wife, and could live with few comforts. I scrounged around in the government warehouses and found him an old camper to live in while he worked on the eagle project. He promptly lit the pilot light in the camper's furnace and blew himself out the door. He recovered in about a week, but soon discovered that the camper was full of mice, which consumed his groceries, burrowed through his suitcase and ruined his clothes. When I paid him a visit, he smiled and told me he'd already solved the problem. He'd trapped them and made several jars of bait out of their little carcasses.

Shipe was a natural-born trapper; he just had a little bad luck now and then. The first vehicle I assigned to him was Miner's old government-issue Suburban. It caught fire and the engine melted. I arranged to get Shipe another truck only to have Carp call and tell me that Shipe had broken down 40 miles outside of Dillon. Instead of waiting for help, Shipe decided to start walking. He met a horse somewhere along the way and commandeered the animal, making a set of reins out of his shirt and tying it around the horse's neck. Shipe climbed on and the horse bucked him off. That was when Carp happened to drive by.

"Where's your shirt, Shipes?" Carp couldn't ever get the name right.

Shipe pointed off in the distance. "A goddamn horse is wearing it."

Another fellow, Gary Evans, came to the eagle project from the U.S. Forest Service, but had no trapping experience. He was paired with Shipe, and they were so busy not getting along that I thought I'd better pay them a visit to see if either of them was getting any work done. We piled into my truck and drove to the pasture above Rock Creek, where the eagles made trouble every year. We were looking things over when two coyotes darted in front of me and slipped over a rock rim and disappeared. Coyotes were public enemy number one around sheep. (I'd been trained to think this way.) I hit the gas and peeled after them. I could see them a couple hundred yards away, running down a long grassy basin. I could parallel them from above and cut them off if I got there fast.

I sped up to 50 mph and my passengers bounced all over the cab as we skimmed down the ridge road. My rifle hung behind me on the gun rack and Shipe grabbed it, knowing I'd want it in a minute. Evans gripped the door with both hands.

I caught up with the coyotes, but they made a wide circle trying to avoid the truck. I skidded to a stop and jumped out of the truck. Shipe tossed me the rifle and I jacked in a round, took careful aim and fired. One coyote dropped, but his pal kept running, disappearing over the hill. Dammit!

Later on, Evans wanted to talk. In good conscience, he simply had to report me for reckless driving and misuse of a government vehicle, he said. Also, he was going to file a few complaints about Shipe's insubordination, and once that was done, he planned to resign. I bit my tongue. Evans took his complaints to Miner and I waited for my reprimand, but Miner told me I had done nothing wrong. Chasing coyotes safely in my government pickup was totally appropriate unless I wrecked the truck doing it, he said.

"What that guy needs is a good, old fashioned spanking," Miner said, adding that he gladly accepted Evans' resignation.

Meanwhile, I wasn't done with Shipe's problems. He called me shortly before his trapping gig was up.

"Carter, what do you do when the bed of your pickup falls off?" he asked.

I couldn't imagine how this happened, but he explained that he'd been driving down a washboard road pretty fast when he glanced at the eagle boxes in the side mirror, spilling and busting in the roadway one at a time. The truck bed had been vibrating so badly that first the tailgate fell off, then each side panel fell away, leaving only the flat portion of the bed. Plywood and truck parts were strewn for three miles behind him. Despite the wear and tear on government equipment, I liked Shipe so well that I hired him to trap eagles in 1979, too. I don't think he wrecked anything that year.

Lots of trappers got their start by following in their dad's footsteps (actor Sam Elliott is an exception) and Carp's son, Dean, wanted in on the eagle trapping experience. Dean Carpenter looked a lot like his big, tough father and had eagerly learned a bit about trapping from him.

"I caught this big ugly eagle today and it's one mean s.o.b." he called me to report. "It tried to attack me. It's brown and got this big long beak and ugly head. What the hell's the deal here anyway?"

It was a bald eagle, often mistaken when young for a golden eagle. The demeanor of our national bird is about like that of a grizzly bear: cranky. I'd worked with Mike Lockhart once to get one out of a trap. When we approached it, the bird flipped on its back and threatened us with its long, razor-like talons. When we finally got its feet under control, the baldy tried to bite us and screamed incessantly. The eagle finally won when it managed to sink a talon into Lockhart's hand.

"Look at its legs, Dean. I bet there are no feathers on its legs and it has a long bill that gives its face a flat profile."

"By God, you're right," he said, as though having an epiphany. "It ain't no golden eagle, that's for sure."

"Be careful. Those damn things will take a chunk outta you." At least he'd been forewarned.

I drove down to check on Carpenter the following week. Like a good supervisor, I wanted to see if he was following procedures. While checking traps we saw a golden eagle eating on a sheep carcass, so he drove us toward the huge bird. It was so full of sheep meat it hobbled away and tried to take off, but couldn't do it. So it headed downhill to get a running start. We could catch it with a dip net if we hurried.

"Speed up, speed up!" I opened the truck door slightly. "I'm gonna jump out and get him."

Carpenter accelerated until we were next to the eagle that was now hopping across the field. At the right moment, I bailed out of the moving truck, grabbed a net out of the back, and ran after the eagle. The bird was nearly to the steep edge where it could get airborne.

I was almost ready to put the net over the eagle when Carpenter suddenly appeared beside me, running. I looked behind us. The truck was ambling along, driverless, doors open, heading toward the same slope as the rest of us.

"Holy shit!" I threw down the net and maneuvered to the driver's side. As the truck rolled by me I made a leap into the seat, using the steering wheel as a grip to keep from falling under the wheels.

I brought the truck to a stop, but Carpenter was still running after the eagle. The bird beat him to the edge and lifted off. He slogged back to the truck.

"Sorry, Carter. Guess I wasn't thinking, huh?"

I hired Jim Rost, a real trapper, away from Wisconsin, in 1981, and he came up with an ingenious way to find out if the released eagles were simply making a u-turn and coming back to the sheep grounds – and how long eagles tended to hang around once they discovered the sheep in Rock Creek.

Rost caught 25 birds that spring, and after recording data and banding them, he released 11 near the sheep and I trucked the rest to Yellowstone. Rost marked the 11 by cutting the tips out of four of their tail feathers, which created a notch that could be seen when the eagle was soaring. All 11 birds disappeared within a few days, which indicated they were not targeting the area, but migrating through it. This small experiment showed that all of the trapping and moving we'd been doing may have been unnecessary. On the other hand, the weather was good that particular spring, and because of it, the eagles weren't pressed for food – they had yet to kill a single lamb. Still, it illustrated that Animal Damage Control's original idea, killing the eagles, was flawed. We figured out that most of the birds doing the killing were year-old migrants that stopped and helped themselves to a few lambs on their way somewhere else.

By 1983, the entire concept of stopping golden eagle attacks on sheep at Rock Creek was turned on its head. The University of Montana, under the direction of Dr. Bart O'Gara, proposed scaring the eagles to get them to move and keep them away. I was given the job of developing a prototype scarecrow, so I used myself as a model, putting together two-by-fours and chicken wire and dressing the body in my old flannel shirts and holey Wranglers. Then I went to a hairdresser and bought a Styrofoam head so that my scarecrow could wear an Animal Damage Control hat. It was a hit, so I made several more. I dug holes on the ridge tops in the middle of the sheep pastures and fixed the scarecrows in place, bracing them with rocks. As a final touch, I added fluorescent orange vests and suspended pie tins from each scarecrow for a little flash and movement. Eagles avoided them and the incidence of dead lambs declined even further. O'Gara even bragged up my scarecrows in a publication or two.

"**D**on't you have a college degree?" Norton Miner asked over the phone. I was suspicious, although nothing that came out of Miner's mouth should have surprised me. The eagle project had ended for the year and I was waiting for another job to materialize.

"Yeah, I have two," I said.

"Well, how'd you like to be a district supervisor?"

The question lay there like a dead mouse.

"Uh, sure, Norton. I need a job," I hesitated. "What's a district supervisor?" I thought about Paul Bunke being a district supervisor flying his trappers around in eastern Montana, but had no idea what else he did.

Miner barked a bunch of details at me, but I didn't hear him. I was preoccupied with how he could give me a job without having me fill out a bunch of paperwork and without asking anyone. On the other hand, I didn't want the details. I needed the work and this offer must have meant that Miner liked me and was giving me a chance to move up.

Being a district supervisor, I discovered, meant I was in charge of a bunch of men that were old enough to be my dad, and that I had to keep track of everything they did in the western half of Montana. I also had to move again, this time to Helena.

I still considered myself a greenhorn and tried not to act overwhelmed at the prospect of suddenly being crowned a supervisor. I didn't know anybody in Helena, and hadn't learned a thing about the day-to-day operations of Animal Damage Control. Before I left Dillon for good, I finished the final report on the eagle project. Miner, meanwhile, wrote a letter to the crusty bunch I'd be supervising, telling them to go easy on me until I had my feet on the ground.

I took a bus from Dillon to Lewistown, Montana, to pick up my first official government truck. I was finally done using my poor old Blazer, which I'd beaten up pretty bad in the mud and snow over the past couple of years. I'd spent several hundred dollars that I didn't have getting one thing fixed, then another, none of which the feds offered to cover. I smiled the whole way from Lewistown to the Animal Damage Control headquarters in Billings for my official indoctrination. I was burning their gas in their truck and had a government credit card for expenses. I finally felt like I was making some headway.

After I met a few people and shook a few hands, Miner escorted me to his office and pointed to a chair. He plopped down behind his desk and leaned back, observing me.

"Carter," he began, "you need to broaden your shoulders and callous your ass because I'm going to be all over you like stink on shit."

Maybe he hadn't noticed that this had been the case since I'd met him. Miner was nothing short of a human hand-grenade.

"We've got a lot of good men working for us in Montana, and some of them have been at it a long time," he continued. "If you ride along with those old boys and you see them dig a hole two feet deep and put their trap in it upside down, I don't want you to say one goddamn word or question why they're doing it because they know the business better than you and they've got their reasons."

I nodded and hoped what I thought of him wasn't apparent on my face. Once Miner had set me straight, he sent me down the hall to fill out a bunch of paperwork, then gave me a stack of books about policy and how to be a supervisor. Read these, he ordered. He arranged to have my new truck outfitted with a two-way radio, a topper for the pickup bed and a new set of all-weather tires. The ladies who worked in the office showed me how to fill out forms and gave me a new credit card just for gas. The rest of my basic equipment included an 8x8 teepee, a 12-gauge shotgun and ammunition, an electronic siren for howling up coyotes, traps, and a few wooden stretching boards. I had a whole set of papers that were included in my field gear, too: landowner agreement forms so that we could do predator control on private ranches, field itineraries to document daily work, predator damage report forms to document livestock loss, and an array of colorful signs warning people about our traps, snares, or toxicants that could be dangerous or deadly.

In the mid 1970s, about three million beef cows and calves and 675,000 sheep and lambs munched on private and public rangeland in Montana. The predators that routinely killed livestock included coyotes, domestic dogs, black and grizzly bears, mountain lions, bobcats, red foxes and golden eagles. Coyotes were the worst offenders, according to Animal Damage Control.

Every once in awhile, beginning in 1978, I'd get a call from someone in northwestern Montana saying they saw a wolf. But there weren't wolves anymore – at least I didn't think there could be. There wasn't any proof to go with the sightings, anyway. The government had extinguished the last one of those livestock-killers in Montana by the 1950s. It must have been a coyote.

I wasn't worried about wolves. I had plenty of other real distractions. It was my job to grease the wheels of Animals Damage Control in western Montana. Norton Miner made it sound simple: Keep the ranchers happy and my trappers willing and able to kill as many predators as possible.

I joined the federal predator control business just as a wave of environmentalism was sweeping the country. The new mindset forced changes to old laws, sheltering rare plants, animals, birds and insects with mammoth protections that Animal Damage Control couldn't ignore, no matter how much it wanted to. The federal agency was, in fact, turned upside down. There was now a thing called the Endangered Species Act, passed by Congress and signed into law by President Nixon in 1973. Gone were the days of government hunters shooting grizzlies caught in bone-cruncher traps and throwing them down defunct mineshafts to get rid of the carcasses. The now-rare bears must be caught by foot snare to reduce injury. On top of that, the grizzlies would be moved, not killed. The old standby poisons, including strychnine, 1080, and thallium sulphate, highly effective at killing predators as well as everything else that fed on the meat down to magpies and other scavengers, had been banned in 1972. Believing that predators could not be controlled the old-fashioned way by trapping problem animals, Animal Damage Control successfully lobbied Congress for a full-time federal aerial hunting program in the West to make up for the loss of poisons. It was an easy, if expensive, way to kill large numbers of coyotes, especially.

I read with morbid fascination that, prior to my employment, Animal Damage Control had been putting out more than 2,000 1080 bait stations in Montana every fall, winter and spring to kill coyotes. Throughout the state, about 100,000 pounds of horsemeat was injected with 1080 every year and placed at these stations, resulting in 18,000 to 20,000 dead coyotes annually. The reports said that trappers picked up the uneaten meat each spring and destroyed it.

Then there was strychnine. Trappers in Montana put out 50,000 to 60,000 tablets yearly to kill coyotes. Before it was banned, tons – literally – of grain treated with 1080 (strychnine and zinc phosphide) was spread over public and private lands to kill various rodents, including ground squirrels, prairie dogs, meadow mice, pocket gophers and porcupines. I couldn't imagine how any birds or other animals could be alive after an assault of that magnitude. Even more unbelievable was that the federal campaign against predators was going on in every western state. The figures on the pages in front of me represented a fraction of the all the poison used in the United States. The programs that made it all possible were, for the most part, financed by taxpayers.

Standing in the middle of scenic meadows in Montana are four-inch diameter poles about 10 feet tall. Their tops were once bright orange, but the paint has faded over time. The first time I saw a pole like this, I couldn't imagine what it was for, so I asked the trapper I was with. It was a 1080 bait station, he said. A pole like that stands in the center of every township in Montana. It marks the spot where, every year, chunks of horseflesh were injected with poison and dumped. In the spring, dead coyotes would litter the area.

Because I'd been appointed a supervisor, I needed to know everything I could about what my trappers were allowed to kill and how they were allowed to go about it. Shooting (on the ground and from aircraft), trapping, foot and neck snaring, gas cartridges, 1080 collars and M-44's containing sodium cyanide were allowed. Poison grain could be used to kill certain animals, such as pocket gophers and ground squirrels, on private and public land to protect grain and crop fields as well as seedling trees on reforestation projects. I rationalized that predator control must be less barbaric these days. Still, I couldn't imagine learning about all of this stuff. Killing predators was a full-time operation.

I had to take a course on how to operate an M-44, a device that shot cyanide into the mouths of coyotes and foxes. I took training courses for certification on anything that contained poison. I also had to take a course to become a certified aerial gunner.

Every government trapper was authorized to carry a rifle, shotgun and handgun in his truck. Using any of them to kill problem predators was encouraged. Many trappers used dogs and predator calls to kill coyotes, luring them into the open where they could be shot. To Animal Damage Control, aerial hunting and the concept of preventative control meant killing every coyote in sight, no matter how far from livestock it was. Killing from the air had been gaining popularity over the more difficult and time-consuming task of trapping.

While the state retained statutory authority over predator control, Montana hired the federal Animal Damage Control to do the actual work. Norton Miner told me to get on the stick and meet with every county commissioner in western Montana to negotiate predator control fees. Without them, I had no budget. The counties and the livestock within their borders were what made the predator programs tick.

The trappers that were suddenly under my supervision weren't excited to have a 28-year-old boss, especially one that had been to college. The men were ornery and bullheaded and many of them were war veterans. I could have just called them up and introduced myself, but I decided to drive out to meet each one in person. It seemed like the respectful thing to do.

I liked them and even got to where I trusted them, but I learned fast that they didn't like the idea that a youngster from Iowa was in charge. George Good told me when I moved to Montana that I'd be wise to put my books away and forget all that college bullshit. Once I met the men I'd be supervising, I understood what he meant. Most of them got as far as high school, but took a dim view of the educated. Miner had a bachelor's degree in wildlife management, but it was almost unheard of for someone with more than that to knock at Animal Damage Control's door.

When I showed up at the trappers' homes, they were all nice to me, but I could tell that they were waiting for me to show that I was just a pencil-pusher. Their wives cooked for me and I met their kids and grandkids as well as their hounds and mules and horses. Each man showed me his "trapper's shed" where he kept everything from bait and stretching boards to horse tack and camping gear. We made small talk and I slipped in a few things I knew about trapping. They weren't sure what to make of me after awhile.

A trapper's place was easy to spot from the roadway: His government truck was parked in the front yard, and a shovel and a jack stuck up in the truck bed among toolboxes, buckets and maybe a 3-wheeler. Scattered around the house were outdated, butt-sprung snowmobiles, kennels, horse trailers and campers. Rusty traps hung from fences and shed walls. Firewood was stacked everywhere. Whether the trapper used them or not, government-sponsored hound dogs barked and yowled in their pens until the trapper finally yelled for them to shutup, goddammit.

I discovered that manipulation was the best way to deal with these men. I knew I couldn't just come out and give them orders. Instead, I made things worth their while or convinced them that my idea was really theirs.

Charlo, Montana, was where my predecessor had stored everything relevant to Animal Damage Control's western Montana district, in a government warehouse on the Ninepipe National Wildlife Refuge. I had no idea where to find this place, so I called trapper Jerry Lewis in Florence and asked him to go with me. Lewis was one of the younger men in my district. He was an Air Force veteran and had the world's most perfect poker face. He liked to give me horrible news, then wait until I looked good and distressed before chuckling, "Aw, I was only shittin' ya." He did it to ranchers, too, telling them he just saw a bunch of their sheep lying in a pasture dead. They never learned to disbelieve whatever Lewis said.

We found the warehouse. It was nothing more than a building with broken windows and bullet holes in the ceiling. I pulled out the inventory list Miner had given me, and Lewis and I began searching. We found a few boxes of maps, broken chain saw parts, a demolished Bombardier snowmobile and a military-issue camper designed to fit in a pickup bed. The camper was full of straw and sheep shit. I checked my list against the stuff in front of me and couldn't find anything that matched except the broken snowmobile and the camper. (Animal Damage Control obtained a lot of surplus goods from Malmstrom Air Force Base in Great Falls. Since the feds got first dibs on everything the military was getting rid of, I visited regularly in the years to come, signing in on the clipboard and scrounging everything I could get my hands on.)

A refuge employee found us rooting around in the building and shook his head, offering to show me what he knew about the warehouse. I'm warning you, he said, it's a mess.

Into the side of the refuge's big grain bin, which stood next to the warehouse, someone had created a softball-sized hole using a metal rod, letting feed spill all over the ground. I looked at the hole and wondered how much the bin cost. We walked next door to the house. Maybe some of the inventory was in there. Among other useless things, I found six inches of dog shit in the basement.

I called Miner, expecting him to tell me to call the sheriff. Instead, he let the situation go with some rapid-fire expletives and told me to salvage whatever I could and junk the rest. I was dumbfounded, but I did what he said. I wondered if I should get used to this kind of thing.

I found more remnants of the Animal Damage Control practices from days gone by: fat stainless steel hypodermic syringes used to inject 1080 into horse flesh during the poisoning years, trap parts, snare cables used to capture bears, and clamps used to set old bear traps. Handbooks from the 1950s that described the duties of a government hunter were stacked on a shelf alongside maps of old ground squirrel poisoning sites. A huge anvil and a vise sat in one corner of the room. A 50-gallon barrel of seal oil for making lure leaned cockeyed and ready to collapse against the outside wall. I pointed to a device that looked like a one-row metal corn planter. It had been there a while and weeds grew through it. Lewis told me it was a burrow builder used to deposit poison peanuts or grain to kill pocket gophers.

We hauled the camper to the landfill and took the rest of the stuff to Lewis's place and stowed it in his barn.

I found our small family a place to live in Helena: a double-wide mobile home. It was cheap and sat next to two others just like it on a farm about five miles northeast of town. Pam's mother and sister had moved back to Iowa once Shadron healed, so a mobile home was fine for a couple with a young daughter. I signed up for an option to buy it and paid 50 dollars a month to rent the dirt it sat on. Shortly after we were settled, our son, Jason, was born. Thankfully, he was a healthy kid and went straight to growing up fast.

Shadron loved animals, but Jason wasn't so sure about them. His sister made every orphaned animal I brought home into a pet, even sleeping on the deck with coyote pups – all of them together under a blanket. Jason distrusted the animals' motives and tried to keep his distance. One coyote, wanting to play, chased Jason around the kiddy pool in the front yard and latched onto the kid's diaper, yanking it right off of him. A chicken scared him nearly to death by following him into a fence corner and staring at him. Jason took to skateboarding instead and later, ironically, bull riding.

Our new landlords were Bill and Myrna Summers. I met Bill for the first time when he was unloading a dead elk from his truck in the middle of the night. Several hunters were involved and a small crowd struggled to drag the elk to the Summers' red barn. I watched this circus from the top of the driveway, slowly meandering over to get a better look.

Bill Summers had done a little of everything in life. He was an ex-Marine, farmer, pesticide applicator, volunteer fire chief, carpenter, and collector of junk. In the fall, he was a guide and outfitter for non-resident hunters, usually from Wisconsin. In the summer, he farmed as more of a pastime than a job. He owned 30 acres and, among other animals, a huge sow named Pigley.

I needed a warehouse in my new capacity as district supervisor. Summers offered to build one on his property, if the feds would rent it. Or perhaps I'd be interested in the building that was already there. He took me around back and showed me a collapsed plywood building that looked like a tornado had ripped through it. Summers opened the door and we tried to step in, but there wasn't room for both of us. Every conceivable household item known to man was entangled in a kind of trash-art sculpture in the middle of the floor: A four-man rubber raft was woven between pots and pans, rope, wire, appliances and furniture. Summers said that somewhere underneath all this crap was a coin collection that had gotten spilled. He planned on looking for it someday.

"Pigley did this," he said apologetically. "She was looking for a place to have her piglets and broke in here." He kicked at some of the junk. "She made a pretty good nest, don't ya think?"

I would have made sausage out of Pigley, but Summers acted like this was part of everyday life.

Norton Miner agreed to let Summers build a warehouse. Because it needed to happen fast, I spent most of my time for several months helping sift through the mess that Pigley made. We tore down the old building and chewed up the foundation with a tractor. Then we built it back up in the same place. When it was finished, it even had a bathroom. I set up the vise and anvil from the Charlo warehouse. It was almost the only serviceable item I'd found.

Soon supplies began to roll in and the shelves in my new warehouse were stocked with new Victor 3N coyote traps, cases of 12-gauge shotgun shells for aerial gunning, and cable for snare construction. I ordered a deep-freeze to store animal carcasses and bait components. My pride and joy, however, was a brand-new IBM Selectric typewriter. It was a revolutionary breakthrough in technology for me compared to the manual typewriters I'd been using. Once I was done with my reports, however, there was no way to make copies. I spent a thousand dimes over the years making copies at the library.

I aspired early on to spend a lot of time with my men. Because of that, I got to know a lot of the ranchers and farmers in western Montana. I couldn't think of a better way to be in charge of the unruly bunch, especially since they didn't look for reasons to listen to me.

The simplest way to know whether one of my trappers was doing his job wasn't to read his itinerary, which he was required to fill out and mail to me every Friday, but to tally up the complaints I received from ranches and farms. A trapper who killed a couple of coyotes that were killing sheep meant more than a trapper who killed a hundred coyotes without solving a problem. I took a lot of poking and jabbing from other supervisors about this, but I didn't care. I wanted meaningful results, not just a lot of dead animals.

The trappers' itineraries, which were copied to the state director, showed what they'd been doing to earn their pay. It showed their hours, mileage and destinations, and was supposed to contain a short narrative of whom they visited, what they did. But the most critical section, as far as the state director was concerned, was *Animals Taken* and the corresponding number, species and method of killing. This was the entire reason for Animal Damage Control's existence; the state director wanted to see big numbers, particularly of target varmints like coyotes and fox. Managers also wanted details: whether the animal was shot, trapped, snared, poisoned, aerial gunned, released, or relocated. Animals were identified as target or non-target, government talk for "intentionally killed" and "accidentally killed." A non-target animal in a trap was supposed to be released if it was alive and not seriously injured, and it was supposed to be noted on the trapper's weekly itinerary. A lot of the men didn't report non-targets, thinking they'd get in trouble or that environmentalists might find out. The fact that the agency used – and still uses – the word "take" instead of "kill" on its reports showed that it was somewhat self-conscious of its mission.

Unfortunately, field itineraries often were used to judge a trapper's efforts and abilities. The men were pressured to kill a lot of target animals each week. If they didn't, I heard about it.

"What in the hell is he doing?" the state director demanded regularly, thumping on a particular trapper's itinerary. "He hasn't killed a damn coyote in two weeks!" I heard it elsewhere in the ranks, too: My men weren't producing enough dead bodies.

But it wasn't for a single coyote to avoid capture while inflicting hundreds of dollars in losses to sheep. The trapper would burn up dozens of hours in a helicopter or an airplane and run miles of traps and snares. In the process, he would kill 30 coyotes while missing the one doing all the damage. In many instances, the cost of the aircraft and gunner far exceeded the dollar value of the livestock losses.

Nevertheless, killing coyotes was what paid the bills, and each summer, as commanded, I sat down and wrote agreements with all of the counties in my district of Montana that had interest in predator control. The counties in turn collected money from stockmen through a variety of fees on livestock, self-imposed and otherwise, which was put aside to help pay for Animal Damage Control's efforts. At the time, cattle producers were voluntarily paying 25 cents a head and sheepmen 15 cents a head. For the most part, the smaller counties couldn't generate enough money to put a dent in bills that Animal Damage Control racked up killing their coyotes, especially using aircraft. The commissioners knew the feds would foot most of the bill anyway. The volunteer taxes were more of a show than anything. It was silly to drive hundreds of miles to collect chump change from small counties. They knew it and so did I.

Still, Animal Damage Control needed each county to sign on the dotted line before it could start killing predators. I was assigned this bit of deal-cutting and I paid visits to each set of commissioners. They looked forward to this, I think, because we often got side-tracked while talking business and ended up trading hunting stories. Sometimes they reluctantly conducted other business while I was there, motioning me to stay put while they signed papers and gave a few cursory answers to others who were trying to get some work done. They dismissed the intruders quickly so that we could continue telling stories.

Trappers could not legally kill animals on private property or public grazing allotments without a signed landowner agreement. A signature meant that Animal Damage Control could hunt, trap, snare, use toxicants or aerial gun on the property, recognizing that these activities could injure or kill livestock or pets. If there was something the landowner didn't want the trapper doing, it had to be noted in writing. The agreements were good forever, or until one side or the other terminated it, and they were like gold because there were a lot of big ranches in western Montana. There were also agreements between my agency and various federal and state land management agencies to keep coyotes under control.

The final product in a successful predator control program, as far as I was concerned, was the satisfaction of those who wanted it. If everybody was reasonably happy, then we were doing our jobs. Some of the higher-ups, however, didn't agree with my philosophy.

When the sheep and cows were driven from Montana's mountains at the end of every summer, trappers went to full-time aerial assault on coyotes. Their job descriptions said "trapper," even though some didn't do much of it anymore. I used my new position to order them to salvage every animal they shot. If I could do it, they could, too. I hated seeing good fur wasted, and the value of coyote and fox pelts was skyrocketing. To prove that I wasn't a tyrant, I helped them do the skinning.

These old-timers were still sizing me up, waiting politely for me to prove that I was an egghead desk-jockey. I decided to say less and do more. I hung a dead coyote by one hind leg and made small talk while I sharpened my knife. Then I peeled the coyote from tail to nose in just under three minutes. This was all it took to knock down the walls between us. I didn't have to repeat this for everybody; I knew that those who saw me do it would be burning up the phone lines by morning. It helped build trust, but I would have done it anyway because I liked the work. It's what I was used to and I'd become good at it. By the time I left Montana, I'd skinned well over 6,000 coyotes and foxes. Most of those were animals killed by the federal government to benefit ranchers, but I also helped private hunters, private trappers and fur buyers just so I could make some extra money. I found that everybody knew how to kill, but few knew how to skin, and the higher fur prices climbed, the greater was the demand for my skills.

Since finding and killing coyotes was the primary job of my agency and I was a supervisor of men who were doing it, I supported the cause by pulling fuel trailers all over my portion of the state and parking them where the helicopter could land. The state eventually bought two more helicopters just for coyote control, flying a total of three full-time, all year. My agency owned one Super Cub airplane that was based in Billings and flown by Larry Lundquist. All that air power seemed like enough, but Animal Damage Control also hired more fixed-wings and privately-owned helicopters at various times of the year so that its gunners could do even more. Altogether, my agency spent tens of thousands of dollars and hundreds of hours annually pursuing coyotes. It was an efficient if expensive way to deal with a problem that affected few people.

But I was into it. I wasn't political in those days. I didn't question the wisdom of what I was doing or the reasons behind it. It was my job, and besides, it was fun. I spent part of every day setting up flight schedules for the men and coordinating aircraft and pilots. When the weather was good, coyotes were dead. I still think in that direction in winter when the sun shines and there's new snow on the ground. Those were the best conditions a government hunter could ask for.

A normal day for my trappers meant sitting in a helicopter. They shot coyotes, landed to retrieve the carcasses, and hauled 20 or more to me in a single load. I skinned as many as I could in the three hours it would take before the chopper returned with more. Over the years, my right shoulder got bigger than my left from the way I lifted and hung the carcasses. It wasn't unusual for the outside trays on one of the M*A*S*H-style helicopters to be heaped with dead coyotes, unable to carry one more. Soon it was too dark to fly, and we'd get up and do it again the next day – and the next.

The trappers liked this arrangement, I think, because it meant they could usually go home at night and relax. If they didn't get it done during regular work hours, they'd have to skin all the coyotes on their own time because they didn't get paid overtime to salvage the pelts. In winter, the carcasses froze before the men could get to them and had to be thawed before skinning, which often required stoking a wood stove all night just to keep the skinning shed slightly above freezing. They weren't reimbursed for firewood or anything else, not even bug spray, which they needed when they let carcasses lay around too long. Fleas started a mass migration once the carcass cooled off, often seeking whatever warm body was nearby – human or otherwise.

They usually showed up during meals. Trapper Bob Neal and his wife were eating supper one night when a flea crawled into sight on Neal's bald spot. His wife, without warning, slapped it as hard as she could and washed it down the kitchen sink. Trapper Bill Perry had one jump into his salad dressing, which made it easy to catch.

Fleas seldom bit me, although I know I'm guilty of giving rides to hundreds over the years so that they could go bite someone else. The best way to deal with them was when they were still on the coyote: put the carcass in a plastic garbage bag and fumigate it with insecticide. Or, if you already have fleas, do like trapper Steve DeMers: Spray the insecticide on your comb, then run it through your hair.

The result of all the pelt salvaging was that fur buyers bid on them at government auctions and Animal Damage Control made quite a handsome wad of money. If there were hides left over, I hauled them to Pacific Hide & Fur Depot in Great Falls and sold them there. The extremely light-colored coyotes from northern Montana were bringing more than $250. Red foxes were worth $90. Pacific Hide & Fur had a branch office in Helena and brought dozens of dead coyotes to my house for skinning. By doing this, I was on that razor-thin line between legal and illegal. My agency's policy said that trappers couldn't run private traplines, and neither could anyone in their household. The great irony was that everyone wanted coyotes dead and it didn't seem like it should matter how they got that way.

The reps for Pacific Hide & Fur thought they were torturing me when they dropped off a load of stinking, green-bellied, flea-infested coyotes. They even tipped me. I was making the same low wage as the trappers I supervised, so I welcomed whatever brought in money.

In a good year in the early 1980s, Animal Damage Control in Montana salvaged more than $90,000 in furs. The money went into a bank account managed by the private Montana Wool Growers Association to be used to maintain government-owned aircraft and buy fuel. This system was deemed above reproach because withdrawing money from the account required two signatures — that of the woolgrower secretary and of the Animal Damage Control state director.

But when fur prices peaked, the FBI blew in. Agents started rooting around, looking for proof that government trappers were on the take. My trappers and I were ordered to report — separately — to the local FBI office where we were subjected to intense interrogation. They asked two or three questions about whether we'd ever sold furs obtained on the job for private profit. We said no. And we were telling the truth. The federal agents also combed through the books of Pacific Hide & Fur to see if any government trappers were listed. Naturally, they weren't. Montana squeaked by, but several trappers in other states got caught selling bobcat pelts, which were going for more than $500 apiece.

A few years later, after I'd almost forgotten the FBI ruckus, an agent called and left me a message. I needed to contact him right away, he said. I panicked, knowing that he was only calling because he thought I was up to no good. I procrastinated a day or two, then returned the call. He launched into a breathless story about how pack rats had invaded his federal car, destroying the wiring and making a huge nest right on top of the motor. They wouldn't leave.

"Can you come downtown and get rid of these things for me?" he pleaded.

When the phone rang in my warehouse office, things could, and did, change in an instant and often my plans for the day were shot in the butt. Each spring, without fail, predators would attack newborn livestock for a couple of months. Predators didn't respect nights, weekends or holidays.

As July rolled around, the limelight shifted from coyotes to grizzly and black bears, which killed not only livestock, but also got into commercial beehives and tore them apart trying to get at the honey and the bee larvae. Since bees were considered livestock in Montana, all black bears were to be killed for such offenses. If a grizzly call came in, I had no choice but to go because safety regulations said we had to work in two-man teams. I was the second man, no matter where the attack occurred. The trappers seemed happy to have me there because they didn't know a thing about mixing drugs to immobilize a 500-pound bear or finding a place to release it where it could reasonably stay out of trouble. Grizzlies had become so endangered that they were under federal protection even back in 1966. When the formidable Endangered Species Act rolled around in 1973, even tighter regulations, including mandatory relocation of problem bears, made government trappers grumble. Ironically, the state of Montana was still allowing a hunting season on these animals. But as a fed I was bound to follow such laws to the letter, and it was my responsibility to move grizzlies that got in trouble.

I managed to jettison the double-wide and built my dream house. It sat alone on two acres in the Helena Valley, surrounded by quiet hayfields and good fox habitat. My mother had given me money to help buy it.

"You're going to get whatever I have anyway," she said.

My in-laws had come to visit from Iowa, and we were having a nice weekend when the phone rang. It was trapper Ken Wheeler and he had a female grizzly in a foot snare on Joe Ober's sheep allotment. I had to go.

I took my father-in-law, Bud, with me and we drove for three hours, finally arriving in Kiowa, a short distance from Glacier National Park. When we got to the bear, two park rangers helped us immobilize her. The grizzly was timid and offered little resistance. Bud was pretty thrilled and I snapped a few photos of him with the bear before we loaded her into a culvert trap.

At Kiowa Junction, a tiny whistlestop on the reservation, we stopped to call the usual officials. Our standard protocol was to release problem bears far away from the place we caught them, depending on the bear's behavior and offense. The pay phone was tied up; a bunch of women were talking on a party line. The day was getting hotter, and the longer I waited to get a dial tone, the more I worried about the bear's health. A small crowd had gathered and everyone wanted to look inside the trap. I tried the phone again.

An old Indian woman with few teeth tottered over and asked about the bear.

"Where are you taking it?" she looked up at me.

"I'm not sure yet until I make some calls," I said, realizing that I was getting irritated. "People sure talk on the phone a lot around here."

Her brows knitted together.

"You need to use the phone?" she asked.

"Yeah, but I guess I have to wait my turn."

She reached up, picked the receiver off its cradle with her crooked, brown hand and put it to her ear.

"Get off the goddamn line. We need to use it!" she yelled. She listened some more, then handed it to me, smiling. "Here."

Montana's high-powered wildlife officials decided that we should take the bear, which was now fully awake, to Chief Mountain near the Canadian border. While I was making the arrangements, Wheeler borrowed a hose and sprayed the bear with water to cool her down, then held it near her mouth where she slurped at it. The crowd pressed close, trying to get a look.

We left my truck behind and piled in with Wheeler. Chief Mountain was a long ways off, but the grizzly seemed to be doing fine. Wheeler knew the country and had been to Chief Mountain many times, so we settled in and told stories to entertain Bud. He was eating it up after such a dull life in Iowa.

By the time we got the grizzly to her new home, the sun was dropping in the west. Wheeler picked a remote, forested road where we could release the bear without an audience. The culvert trap had a rope and pulley that allowed us to lift its door while staying close to the truck cab. Wheeler pulled the rope and the door slid open. We thought the grizzly would jump out, but she cowered, planting her butt in the back of trap. We tried yelling and pounding on the trap but she wouldn't budge, so Wheeler grabbed a shovel and poked at her through the bars. I moved my shotgun closer in case Wheeler's lapse in judgment failed and the docile bear decided to get pissed. Just as I was telling him to be careful, and after he'd jabbed the bear in the ass three or four times, it bolted from the trap, Wheeler dropped his shovel and we nearly tripped over each other piling into the truck, slamming the doors.

We watched the grizzly hightail it into an aspen grove.

"I hope the hell nobody is up that road," I said.

At night, away from civilization, the roads are really dark. I figured that by the time Bud and I rolled into Helena, it would be well after midnight. I was tired, but I was used to it. Somehow driving like this, at this hour, had gotten to be a way of life. If I'd been able to charge the government for all the hours I'd spent driving in the middle of the night, I might have retired a millionaire. Bud was nodding off as we went down a stretch of new asphalt highway that hadn't had its lines painted yet. There wasn't even a moon to give the pavement some depth and I started feeling hypnotized. Then I thought I saw something. In a split second, Bud was flying across the cab as I hung onto the steering wheel, swerving, trying not to hit something enormous. A black angus bull lay dead on the pavement, its legs sticking straight up. It had probably been hit by a car. I avoided it by inches.

Less than a week later, Wheeler called me again: more dead sheep belonging to Joe Ober, this time north of Kiowa Junction. Back I went, arriving at dusk. I pulled over at the place we talked about and waited. Wheeler said he was going to set a few snares and meet me, but it had gotten dark and he didn't show up. Maybe I was in the wrong spot. I drove slowly down the road looking for shapes in the dark that could be the sheep. They were around here somewhere, but I couldn't find them. The best thing would be to wait right here until morning.

Once it was dark, the wind picked up and was howling through the trees. I wasn't sure where the dead sheep were or if the bear that killed them was still around, but I sure as hell wasn't pitching a tent here. I parked on level ground, put my shotgun on the floorboard and tried to stretch out in the cab of my truck. I closed my eyes, then opened them again, thinking about the stinky bait in the back of my pickup and how good it probably smelled to every bear within a mile. The truck rattled with every gust of wind and big aspens threw shadows back and forth that looked just like bears on their hind legs. By the time it was light, I was exhausted.

Wheeler and I eventually found each other and the sheep. We also found Ober, a perpetually unshaven man with one eye that had been poked out in a hunting accident. Ober had lots of problems with his sheep, grizzlies being only one. His herder was in the sheep wagon early one morning when a grizzly chased the herding dogs under it, scaring the hell out of all of them.

After things settled down, the herder emerged, rode Ober's horse to the highway, tied it to a tree and left.

The sheep were easy snacks for bears. They were on tribal land about a mile from Glacier National Park. The whole situation was asinine. I told Ober that he should really think about taking the band back to his ranch near Fairfield. He'd planned to, he said, but he was having trouble keeping them together. Wheeler and I offered to help, but we'd found four more dead ewes that morning – killed only a few hours earlier, three by a grizzly and one by a coyote. When I howled, four groups of coyotes answered from the hills. Things weren't going to get better anytime soon. Wheeler and I heaved the dead sheep into a pile and set more foot snares near the carcasses. Then I drove to Kiowa Junction to call Norton Miner and tell him about this hopeless situation. Predictably, Miner exploded.

"Tell Ober he has three days to move those sheep or I'm pulling you and Wheeler out of there," he yelled. I was relieved.

At dusk, Wheeler and I went looking for the bears, driving to a point overlooking Glacier's backcountry where we could see into the park. Through binoculars, I spotted a big grizzly digging in a rockslide, probably in search of a marmot. It would take that bear a matter of minutes to walk over and kill Ober's sheep. On our way back to camp, we were exchanging ideas about ways to get Ober's head screwed on straight when we started seeing eyes in the brush and aspens along the road, first a few, then a lot. Wheeler stopped and backed up slowly, turning the headlights into the trees. More than a hundred sheep stared back at us. Who knew how long they'd been separated from Ober's band. We got out and chased them onto the road, then herded them with the truck until they reached their buddies.

We never did catch a bear. None ever returned to eat on the carcasses or kill any more sheep. We fired a couple of shots at a stray dog that was chasing ewes, but nothing more. When Ober showed up again a couple of days later, I announced that we were leaving and he should, too. He grumbled about it, but he finally did, taking his sheep to a safer place. Ober wasn't trying to be obstinate and he wasn't dumb; he was just another rancher who did what he did because that's the way he'd been doing it for so long. If things get bad, they just call Uncle Sam. It's still how things work.

I was thrilled and relieved that my agency wasn't supporting what surely could have turned into an endless snaring campaign where every bear that wandered out of a national park to eat sheep was trucked somewhere else. It was one of the few good decisions the agency made. I remember secretly hoping that the day would come where domestic sheep would be banned in areas where grizzlies might be tempted to kill them. A few years later, as if by divine intervention, all sheep grazing was banned around Kiowa and Chief Mountain.

July 28, 1980

Dear Mom,

Well, when I got home from Iowa, we had some real excitement. A grizzly started killing sheep near Lincoln only about two miles from where our government trapper picnic will be in two weeks. That old bear was a smart one and so I went over to help my trappers, Jim Stevens and Bill Perry.

We tried everything to catch that bear, but nothing worked. He was wise to our snares and wouldn't get into one of them for anything. We weren't even sure it was a grizzly until the end of the first week. I called the Area Manager and the Montana Fish and Game and told them that we couldn't catch it, and tried to get permission to shoot it. At first they said no, but after a phone call or two from Senator Max Baucus (the sheep owner's brother), the agencies changed their minds. Baucus was a conservationist and forbade his herders to shoot bears. He wanted the government trappers to handle predator problems. But Baucus warned that either the government kills this bear or he was going to give his herders the OK to start shooting. In the meantime, the bear killed 34 sheep within a stone's throw of our campfire. We could hear the bear come in at night and stampede the sheep. It was eating them within a half a city block from where we were sleeping.

One night we did a stakeout by parking our trucks near the sheep with rifles at the ready. The bear came in the dark, but knew our trucks were there and moved away before we could see him. We stayed up until about 1 a.m.

A friend, Mike Robbins, and I slept on cots by the campfire while Jim and his friend Doug slept in the tepee. Mike woke me up about 3 a.m., because the sheep were stampeding. Sure enough, the bear was after the sheep and chased them right into camp. Sheep flowed around our cots like a river creating a huge cloud of dust. I jumped to my feet and struggled through all that wool, trying to grab my rifle and spotlight. I got to my truck and drove it into the timber on the other side of camp and flipped on the spotlight. There was a big, juicy grizzly bear standing on its hind feet about 40 yards away near a dead sheep that it was eating. I stepped out of the truck, put my rifle up and aimed, but right then it disappeared and ran into an aspen thicket. We drove all over in the dark looking for that bear, but found nothing.

Well, a week went by and that brings us to last Thursday night. Bill and Jim were on stakeout when the big bear ran through the sheep and killed another one and dragged it off. The guys pursued the bear in the moonlight, but it got away again. Then on Friday night, all of us staked out the sheep again. Mike and I were in my truck and Jim and Bill got into a tree stand that we built. That night, we had a full moon and could see pretty well. The sheep were restless, though. I think they knew the bear was coming for them again. We had spotlights ready and we'd built a big campfire as a decoy for the guys in the tree, and we had radios for communicating. Everybody got set and sure enough, the bear came in. Jim could see it in the moonlight and was able to put the crosshairs on its chest and kill it with one shot. Mike and I raced up to it to finish it off, but it was already kicking its back legs and dying. Anyway, we finally killed the Phantom Bear, as we called him. The same day, somebody killed a grizzly in Glacier National Park because it ate a couple of campers. You probably heard about that one – it was only 185 miles north of where we were chasing the Phantom Bear. So anyway, I got in a thrilling time. I wouldn't have missed that for anything.

Love,

Carter

The Phantom Bear wouldn't have ever stopped killing sheep. Why should it? Sheep were the easiest meal around – and there were lots of them. Researchers had snared that bear so many times that it knew how to avoid being caught. It had eartags and a radio collar and the only way to make it stop was to kill it because the rancher had no intention of moving his sheep.

There was more to this story that I spared my mother: We returned to camp in the dark with the huge, dead bear, dumped his guts out and hung him in a tree. Bill Perry wanted to celebrate, but had no whiskey, so we drove the eight or so miles to Lincoln to get some, and returned to camp to pass the bottle. Perry, once soused, couldn't resist calling Larry Davis, the local game warden, to taunt him about the bear. Perry yelled into the phone, accusing Davis and the Montana Fish and Game Department of lying about the collared bear, knowing all along that it was in the vicinity, but refusing to tell us. The state just wanted us looking like fools, Perry said. Davis wasn't around at that hour, so Perry left his drunken rant on the fish and game's message machine.

"I'm not giving you this bear until you admit you lied," Perry slurred at the warden. "And you're gonna personally show me that the collar works and that you could tell where that bear was the whole time."

It was way past midnight and some of the guys started for their tents. A few of us finished off the whiskey while standing around the fire, feeling pretty cocky that we'd fixed up that bear. It was quite a sight – a full moon, a crackling campfire and a dead grizzly hanging in a tree. But Perry, who refused to go to bed, kept cussing Fish and Game. He stumbled around the fire while he talked, reminding me of a hubcap rolling in ever-smaller circles until it came to rest. Perry did the same thing, except he spun himself into the middle of the campfire, sending sparks into the night.

We lunged at him and pulled him free before he ignited. I cussed him and dusted embers and charcoal from his clothing, but he was out cold. We carried him to his tent and threw blankets over him.

In the morning, I heard a truck pounding toward our camp. The sun was just coming over the ridge. I buttoned my shirt and stepped out of the tent. The truck had a Fish and Game emblem. It was Larry Davis, the warden.

He shook my hand, but he was tense about a certain phone call he'd received last night. I told him about the bear, the whiskey and the campfire that attacked Bill Perry. I figured Davis had no idea that the bear had wandered into his district.

"I want that bear. Is that going to be a problem?" he looked at me.

"Well, the way I see it, Bill's in bed, so there's really no problem," I said.

Davis backed his truck to the dead bear in the tree and we lowered it in and he left.

Jim Stevens got up and fixed a pot of coffee, and gradually we both tore down camp and cleaned up a bit. After awhile, we heard Perry rustling around. He tried to exit his tent grandly, but he looked like hell. He walked over to the tree and stared at it.

"Where's the goddamn bear?"

"Larry came by and took it." I faced him squarely and waited for him to challenge me. "I told him we'd work it out."

Perry sipped coffee and said nothing. He was beginning to perk up and I waited for him to take down his tent and get ready to go. Instead, Perry dumped out his cup and wandered over to his truck. He climbed in, started the engine and crept away on the dirt trail. He switched on the intercom of his truck siren, picked up the mic and began to sing, *"Happy Trails To You, Until We Meet Again...."*

The standard procedure for dealing with grizzly bears was to move them, not kill them. Shooting a bear in the butt with drugs was scary enough, but the paperwork and people could sometimes be worse. My phone rang once a week with reports of bears killing livestock and it seemed there were two common threads in these incidents: bears liked to kill livestock on Indian reservations, and one of the places we liked to let bears go was Canada.

The Canadians didn't want our grizzlies unless we could promise that the big, crabby carnivores weren't aggressive towards people. They had enough naughty bears of their own. Being the supervisor, I was the guy who vouched for a captured grizzly, saying with a straight face that it could be trusted not to misbehave once it was released.

After tranquilizing one particular bear on the Salish-Kootenai reservation, I decided that it was probably docile and I rode with the tribal game warden to the Montana-Canada border. I thought he might like some help filling out the mounds of paperwork required before the bear's release. A customs officer with a clipboard approached us and we handed over the forms. He nodded and flipped through the pages, then stepped to the back of the truck and looked in the trap. The grizzly was sitting on its butt, shoving peaches into its mouth. Dozens more littered the trap's metal floor.

"Are those peaches?" the agent said, coming back to the window. "I can't let you across with peaches. It's illegal."

The warden looked at the man and his clipboard. "I'm not going in there and take them out, are you?"

The agent looked into the trap again and studied the situation.

"Don't ever do this again," he said and waved us into Canada.

The Blackfeet reservation seemed to have constant grizzly bear problems; the latest one was at Ross Williams' ranch. This time, the bear was killing sheep within 200 feet of the ranch house, inside of a corral. We walked the ranch trying to figure out where exactly the bear was coming in and found its huge prints in the mud and wet manure. It had been following a string of aspens near the house, walking past Williams' front door on the way to the sheep.

I was convinced that the grizzly was focused on the dead sheep in the corral and wanted to set a foot snare there. I asked Williams for permission to do it and warned him that, if I caught a bear, the corrals might end up a wreck.

"Hell, my dad does more damage to the corrals in a week with the tractor than a bear could," Williams snorted.

One of the dead sheep was wedged in a corner of the fence. I liked its location. So based on that, I fashioned a V-shaped guide of sorts, consisting of the fence along one side and lodgepole corral panels on the other. The sheep was in the point of the V. I used baling wire to secure the carcass to the fence so the bear couldn't drag it away, and in front of the whole works, I set a throw-arm trap with a foot snare made of quarter-inch cable.

It seemed like it would work, forcing the bear right where I wanted him. I anchored the snare using three massive old railroad ties that had been buried decades ago to brace the corners of the corral. I couldn't budge even one, and reasoned that a grizzly couldn't budge all three.

I impressed myself with my snare set and snapped a photo of it. Out behind the house, Wheeler was setting a foot snare too. We picked up the remaining sheep carcasses and loaded them in Williams' truck so the grizzly wouldn't get distracted.

At 4 a.m., the phone rang. There was a commotion outside, Williams said. He couldn't see much because of the fog. Fred Crossguns, the Blackfeet game warden, met us at the ranch.

The house lights were on and Williams stepped out with his collar turned up. We drove through a gate by the barn and swung our headlights in the direction of my snare. We couldn't see much, but made out a 20-foot section of lodgepole, which was rising slowly into the air, then dropping out of sight.

We waited until it was light to get out of the truck – just in case. When we advanced toward the snare, we saw it: a huge grizzly seesawing on a length of heavy lodgepole. The log was under his front legs with the snare cinched around one foot while his hind legs paddled the air. He heard us approaching and threw a fit, chewing and shredding the one remaining corral panel. The 400-pound bear had destroyed everything within its reach. Only the railroad ties with my anchor cable remained. When he finished his final tantrum, he tried to run off, but tripped over the cable and went down in the slime he'd churned up. A shit-soaked grizzly. Great.

Wheeler got on the phone to do the requisite reporting. I loaded my dart gun. The aggravated bear eyed me and chomped his teeth. I took a step or two toward him and fired a dart into his hip. In 10 minutes, he was out. It took four of us, grabbing fistfuls of wet, matted, stinking fur, to lift the grizzly into a secure culvert trap. He'd soon be on his way to a release site south of Hungry Horse in Montana's Bunker Creek drainage.

"Sorry about your corrals," I said to Williams, snapping a few photos to compare with the pictures I'd taken the day before. He just smiled.

Not long after his release, the bear's radio collar went off the air. Maybe it stopped working. Maybe somebody killed the bear and destroyed the collar. No one really knows. But the bear wasn't heard from again.

When it came to flying in little airplanes, I didn't do it much for one reason: I'm well over six feet tall and not exactly scrawny.

When I first met our fixed-wing pilot, Larry Lundquist, in Billings, he had me climb into the plane to see how I fit. Lundquist, a short guy, smiled and told me to just jump in. Get a feel for it. I complied, squeezing myself into the back seat. I bumped my head and my knees, and when I finally got turned the right direction and could put my butt in the seat, my legs were jammed against the fuselage, making the plane's metal skin bend and pop. Then I put on a safety helmet, which meant that I had to keep my head tilted toward the floor. Lundquist and a couple of other guys stood outside talking. The plane groaned in protest and Lundquist stuck his head inside.

"Get out of my plane before you ruin it."

Often, we used helicopters in Montana; those had more head room. I could have insisted on flying, but besides being too big, I wanted my trappers to do their jobs. I felt better about being their supporter than their competitor; they were still getting used to me. Besides, I didn't really know the lay of the land or where public land stopped and private land began. I was going to have to find out, though.

I'd pulled the fuel trailer to Drummond and waited for trapper Jerry Lewis and the state helicopter pilot, Lou Harris, to show up. It was time to kill some coyotes.

"You been doing much flying since you've been the boss?" Lewis asked, pulling off his flight helmet and hollering over the idling helicopter engine. He was about the friendliest guy I'd met on the job.

"Not at all. I've been pretty busy," I said.

Lewis smiled and handed me his helmet.

"You better get in and do some gunning," he said.

I declined, making up an excuse that I didn't know the country.

"Hell, ol' Lou knows where to fly, so don't worry about that." Lewis slapped me on the back.

I thought that the first time I was forced to shoot things from a helicopter I'd have more time to prepare. I'd never been in a whirly-bird. It was like climbing onto a carnival ride. I didn't know what to do and worried that I would screw up. The only training I'd ever had that seemed remotely connected to this was at the trapper's conference where we shot at targets on a range. Safety training at those conferences amounted to walking around a parked aircraft and having a pilot show us the fire extinguisher, first-aid kit, and how to shut off the fuel line. Then the instructor helpfully told us not to shoot a hole in the gas tanks, propeller or rotor blades.

Lewis insisted and pushed his helmet at me. I took a deep breath, tried to compose myself and climbed in to the Bell 47. Lewis handed me his shotgun and put a can filled with shotgun shells on the floor near my feet. I buckled up and looked at Harris, who appeared to be comfortable with letting a rookie fire a weapon out of his ship. I gave him a thumbs-up, and with a deafening whine, we lifted off.

Lewis waved at me as we rose into the air, then he got smaller and smaller, and was eventually swallowed by the trees and brush. Harris made a wide turn. This was a lot different than flying in a fixed-wing plane. We headed north out of Drummond, Montana. The view was breathtaking and it calmed me down.

Harris pointed ahead and yelled to get ready. We were over legal coyote-hunting ground. I searched the brown landscape, but Harris saw the first one. I couldn't believe how tiny it looked – like a cottontail rabbit. We descended and the chase began. I poked the shotgun out of the shooting port in the helicopter door. I was nervous, trying to remember gun safety at the same time I needed to compensate for the motion of the helicopter. The distance between the chopper and the coyote closed fast and I took aim. I was about to pull the trigger when the coyote jumped into a badger hole in the sagebrush and crouched in a tight ball, looking at us as we passed over it. I pointed at the coyote and pulled the trigger, but nothing happened. I'd forgotten to chamber a shell.

Harris mumbled something and pulled an aerial u-turn. By then I was locked, loaded and ready. The helicopter slowed to a hover as we searched for the coyote in the burrow. It was still there and I shot it. No sport, no challenge, just a simple execution. I didn't like killing a crouched coyote and I felt like an idiot for screwing up the first pass by forgetting to load my gun. But there was no time for reflection; Harris was in hot pursuit of another one. We closed in as it ran for its life and I fired, rolling the coyote end over end. I killed five of them that day. Harris landed near each one so I could get out and load it onto an outside stretcher tray like soldiers in a war zone.

Word spread that I had been initiated and trappers started offering their shooting seats to me. I went, but not often.

I looked at things differently after that. I learned that every winter storm was followed by calm, clear days, making coyotes easy to track. They couldn't camouflage themselves in the snow. Some pilots and gunners were killing upwards of 100 coyotes a day. Those kinds of numbers meant big success, and eventually I became as enthusiastic about it as they were.

Less than a year later, Lou Harris died of a heart attack while flying his helicopter near Glasgow, Montana. He was able to land and shut down, but died before the gunner could run for help.

After Harris, the state hired Bob Schellinger, a Korean War vet who always flew with a cigar stub clenched in his teeth. Schellinger was the in-between guy while the state worked on hiring a permanent pilot. He'd been given all kinds of shiny awards for his heroic rescues of hunters, hikers, climbers and other adventurers who got into trouble in the backcountry. People called him Crash, which made me hesitate to fly with him. Once, in Yellowstone, someone on the ground frantically radioed that his helicopter was on fire. He landed it safely that time. But in 1981, Schellinger was attempting to pick up two surveyors in the rugged mountains east of Trout Creek, Montana, and struck his chopper's tail rotor on rocks. The fire and explosion that followed killed him.

Monte Ballou was the permanent replacement for Lou Harris. He was 27, and gung-ho. Ballou could dismantle a helicopter down to the last bolt and put it back together again. I told everybody I would have flown to hell and back with Ballou.

Unfortunately, I experienced hell more than once with Ballou, not because of his skill as a pilot, but because of his temper. On the ground, I watched many a wrench fly through the hangar when he was knee-deep in chopper parts. That I could tolerate. But his temper in the air was dangerous. Every week, I was trying to mend fences between my trappers and Ballou. He expected all of us to read his mind and exploded when we didn't do it right.

Ballou got permission from the Helena airport to land in my yard and pick me up for work. It was quite a scene, but kept me from having to drive the 10 miles to his hangar. My kids jumped out of bed and hung over the back of the couch at the front window to wave goodbye. Neighbors craned their necks to watch landings and takeoffs. When we returned with a load of dead coyotes, I pulled them off the trays and laid them in the shade of the house.

When it was time for lunch, we'd land at a ranch or take up half the parking lot and kick up a dust cloud at our favorite greasy spoon in the tiny town of Lima near the Idaho border. Because of Ballou, I loved helicopters. They were liberating and convenient. Distances were halved compared to driving, and the endless mountains and lush valleys were thrilling to behold, especially when we went doorless.

When Ballou first came to work, he flew a Bell 47 piston-driven chopper. Then the state bought a Hughes 500 with a turbine engine, and man, did that make a difference. Sometimes in the Bell 47, we could barely get over the Continental Divide for all the wind resistance. Ballou cursed and struggled, trying to find a spot where we could get through. In the Hughes, we buzzed over the mountains like a bee. No longer would my palms sweat in Rimini Canyon as the wind stood us still or pushed us backward. With the Hughes, Ballou just grinned and steered.

"Wanna see something?" he asked me one day. We flew over a spot south of Dillon and he pointed at the ground: the white tail boom of a Bell 47. He'd been flying with a county-designated gunner and they landed to pick up a dead coyote. The gunner stepped out before the helicopter landed, throwing it off balance. The rotor blades hit the sagebrush and the chopper crashed, parts flying in all directions. Ballou was able to free himself and grab the semi-conscious gunner, who had a serious head injury, and pull him away from the wreckage just as the entire ship went up in a fireball.

My experience with Ballou in the air was exciting enough without crashing. I saw a black bear standing on a timbered knob as we buzzed along the treetops one sunny day and I remarked on it. Suddenly we were in a steep climbing turn. The G-force jammed my eyeballs deep into their sockets. Just as fast, we were aimed straight at the ground. I couldn't comprehend what the hell was happening. My brain went blank, my stomach went up to the clouds, and my arms and legs were paralyzed. Ballou wondered out loud where the bear was. At that point, I didn't give a shit. After that, I issued detailed instructions to pilots before climbing in that we were not to go upside down or sideways or any other way but straight.

Unlike some of the trappers, I didn't have any close calls in helicopters. I have always believed it was because I said some good, meaty prayers before take-off. I came close to shitting in my pants only once. I heard a tremendous thud while flying over a chain of craggy, snow-capped peaks. Ballou knew all the sounds and feelings that his chopper was allowed to have. He could detect the slightest imbalance in the rotor blade and somehow knew when a gauge went a certain way if it was a mechanical or a fuel problem. The day we felt the thud, Ballou perked up and scanned his gauges. He whipped a look at me.

"What the hell was that?" he yelled.

My heart fluttered and I froze in place, waiting to die. I watched Ballou concentrate on the feel of the ship. He leaned forward and stared at his gauges. He glanced at the impossible terrain below us. What a lousy place to fall out of the sky.

I waited for something to happen. Ballou poked, flipped and adjusted all the switches, sticks and throttles, then put us in a steady descent – to get closer to the ground when we finally bit it, I presumed. I don't think I was breathing. He found a hilltop with a view most people would give anything to possess and set us down. I couldn't wait to put my feet on solid earth, but Ballou continued inspecting the helicopter. He walked around the ship, eyeing all of its parts and running his hand along the tail section. Then he opened the back door.

"Sonofabitch!" He was almost hysterical with relief. A shotgun had slipped from its fastener and hit the floor.

Jim Stevens and I ambled through the Milford Hutterite colony in his battered government truck after a fruitless day on our trapline. We'd been after fox and coyotes that were killing sheep and chickens on their farm, but our traps were empty again and the sun was going down. We were almost past the community house when Andrew, the sheep boss, waved us down and asked us to stay for supper.

As farmers, the Hutterites are some of the best, probably because they don't have televisions or radios or other frivolous distractions, and their colonies are totally self-sufficient. We didn't really know the names of the men we dealt with. To us, they were the sheep boss, the pig boss, the poultry boss, the wheat boss and the other bosses. They didn't know a thing about predator trapping, so they called Animal Damage Control when the varmints got too thick.

Several Hutterite women, in their pastel ankle-length dresses and headscarves, were busy cooking. The tradition was that the men ate first, then got up and left abruptly, so the women and children could have a turn. We washed up using a bucket of water and a homemade towel, then were ushered to the table and poured some high-octane rhubarb wine, which traveled directly to my brain and eyeballs and made them float. Then the men, with their ear-to-ear beards, sat down. The women set steaming bowls of meat, potatoes, vegetables and rice on the table and we bowed our heads while they prayed. There must have been 25 men at the table, which took up the whole room. They had thick German accents. Over time, we'd discovered that these particular Hutterite men owned guns, even though they weren't supposed to, and traded their wine for whiskey when they were in town. They even enjoyed a good cuss word every once in a while.

The Hutterite women continually peeked at Stevens and me as we ate. I caught them once or twice and it made me nervous. I'd heard the Hutterites were always looking to add new blood to their families and that they'd pay $50 for it. I wasn't sure if it was true, but just in case I looked down at my plate and asked Stevens to pass the potatoes.

Things were going along great when a high-pitched squeak came from my end of the table. Then it happened again. Everyone stopped chewing and looked at me.

"What is that sound?" one of the old, bearded men asked, breaking the silence.

I hesitated.

"You wouldn't believe me if I told you," I said.

Stevens snickered and kept eating. The men stared at me, some in mid-chew. The whining started again, but louder this time.

"I've got a porcupine in my shirt." I'd forgotten about it, but now I had to tell how it got there.

Earlier in the day, Stevens caught a big female porcupine in a trap and killed it, tossing it along the road. Most ranchers want porcupines dead because dogs, horses and cattle invariably get quills in their noses when they encounter one. I looked at it lying there and thought I saw its belly move. I took a step closer. Then I took out my knife and cut open its belly. Inside was a full-term baby. I carefully removed the placental sack, opened it, and laid the little creature on the ground where it gasped his first breath of air.

I found the string from a sack of dog food in the back of Stevens' pickup. I cut off a length and tied off the porcupine's umbilical cord. The tiny creature fit in the palm of my hand and had soft, wet quills. I didn't think it would live long, but I tucked it inside my shirt to keep it warm.

The Hutterite men were silent, trying to decide if this was true, I suppose. I put my fork down, unbuttoned my shirt and reached inside. The baby porcupine squirmed in the light. It was warm and dry and its quills were now like a soft hairbrush. Once everyone had a look, I put it back in my shirt and finished my supper.

At home that night, I rummaged through my junk drawer and found one of several miniature baby bottles that I'd used to nurse other small animals. I mixed up milk and baby formula and tried to get the porcupine to eat, but it wasn't interested. A vet suggested that I add some Karo syrup. That did the trick and the porcupine calmed down and slept. It grew and was doing well, but one day became ill and dumpy. The vet diagnosed it with overeating sickness. I'd never heard of such a thing, but pills fixed it and when my little pet weighed about a pound, I named it Pucker P. Pine, or Puckerpine for short. It was a "he" and he liked nestling around my neck and sucking on my earlobe. I talked to him in a high-pitched voice. Having Puckerpine was better entertainment than any television show.

I built a plywood box and put it in our basement; that was Puckerpine's house. He stayed there, content, with the lid closed at night or when we weren't home. Puckerpine liked homegrown vegetables, but refused store-bought produce. I was mystified by his food habits because he also loved junk food and candy. Once I let him outside, he started acting like a wild porcupine and found his own food, but he scratched at our sliding glass door when he wanted back in. He was mostly housebroken. When nature called, he ran frantically down the basement steps, climbed into his box, backed into one corner and did his business. The few times he mistakenly peed on the floor, he always managed to do it on the linoleum.

I never put him on the scale, but I figured he weighed 15 pounds by the time he was almost a year old. He could have hurt us, but he didn't. Just in case though, I had my kids wear a leather electrician's mitt when they roughhoused with him. His worst offense was shedding quills into the carpet, which had me screaming and hopping a few times.

As he got older, he got stinkier, and everybody took turns cleaning his box every day. Like other creatures I've raised, Puckerpine was starting to act like, well, a wild animal. He roamed our garden and found the raspberry patch, chewed on the woody stems and returned to his box for a nap. One evening, he didn't wake up for his evening romp, so I went to check on him. He sat humped up and refused to move. Normally, I could reach down and he would grasp my arm, step onto my hand with his hind feet and let me lift him, but this time he screamed and tried to bite me.

I called the vet and recited the porcupine's symptoms.

"Sounds like he's bloated. He probably needs an enema," Doc Painter said.

"You're kidding, right?" I responded, looking at my pet, now a rolled-up mass of quills.

"You'd better get on it, Carter. If he's blocked, it could kill him. Go buy a douche bag."

When I decide to adopt animals, I never envision this kind of emergency. I wondered about myself the whole way to the drugstore.

I bought the cheapest douche bag I could find and hoped not to run into any neighbors. My family speculated about what might happen when I tried to hook it up to my pet.

Puckerpine still hadn't moved, so I wrapped a heavy coat around him and put him on the floor. He squealed and fought furiously. All I could do was avoid his teeth and quills.

"Stand back," I ordered everyone. I handed the douche bag to Pam, who looked unsure about this procedure. I wrestled my way to Puckerpine's tail and lifted it while he fought to keep it wrapped around himself. He squealed in protest while I pushed the plastic tube up his butt a couple of inches and told Pam to squeeze on the bag of warm water.

I let go of him and pulled out the tube all at once.

"Now we wait," I said.

If the problem at hand was constipation, the results were gratifying: hard chunks of rolled raspberry vines plopped onto the floor, along with an occasional fart and a couple of happy-sounding grunts. Puckerpine looked almost like he was smiling. He climbed back into his box and I began the disgusting job of scrubbing porcupine shit off the floor.

At Christmas, Puckerpine was still living in the basement, but the good will of the season was the only thing keeping him in the house. He stank and had developed a habit of sniffing people, then humping their legs while pissing all over them. He even bit a good size chunk out of a friend's new cowboy boots.

Puckerpine liked the Christmas tree and wanted to climb it every chance he got. I told Shadron it was her job to keep him out of it. She found out that it wasn't the tree he was after, but the candy canes hanging in it. He sat on the couch and gnawed his peppermints and I wondered what to do. When spring came around, I told myself, I'd put him outside for good. He just wasn't so lovable anymore – even though he liked to be held and still wanted to nurse on my ear.

The afternoon that Puckerpine escaped from his box and chewed up all of Pam's shoes, he was banished from the house. He never touched my shoes or boots, only Pam's. I carried his box outside to a sheep shed that I had fenced with woven wire. He promptly crawled underneath and dug around under the floorboards. Puckerpine paced the fence, but because he'd never really been much of a climber in the house, I didn't think he would climb the wire.

But one morning he was gone. We searched adjacent hayfields, buildings and junk piles, and I even put an ad in the paper offering a $100 reward. I got a lot of calls from people with porcupines in their yards, and I went to their houses with my catchpole hoping to find Puckerpine. Instead, I ended up moving wayward porcupines to nearby forests to get them away from people who might kill them for no good reason. Eventually I gave up and canceled my ad. Puckerpine was gone.

I was sick about losing him, but I also knew this would happen eventually. It happens with all animals, but especially those that we have no business making into pets. Still, Puckerpine had a longer life than most of his species simply because he was a captive. Many wild animals die before they are a year old. It's just nature's way.

Later that year, I heard rumors that a porcupine approached a man's trailerhouse in the Helena valley not even a mile from me. It scratched at the sliding glass door and the man, thinking the creature must be rabid, grabbed his gun, opened the door and shot it.

When I got more than a couple of phone calls from people up near the Canadian border saying they saw or heard wolves, I jotted a few notes and slid them under my pencil cup, then promptly forgot about them. But 24 miles north of Glasgow, Montana, on October 12, 1978, a rancher found a dead wolf in his sheep pasture. It was charcoal-colored and weighed 83 pounds.

The man was checking on his stock when he came upon the canine. The wolf's carcass was full of shotgun pellets. The last time a wolf had been killed in this country was in 1956, the same year my dad showed me how to trap pocket gophers.

If they were coming from Canada, which is what everyone suspected, the wolves weren't getting very far. The majority of reports I heard about third-hand were of lone wolves, maybe a few pairs. There was no evidence that the ones who made it through the gantlet of ranches were reproducing. Government killing programs ensured that lone wolves that migrated in weren't going to find romance here. Most of North America's wolves had been wiped out a generation ago.

In 1981, three years after the Glasgow wolf, Animal Damage Control killed its first wolf on purpose. The animal was a loner, according to reports, roaming the Bear Paw Mountains in northern Montana. After tracking it, trapper Gene Bucklin shot it from an airplane on New Years Eve, but not before the wolf was credited with killing 26 sheep and lambs, one ram sheep, one cow, 25 calves, 11 yearling cattle, two colts and one 30-pound turkey. The total value of the dead livestock was put at $18,620.

I was skeptical that this wolf even existed until the trapper found it and shot it. Even then, it seemed a little weird. It weighed 110 pounds and stood 31 inches at the shoulder, standard size for a wolf. I only saw photos, but there was something odd about it. If I could have found someone to bet me, and an impartial third party to run DNA tests (which didn't exist at the time), I would have wagered it was a hybrid dog. It was tawny-brown, nothing like the lead color of the one in the sheep pasture, or the more typical gray. The Bear Paw wolf, as it became known, was stuffed and put in a glass case at the Fish and Wildlife Service office in Helena. Somehow its tail was damaged with all the handling, so the taxidermist sewed on a coyote tail instead.

Whatever it was, it sparked stories of a blood-thirsty, lone predator wandering from ranch to ranch, killing everything – often near houses. The newspapers loved it. They wrote about it for weeks, stirring people up and stoking bitter divisions between ranchers and pro-wolf groups, including the Fish and Wildlife Service, which had been murmuring about wolf reintroduction.

Even before the Bear Paw wolf, researchers with the Wolf Ecology Project from the University of Montana had been working around the North Fork of the Flathead River near the Canadian border. In 1979, they captured and radio-collared a female wolf. They'd been looking for evidence that wolves were crossing into Montana – and staying – but this one didn't seem to have any associates.

In 1982, researchers found a litter of seven pups, but they were on the Canadian side of the border west of Glacier National Park. Turns out there were 12 wolves in that pack, which was dubbed the Magic pack, and the places they wandered were in my district of Montana.

In May 1986, Mike Fairchild, a scientist with the Wolf Ecology Project, was nice enough to show me, along with a couple of biologists from the Fish and Wildlife Service, what he and his team were up to. They'd kept a low profile long enough to actually learn something about the wolves that lived on the border of Montana and Canada.

We drove to Tom Ladenberg's ranch near the North Fork of the Flathead River. It was a tamed place in a wild area. Ladenberg didn't hate wolves and had even developed accidental friendships with Fairchild, his fellow researcher, Bob Ream, and graduate student Diane Boyd, all of whom were looking for wolves, studying the ones they'd seen or speculating when more would arrive. Tom saw wolves regularly and noticed the tracks they'd left in his pastures, but he never lost his head over it. He told me he had a live-and-let-live philosophy, adjusting his Stetson as he said it.

The Magic pack hadn't committed any sins against Ladenberg's cows and horses, so there was no reason for my agency to go after them. Besides, the wolf's legal status as endangered made my supervisors nervous. Across the border, however, wolves had virtually no protection; Canadian trappers and hunters regularly took out any wolf they saw. Others who couldn't fathom a reason for a wolf's existence killed them with poison. Diane Boyd conducted her studies out of a primitive cabin near the border and demanded that the wolves be left alone. I could tell I made her nervous, being an Animal Damage Control killer and all. I hoped that I wouldn't end up spoiling this research Utopia should the wolves cause problems.

Because it's the way things are, the federal government wasn't ready for wolves to show up all by themselves, without permission. This was complicated by the gray wolf having been high on the list of imperiled species ever since the Endangered Species Act was invented. Wolves were endangered in all of the lower 48 states except Minnesota, where a reasonably healthy population managed to weather extermination campaigns earlier in the century. They were never listed in Alaska because there have always been lots of wolves there.

One of the Endangered Species Act's requirements, besides prohibiting federal agencies from doing things that jeopardized a species, was that the Fish and Wildlife Service had to physically do something about the status of threatened and endangered animals (and plants, bugs, and birds), not just keep adding to the list and wiping their tears away. The agency was required to come up with a recovery plan and put it into action. But when it came to wolves, probably the most reviled creature on four legs, politicians weren't eager to help. And because recovery plans, unlike the Endangered Species Act itself, are not legally binding, it became easy for the Fish and Wildlife Service to write a plan for wolves and shelve it for lack of popularity. It's all very complicated, but it gets worse: Politicians control the purse strings of the Fish and Wildlife Service. If they don't like something, they just suck the money away and indirectly punish forward-thinking regional directors by perhaps reassigning them to fish hatcheries or weather stations in the Arctic. It took bravery in the ranks to move the Northern Rockies wolf recovery plan forward – even inches at a time.

At about the time the Magic pack took up housekeeping in northern Montana, the Fish and Wildlife Service was working on a document called *Wolf Control Guidelines, Northern Rocky Mountains*. It was still a draft. It was supposed to be the guiding light for all federal agencies when wolves were naughty and had to be disciplined – that is when they killed livestock or endangered humans and had to be moved. Killing them was not yet an option. Having such a plan was essential because it showed politicians that the feds realized everything with wolves wasn't going to be sweetness and light. Having a hard-nosed document that ranchers could get behind was going to help pave the long road toward reintroduction.

For my part, I just knew that when a wolf attacked livestock it would happen in my neck of the woods.

Because I was a district supervisor and I was in Helena, I'd been informally given the job of liaison between Animal Damage Control and the Fish and Wildlife Service, which headquartered its Northern Rockies wolf program there. I went and met Wayne Brewster and Dale Harms, who were in charge of the program. We had a big discussion about how nobody was ready for all this wolf stuff. No one was ever going to be ready, I thought. The men had prepared yet another sizable document outlining timetables for ordering wolf trapping supplies, getting drug training, and obtaining the piles of equipment we'd need if we expected to catch these animals and put radio collars on them.

Not long after, I pulled an oversized envelope from my mailbox. It was from the Patuxent Wildlife Research Center in Maryland. Inside was a manual, *Directions for Drugging, Holding, and Transporting Wolves*. The author, Dr. Dave Mech, had scribbled a note on the front, "You'll probably get a crack at this sometime."

We received the drug and wolf-handling training we'd been asking about. Afterward, I got a note from trapper Bill Paul in Minnesota. Quit worrying about trap injuries, it read; overheating is the biggest problem for a caught wolf. As the months rolled along, we pieced together a field kit until we were ready for action. While trappers attempted to understand the many rules and regulations behind potential wolf captures, the Washington Post published a story about the Fish and Wildlife Service's big plan to reintroduce wolves, outlining in detail the positions of pro-wolfers versus angry ranchers. One old boy compared the wolf to the dinosaur: "Its time has gone," he said. The story also touched on a plan by Defenders of Wildlife to pay ranchers for livestock that wolves killed. The hitch, of course, was that someone had to prove a wolf did it.

By 1986, a good share of my time and attention had been hijacked by wolves – or rather the people who were panicking about them – though, for the most part, the animal didn't exist in Montana. I was overwhelmed by all the wolf rules and regulations. Handling a wolf sounded kind of interesting, but I also hoped the whole thing would go away. There were so many ways that I could screw up that it seemed dangerous even to look at one the wrong way. The focus was on each wolf and how valuable it was in reestablishing a population. The whole thing was contrary to Biology 101, which stated unequivocally that populations matter, not individuals.

There was a huge discussion on paper about which traps to use and why and how. We were supposed to use No. 4 Newhouses with offset jaws and a drag – not too rigidly anchored, checked at regular intervals not to exceed 24 hours. There were other passages about using tranquilizer darts shot from a moving vehicle to immobilize a wolf, and even a couple of pages about putting drugged wolves in *"a sturdy transport cage that was three feet high, four feet long and two feet deep ...."* Another section read: *"other equally safe methods may be developed and used, keeping in mind the safety and comfort of the animal."* I thumbed through the pages looking for the part about the safety and comfort of the trapper. There wasn't one.

I was relieved to find that I was covered under a federal permit, which I had to carry with me all the time. The permit essentially said that I was authorized by the U.S. government to investigate nuisance wolves, capture them, move them and release them. If one died while on my watch, well, I couldn't be personally liable. The permit didn't allow me to kill wolves; that permission had to come from the Fish and Wildlife Service exclusively and only after the wolf had proved itself incorrigible.

Animal Damage Control had heartburn with the Fish and Wildlife Service's starry-eyed preoccupation with wolves. It was screwing up our coyote-killing program. What if a wolf clamped its mouth around an M-44? The Endangered Species Act said that a federal agency couldn't do anything to jeopardize wolves. But being an agency that didn't do much but kill, Animal Damage Control was beginning to feel like the bastard child at a family reunion. If wolves couldn't be released where the deadly M-44s were waiting to shoot cyanide into the mouths of whatever bit them, that meant wolves couldn't be released in a lot of places.

Things had to change, but those fights were for the big shots. I was busy trying to figure out how to make a trap that wouldn't mangle a wolf's foot. (It's been almost impossible to convince John Q. Public that toothed traps – at least the kind of button-like teeth I'm talking about – are easier on an animal's foot than smooth jaws, or foot snares for that matter. The offset design keeps the trap from closing so tightly that it cuts off circulation. It doesn't feel good, I'm sure, but it also won't kill the tissue.) Wolves hunt with their feet as much as their mouths, and they have to be able to run to survive. At first, I thought I could just buy some of the old Newhouse No. 14 toothed traps, but I discovered they'd become collectable and therefore expensive. So I went to work converting a No. 4 Newhouse wolf trap with no teeth to one I could use.

A foundry in the Midwest sent me about four dozen pairs of trap jaws from a mold of an old No. 14, so I had something to go by. The mold didn't have holes where the jaws hinged with the trap frame so, using my drill press, I made them myself. It took an hour of cursing and throwing trap parts across the room, trying to get things to fit. I did it, but there was something wrong. I went at it again and thought I might wear out my drill bits and bench grinder. My replica still didn't look right, but I made more and used them anyway. Months later, after I heard about wolves escaping from my traps, I learned that the Midwest mold was based on an original that had been run over by a truck.

The few of us assigned to the wolf issue learned a lot in a short time, not the least of which was how to shoot a wolf with a net gun from a helicopter: There's no safety on a net gun, so try not to shoot it into the rotorblade, our instructor said. All of my trappers knew how to kill things from a chopper using a shotgun, but this was different because it was difficult, and difficult because it was different. Most of them didn't want any part of it.

It was Ross Williams' ranch, the same one with grizzly problems a few years earlier, where one of the first wandering wolves in Montana killed a cow. Wheeler examined the dead bovine and pronounced it killed by wolves. The wolf left tracks going every direction, but disappeared before it could be caught. No matter. A couple of months later, on a ranch nearby, the shit hit the fan.

"Carter, over here," trapper Ken Wheeler shouted from the trees.

We were looking for wolf tracks on the shores of Horse Lake on the Blackfeet reservation. Over the past few years, I kept finding myself somewhere on this particular patch of Indian land. It seemed to attract big hungry carnivores, probably because of its proximity to the rugged and wild Glacier National Park and Canada.

Wheeler had arrived days earlier to examine a dead cow that belonged to rancher Jim Hall. Hall's wife and daughter had watched as two gray wolves attacked the cow. We worked circles around the ranch for miles, looking for the place where the wolves emerged from the woods and where they'd gone back in again. We'd heard that wolves were hanging around the lake, and Wheeler believed there might be a den nearby. It was 1987, and my first real wolf investigation.

Wheeler was studying the ground in front of him. Something had excavated a hole two feet wide and several feet deep, and there was dirt strewn everywhere. It looked like it could be a wolf den, but it was old; spiderwebs crisscrossed the entrance. But Wheeler wasn't looking at that: suspended on twine and wrapped around a downed tree limb were three sticks of dynamite, their wrappers tattered and faded.

Fred Crossguns, in uniform, came through the pines. We stood silently, staring at the dynamite.

"Do you think this stuff will blow if we shoot it?" I said. The men shrugged.

I picked up the branch and walked it gingerly to the opposite side of the meadow where we'd parked our trucks. We loaded our rifles and blasted away, but we only pulverized the sticks and blew powder everywhere. I thought about the old westerns where shooting the dynamite was the only way to fix the bad guys and bring the movie to an end. Maybe theirs was fresher.

The dynamite was meant for whatever was using that hole, which convinced me that it had to be wolves. If the plan had worked, it would have saved everyone a lot of trouble.

Our orders were to find and collar at least one wolf in this troublemaking pack. But we searched for weeks and the animals had simply disappeared. By then, it was mid-summer and I had vacation to burn, so I gathered up my family and drove to Iowa for the Fourth of July.

As was always the case when I went on vacation, something happened. Wheeler caught a black wolf the day I left, then a gray one. The black wolf was missing half of one hind leg. I'd left my drug kit with Wheeler because he didn't have one of his own. But he didn't need it. Wheeler was not the greatest trapper, but he had other talents, some learned as a cowboy. When he caught the two wolves, he didn't go for the syringe. Instead, he roped and hogtied them, then wedged sticks in their mouths before taping their muzzles shut.

The black male wolf was judged unfit for release and placed in permanent captivity in a facility in Minnesota. The large, gray male was ear tagged, lip tattooed, radio collared and released back into the wild.

I was still in Iowa when the pack attempted to kill another cow on the Hall ranch. Then they killed nine adult sheep and a lamb on the Dan Geer ranch near Browning. On top of everything else, Wheeler was risking his life by trying to catch wolves in the middle of prime grizzly country. There hadn't been wolves in that area for a generation, so there were understandably few traps of the correct size available. The ones we used could, and did once, catch a grizzly.

When I returned from vacation, it seemed like I'd been gone a year. We had to get our hands on those wolves. Kemper McMaster, a field supervisor for the Fish and Wildlife Service in Helena, was calling the shots and he wanted them alive. But the pack was wary, staying hidden in the underbrush and scampering to the safety of dense aspen groves. Wheeler did the flying and took a shot with the netgun that he thought was reasonable, but the net tangled in the trees. If the wolves weren't wise to us before, they would be now.

Wheeler and Ballou kept flying and were following the collared wolf when, one morning, it stepped out into a meadow, blood staining its chest and face. Dan Geer's cattle were nearby. The air team flew back to the ranch and told what they saw. Geer and his wife jumped on motorcycles to go check their cattle. I followed. One steer had gaping holes where wolves had been eating it. It couldn't stand but was still alive. Geer shot it in the head to end its misery. The remains of another, a week dead, lay nearby.

We backtracked a bloody trail along a barbed wire fence where the wolves had slashed and torn at the fleeing animals. Geer was usually an unflappable man, but now he was angry. I took a few photos to document the attack. In one, Geer lifted the steer's leg to reveal the extensive, irreparable wound. Within a few weeks, copies of the image were passed around Washington D.C., and certain congressmen started calling the Fish and Wildlife Service. Only then, did McMaster give me permission to kill two adult wolves – but only gray ones.

"We've got another kill out here," Wheeler radioed me the next morning, mere minutes into their helicopter flight. I was parked on the shoulder of the road, idling, waiting to hear what Wheeler would find today. I hated to lose the radio collar out of this pack, but I suspected that one wolf – the one that Wheeler was seeing now – was doing most of the killing.

"Shoot it," I said, switching off the ignition. I opened my door and listened. The helicopter, a half-mile away, made a turn and droned as it slowed. *Boom, boom-boom....*

When I reached them, Wheeler and Ballou were smiling, taking turns posing with the dead wolf and snapping photos.

"Stop it," I said. "You want those pictures to end up in the wrong hands?"

I turned the limp, bloody animal onto its side. Its tongue rolled around in what looked like an ordinary dog's mouth. I'd never experienced a wolf up-close and this circumstance wasn't what I had in mind. Its thin summer pelt was ratty and its head looked huge. A radio collar hung loosely from its neck. Its feet were enormous. It weighed 108 pounds.

If there was a good part to this, it was that Wheeler shot a gray one this time. There had been two times during our quest to find these wolves where Wheeler had shot black wolf puppies thinking they were adults. Those incidents drove an even bigger wedge between McMaster and Bill Rightmire, the state director of Animal Damage Control in Montana, who was present during one of the shootings. McMaster forbade any more helicopter work to find the pack. We had to use traps. So we did. Wheeler caught one gray pup and the alpha female. She went berserk, chewing up trees, finally dying of stress while still in the trap.

Dan Geer, understandably, wanted all of it to end. Wheeler spent 1,124 trap nights on the ranch and Rightmire was having a fit that three of his employees and a helicopter were tied up because of wolves. The price tag had skyrocketed. The smartest thing to do would be to kill the wolves and be done with it, he said. Two weeks later, when Montana's only known wolf pack was dead except for one animal, McMaster called off the operation. That last wolf, Geer said with a grin, wouldn't ever be any trouble.

After the Browning disaster and the loss of one of Montana's only known wolf packs, I jotted a few notes to myself in case anything like it happened again: Wolves had their pups in April when elk and deer were wintering at lower elevations. With spring green-up and snowmelt, a meager population of game moved out of the area and the wolves were unable to follow because of their pups. So instead, they ate sheep and cattle.

While I spent time in 1987 trying to get a handle on where wolves might strike next in my district – and why they did what they did, the brass at my agency were jockeying for position in case wolf reintroduction became a reality.

Animal Damage Control managers felt slighted. On the Geer ranch, they'd been reduced to the level of "concerned citizen." They wanted a bigger role in deciding whether problem wolves should be snuffed out, and they took their case to the U.S. Fish and Wildlife Service. Wolves were going to be a problem for my agency and its unbridled campaign against predators, forcing up costs because its trappers were going to have to be more careful. The irksome presence of wolves would force frequent, inconvenient trap checks and maybe even the end of widespread poison meant for coyotes and the like. Animal Damage Control wanted complete involvement in developing strategies to deal with naughty wolves, pushing aside the stated policy of the Department of the Interior that, in the beginning, bad wolves were to be moved, not killed.

Far away from the quibbling in Helena, Defenders of Wildlife with its thousands of members, had seen how things had gone at Dan Geer's place. Hank Fischer, Northern Rockies field representative for Defenders, hatched a plan on behalf of the group to pay ranchers for livestock lost to wolves. In short order, the organization raised $100,000, catapulting the Wolf Compensation Fund into existence. Fischer asked me who exactly lost livestock during the Browning wolf invasion. I sent him a list and he mailed checks the next day. Geer called the money a joke, but he cashed the check anyway.

Though they were scroungy, I sent the four Browning wolf pelts to a tannery. I boiled, cleaned and bleached their skulls. Then Wheeler and I delivered them to the Blackfeet Nation, who considered wolves sacred. The tribal council said thanks, but the religious leaders were so angry that they almost couldn't speak.

Newspapers couldn't write fast enough about the presence – followed quickly by the absence – of wolves in northern Montana. Reporters recycled stories, mixing and matching fact, hype and rumor, depending on their readership. A few papers outlined the pissing match between McMaster and Rightmire, calling all of them meddling bureaucrats. By the time it was done, the Browning boondoggle cost taxpayers a shameful $40,000. I didn't recognize it as an initiation until after it ended and my reaction was probably too simplistic – but maybe not: 1) why don't we just write the rancher a check for $40,000, if the wolves are going to be killed anyway, and 2) we need to get a plan in place for the next time this happens, which could be as soon as tomorrow.

After the wolves visited, Dan and Patty Geer became their most outspoken opponents. Dan had a biology degree from the University of Montana, which should have afforded him some understanding of wild carnivores and what happens when they meet domestic prey, but he told Range magazine, "As long as there are wolves, there will be problems." Their 2-year-old son was traumatized by the wolf attacks and suffered nightmares, Patty said.

For the first time, I started getting calls from people who thought that killing predators was akin to drowning babies. "Leave the wolves alone!" a woman from Arizona yelled in my ear. "They were here first!" After a dozen ass-chewings along these lines, the specter on the horizon started to take clearer shape. I dug out my journal. *Wolves have lots of friends,* I wrote.

In December 1988, I took my family back to Iowa for Christmas. My mother had been diagnosed with advanced breast cancer four years earlier, after Velva Niederfrank saw her bleeding through her blouse while they sipped coffee together. She drove my mother straight to the hospital in Mason City.

"Why didn't you do something sooner, Ma?" I asked her after the surgery. She had to have known, a lump that size.

"I just wanted to go to sleep and never wake up," she said.

She'd been totally and irreversibly depressed since my dad died nearly 22 years earlier, and there was no way to snap her out of it – not even with the Yogo sapphires I could scarcely afford, or the muskrat cape I made for her, or with encouragement or an offer to pay for a plane ticket for her to come visit. The cancer was perhaps a manifestation of her state of mind. I wanted to spend Christmas with her because I knew that soon she'd be gone. She was mostly bedridden, weak and in pain. It was hard to watch. In April, she had a bowl of ice cream, then took a nap and never woke up. Before the service, Rose Klemm closed her beauty shop and walked over to the funeral parlor to fix my mother's hair as she had a thousand times before – one last gesture of friendship.

My mother died not having to know that later that year I would be divorced, leave my family and end up living like a dog. I wonder sometimes if I timed it that way.

Wolves had a way of working their way into my life, like a worm through an apple. They are just animals, of course, but they have a way of making people nuts, and for that matter, attracting nutty people. No normal person could do the job I was doing, and normal people wouldn't want to be involved in something this controversial, at least not on purpose. But here I was.

It was 1989, and I was on the road more than I was home. When I pulled into the driveway, Pam would practically meet me at my truck, wanting the kids spanked for whatever they did that week, wanting to know when the goddamn washing machine would be fixed, reminding me that she had to handle everything because I was always gone. She was probably right. I had my reasons, though. When I was home, I'd discovered that I just wanted to get along, so I stayed out of the house. I hacked at weeds in the yard or went over and did busy-work in my government warehouse next door. Her anger and depression were contagious and I wondered if this was going to be the sum total of my family life. If we had ever had anything in common, we'd slowly lost it somewhere along the way.

The paperwork was done in 1989, almost exactly on what would have been our 20th anniversary. I'd always admired married couples that stay together forever, but now I had to live with the reality that I wouldn't have that to brag about. I was ashamed and guilt-ridden, though I tried to be at every school and sports event my kids were in, and when their mom wouldn't give them the money, I bought their graduation caps and gowns and class rings even though I barely had enough money to buy my groceries every week. I gave Pam everything except my retirement money. The aftermath of divorce combined with the stress at work almost ground me to dust, but what does not kill us....

The following summer, I attended the annual trappers conference, eager for a break in the routine and to kick back with my friends. Each year, the conference was held in some breathtakingly beautiful place in Montana. This year, it was at a church camp, Camp-On-The-Boulder, south of Big Timber. Trappers came from every corner of the state, arriving early so we could all have our hearing tested (federal regulations). The hearing specialist announced that as a group we had the worst hearing he'd ever witnessed and there was really no hope, and left. It was an occupational problem. Spend a couple of decades around airplanes, helicopters and firearms, and that's what you get. I couldn't make myself remember to wear earplugs.

The real reason to show up at the conference, camaraderie aside, was the shotgun shooting contest. The first prize was always a big, silver belt buckle made by Montana Silversmiths with the year of the conference engraved below a brass grizzly bear. It was beautiful and I wanted it. There must have been 25 or 30 guys vying for it as we fired away on a makeshift shooting range. One by one, the trappers missed targets and were disqualified, but I hung in. These guys were good shots – better than I was, I believed – from spending a lifetime hunting predators, target shooting and being gun buffs. I wouldn't have wanted to be a coyote running across an open field when they were around. What I was discovering, however, was that the contest was about keeping your cool and staying focused, more than it was being a good shot. When it got down to just a few of us shooting, and everybody else watching, the heckling began. I wanted that damn buckle. I'd had a shitty year: divorced, depressed, overworked, underpaid and getting deeper into new territory working with wolves. I felt like I deserved something nice. My heart rate was up, my palms were sweating, my shoulders were tense. I had to remember to control my breathing.

Each shooter had to hit a clay target – a "pigeon" – when it came flying out of an unseen chute below and in front of us. It was down to three pigeons. The command by the shooter, when he's ready, is "pull!" and the target goes slinging skyward. It could go left, right, or straight up the center, low or high. I advanced to the next round, and the next, never missing. I was finally with three other shooters, then two, and finally, it was another guy and me. There was tremendous hooting and hollering behind us.

I leveled my shotgun at the open sky.

"Pull!" I yelled over the crowd. Whatever I hit exploded into powder and a roar went up. "What in the hell?" I mumbled.

Someone had slipped an old dried-up biscuit from breakfast into the thrower. I was so keyed up that I shot it. Now I was kind of rattled. My competitor made his shot and it was my turn again.

"Pull!" I followed another biscuit and turned it into a white puff. I wasn't sure what they'd put in there next, but my competitor was even more shook up than I was at all the commotion and blew his next shot. The next target was a plain old clay pigeon. I shattered it, too, and the crowd went nuts. After 20 years of wearing it, that buckle still shines up pretty good.

What I wanted in a wolf "control plan," as we were calling it, was something that resembled protocol – not that anyone cared what I thought. I'd been spending more and more time checking out wolf reports. It was classic, like mountain lions in Iowa: When my friend, Ron Andrews with the Iowa Department of Natural Resources, went around talking to groups about lions, people suddenly started seeing the big cats in their gardens, in the parks, maybe on their back porches. I didn't know much about wolves, but judging from our collective record so far, the Fish and Wildlife Service and my agency, Animal Damage Control, were wading steadily into some deep shit. Those of us at who were in the predator control business needed to nail this stuff and fast before we were dragged into the spotlight for accidentally killing an endangered species. While I was worrying about this and telling people in my agency who cared, the U.S. Fish and Wildlife Service hired Ed Bangs, a biologist who'd worked with wolves in Alaska for 13 years.

I met Bangs in his new Helena office on July 25, 1988. We talked for a long time about how to fix things. Wolves had only recently arrived and already our agencies couldn't agree on anything. Bangs seemed to know wolves, which thrilled me because my agency knew nothing – and wasn't eager to learn. More importantly, he seemed like he *wanted* to be in charge, ready to put the bulldozer in gear. There were meetings every week regarding wolves, and since my half of the state was the half that the wolves liked to visit, I ended up going to a lot of these hand-wringing sessions. I found myself talking wolves with Bangs several times a week, but we didn't really get to know each other until another marauding pack showed up, this time in Marion.

I'd trapped a hell of a lot of predators in my life, but never a wolf. The idea of wolves hadn't ever crossed my mind except when I was a kid watching that newsreel in the darkness of the Avery Theater. Wolves had been mostly fantasy, the subject of movies and history books and idle dreams. I thought they were fascinating animals, but I never thought I'd get a chance to work with them. Anyway, they were extinct now in most of the United States – except that slowly they were trying to return. As the years passed, more and more wolves crossed that invisible border between Canada and United States, and the more they did, the more I wished they'd just stay away. People were going to be their worst enemy, myself included.

When I caught a pup in August 1989, on the operation at Marion, I didn't go around bragging about it. She only weighed 40 pounds. I found out that it was a lot easier to catch the pups than the wise old adults. The pack, which we could never count accurately, had wandered down from Canada a hundred miles from the Browning incident and started killing cattle – at least that's what the rumor mill said.

I drove to Marion, where a wolf had been shot days earlier for hanging around a sheep corral. It was going to be my job to determine if wolves were to blame for the five dead Holstein calves on a ranch outside of town. If they were, they'd have to be moved, something no one had yet attempted. Bangs was heading there, too, as were a couple more wolf experts hired by the Fish and Wildlife Service, Dr. Steve Fritts and Joe Fontaine. I was grateful to have the help. These guys probably knew everything about wolves. The lines were clear now: The Fish and Wildlife Service was in charge of live wolves, and Animal Damage Control was in charge of the dead things and of catching problem wolves.

The Marion rancher and his five dead calves looked like they'd hit on hard times long before the wolves arrived. The word *calves* is really a misnomer, for they can weigh upwards of 500 pounds. He pointed at a live one, telling me that the wolves attacked it and wounded others as well.

I bent down to take a look, but I couldn't see anything but maggots wiggling in a wound on its hip. Next, he led me to a group of calves standing in a corral. They were weak with illness and had pinkeye. One calf's rectal area was nothing but a hollow cavity infested with maggots extending all the way into the hair and skin on one hip. Time to shoot this one, I thought.

"Sir, as far as I can see, these calves haven't been bitten by any predator," I said, adding that it would sure be interesting to know where all the maggots came from.

This didn't go over well, and he insisted we go kill some wolves. He also wanted to be reimbursed for his dead calves and, oh yes, he wanted me to help him get a government loan to help with his farming expenses.

Bangs and Fontaine took over nodding and listening while I headed out to the pastures, looking for signs that wolves had been around. I checked the fences for hair and the pasture for tracks, and found only dog tracks and dog shit with Holstein hair in it. The rancher's dog was probably doing the biting and killing, if it was happening at all.

Four more calf carcasses lay along the tree line of the pasture, but nothing remained but greasy bones. The bones were undisturbed and the skeletons were complete, meaning that they died and rotted and nothing scavenged them. Wolves were not to blame in this case, but I wasn't ready to say that out loud quite yet. I returned to the corrals and studied the injured calves for an answer. Then it came to me: the rancher was branding his calves on the right hip and the brands burned too deeply. Flies were depositing their eggs in the bloody wounds and in turn the maggots were eating the calves alive.

That night I shared my theory. Bangs agreed, but had already concluded that things had spiraled into a public relations nightmare before we'd even arrived. The local newspapers had convicted the wolves, and so had the neighbors for miles around. Bangs was worried that if we didn't move the wolves, people were going to start shooting them.

We put our plan into action the next morning, and we were a good five minutes into it when Paul Mangini, the foreman of the Lost Trail Ranch who'd come by to check things out, pulled me aside.

Did wolves kill those calves?" he asked.

"No sir," I said.

"Do you want to know where the wolves are?"

I expected some crazy theory.

Paul leaned close and whispered. "They're nowhere near this place. They're on some private land right behind the ranch I manage."

He stood back and looked at me, waiting for his words to take hold.

While Bangs and Fontaine took a butt-chewing, I slipped away with Mangini, saying I was following up on a lead.

I followed him back toward Marion and north to the Lost Trail Ranch. A light rain was falling when we turned onto a timber company road and through a green gate. *No Trespassing*, the sign read. The road took us past scattered groups of cattle between thick stands of trees and old clearcuts. Mangini pulled over and shut off the truck. We got out, careful not to slam our doors, and walked quietly down the road. He stopped us when we came to a huge clearing, an island of aspen in the middle.

"The wolves come out of that heavy timber and hang out in the pasture by those aspens," he whispered. "I watched 'em all summer when I was haying."

I was skeptical. Who was this guy, anyway? I turned to talk to him. I wanted to know a few things.

"So how many you think are in this pack? Do they have pups...?" I was going to quiz him if he knew so much and had been keeping quiet all this time, but he pointed around me.

"Look right there!"

The slim, black animal trotted across the pasture and disappeared into the aspens. I couldn't believe it.

"Damn, I should have tried to use my predator call," I said. Mangini urged me to do it, but I shrugged it off. It was a gamble getting its attention from this far. The trees where it vanished were 500 yards away.

Suddenly another black wolf appeared, trotting in the same direction. I fumbled through my coat and found my predator call.

All we had to hide ourselves were low tree branches and knee-high grass.

"Don't move," I said, and blew on the call, imitating the sound of an injured rabbit.

The wolf stopped and looked in our direction then began to lope straight toward us. I paused, thinking about all the whitetail deer we'd seen on our way into this area. Why would wolves kill cattle when they can eat deer?

The wolf slowed, coming within 200 yards, then it stopped and stood motionless, looking straight at us, but not seeing us. I blew again and the wolf started toward us. I pulled out my camera. It was within 30 yards but wouldn't come any closer. I snapped a picture. It wasn't yet a year old. A pup by my estimation. Slightly bigger than a large coyote. It turned and hurried to the safety of the aspens, its ears back.

I stood by my finding that no wolf pack was anywhere near the other ranch – because I knew exactly where they were living. But to cover myself, I set traps there anyway. I caught and killed a few coyotes and shot another that came close when I blew on my predator call. The calves had some abrasions and minor wounds that could possibly be blamed on coyotes and that was the justification. Something needed to die while Bangs was drawing up a plan. It was a shameful reality that this was the only way to get pressure off the wolves.

Bangs decided that the wolves hanging around the Lost Trail Ranch should be moved. It was time to start trapping. I figured he knew best. He'd persuaded the locals to back off for another month so that the pups could grow a little more and stand a better chance of surviving relocation.

The wolves showed themselves one rainy day when I was shoveling the only dry dirt I could find from under an old hay shed. Bangs and Fontaine showed up to get dirt for their trap sets, too. All of us saw the wolves, walking around in a pasture about two football fields away, sniffing the ground. A big black wolf slipped into the trees, but two puppies sat and watched us.

When the rain finally let up I set a few traps, dressing my sets with delicate globs of my own homemade bait that I called Carter's Kitty Kandy.

My special, secret bait was revealed to the world quite by accident. While doing research for his novel, *The Loop*, author Nicholas Evans flew all the way from England to ride around with me for a week. There were others in Montana he needed to interview as well, but he wanted to go with me to see what made a trapper tick. I was thrilled to get to meet a real author, but kind of nervous. He'd been catapulted to stardom for his book, *The Horse Whisperer*, and for that reason, and because he's English and therefore sophisticated, I was baffled that he'd want anything to do with me or a trapline. All the same, I put on clean clothes.

Evans pulled his rental car into the gravel driveway of my warehouse, and in my eager state, I threw the door open and greeted him just as he was approaching the threshold. He staggered backward slightly, slapping a hand over his nose.

"How can you stand being in there? What is that horrible stink?"

I was immune to Carter's Kitty Kandy. I'd almost forgotten that I was fermenting a new batch. I closed the door and we stood outside where the air was fresh. Nobody ever asked me much about the bait I made, especially a famous author.

"That's my own personal recipe!" I said. "First I get some bobcat carcasses and grind them up into five gallon pails...."

Evans' color had become sort of green. I thought I should get him a chair or a maybe a belt of whiskey. Instead I kept talking, "...and then I burp it when it's fermenting, you know, to let the gasses out...."

Kitty Kandy caught wolves like crazy and was a great icebreaker when I drove out to ranches. "What the hell is that smell?" they'd ask before I could even turn off the engine.

After a few minutes, the author gathered his senses and even asked a few questions about Kitty Kandy. It was as good a way as any to get to know me. He dreaded asking where I got the ingredients for such foul concoctions. I hesitated. I didn't want him giving my bait recipes away.

"I get bobcat carcasses from fur buyers, but sometimes I substitute mashed kitty cats from the highway. It's kind of like an O'Gorman lure, but not nearly as delicate, so to get it just right, I need to put my nose right up to it when it's fermenting to see what else it needs."

Evans stared at me.

"The bouquet has to be right," I added to the silence that had suddenly fallen between us.

Because it was a secret recipe, I shared Kitty Kandy with only a few trappers. I still have 50 gallons of the stuff stored in a secret location in Idaho. Because it's rare, it catches a lot of wolves. I told Evans all of this. Then I decided to change the subject. He ended up writing my bait into his novel's storyline.

But now it was time to put Kitty Kandy to work for real at the Lost Trail Ranch. I was sure no wolf could pass it up. Flies landed and rubbed their tiny legs in approval. I carried my pails and traps past Fontaine and Bangs, who were on the ground not far from me, excavating like badgers, presumably to set some traps, too. What were they doing? I did my best to contain my annoyance, but as I finished my next set, the two men strolled past me with their traps and bait buckets. We hop-scotched like this all day. There was no way we were going to catch an adult wolf in any of these traps with all this human scent around, I grumbled to myself.

I was extremely particular when it came to scent around my trap sites. George Good had taught me well and over the years it paid off: no walking around, no spitting, nothing that flashed *humans were here* in the nose of a canine. To complicate matters, Mangini, the ranch manager, had become my shadow, murmuring insults about my cohorts all day long.

"You want me to run them off so you can work better?" he asked.

While we tried to catch the wolves, the locals were getting lathered again: There was another dead cow, this time at Mangini's. I examined it while he stood over me. Yes, the wolves had been eating it, but the carcass was too far rotten to tell how it died. It was laying in a meadow where the wolves hung out a lot, outside of the fenced pasture.

Mangini invited us stay in a tiny house on the ranch. At least we could cook something, plus it saved us time and money and, best of all, we'd be able to hear wolves when they howled and announced that they'd not up and left. We found, however, that staying there wasn't without cost: Mangini expected a daily briefing – but at his home where we sat around a huge oak table with him at the head. We started calling him The Godfather, but not in front of him. When he had time to ride along, he only wanted to go with me. I never knew exactly what his beef was with the other fellas, but he really got a kick out of picking on Fontaine. When Dr. Steve Fritts, the brains of the impending reintroduction, showed up, Mangini started in on him, too. The Godfather held all of us hostage, but we realized it only after we'd been there a week, using the handy ranch house and trudging over to his place every night to give him the latest while he nodded slowly and worked a toothpick.

Bangs and I each caught a pup, but those don't really count. What mattered was the adult male that I eventually enticed into one of my traps. It was the first one of my career.

On Mangini's ranch we used the Braun trap, an ugly monster of a thing that weighed eight pounds. With the chain and drag, it weighed 11. The jaws – the business part of the trap – were lined with hard rubber pads which looked nice, but the trap was mean enough to snap and hold the foot of a calf, a cow, or even a horse. It took all of my 240 pounds and a tough set of boots to step down on the springs and open it. I hoped no one's dog came around and stepped in one of these because I was pretty sure the average person couldn't open it. I sure as hell hoped it wouldn't splinter the leg on a wolf. Wouldn't that look nice in the newspapers?

Wolf traps had been a major issue since 1986, when I first approached the two federal agencies about acquiring an acceptable wolf trap. Ed Bangs rolled his eyes the first time he laid eyes on the Braun. The high, square crown of the closed jaws meant it would likely snap on the leg rather than the foot. The foot is where you want to catch a wolf, if there's a humane way to trap one. Brauns were bone busters. But expediency was the name of the game and our agencies didn't have anything else on hand. Besides, they were originally designed for wolves, the Animal Damage Control supervisors said. The difference was that, back then, no one was trying to keep the wolf alive.

We caught wolves with Brauns, and the traps hurt them, but luckily none of the animals suffered broken legs. The plan, which we formulated as we went, was to take the pups to the vet clinic in Kalispell and keep trying for the adults. I set more traps and so did Fontaine and Bangs. Then Steve Fritts decided to set some, too.

True to its nature, one of my Brauns caught a coyote and gave it a compound leg fracture. I shot the poor thing. A day later, Fritts was missing a trap. We searched for hours before Bangs found it clamped on a dead deer's slender leg. A few days later I snapped a deer, too, but a mountain lion finished that one off before I could find it.

Checking traps became nerve-wracking; I was out before it was light every day waiting for the next disaster. One morning, the rancher at Marion waved me down. I rolled down my window and he shoved a newspaper in my face. The headline said something about coyotes being responsible for his dead calves.

Who had time to think about reporters?

"I'm sorry, I said. "I'll get to the bottom of it."

I was seething. I wasn't sure where the reporter got his information, but it wasn't from me. I decided to head to Kalispell and straighten out Mark Armstrong at the Daily Interlake. Bangs and Fontaine could check my traps while I was gone. On my way, a radio news flash told of government trappers who had more than 30 wolf traps set near Marion.

Armstrong wasn't at the office yet, so I looked him up and knocked on his front door. He let me in without hesitation and gave me a cup of coffee. I vented and he listened.

"I got my information from the Fish and Wildlife Service in Helena," he said, and apologized for the hard feelings. I had a reporter on my side of things when I left. For years afterward, Armstrong called me before he put a story to bed.

On my way back, I saw Fontaine talking on a pay phone at a highway gas station. He waved, and I pulled in next to him and sat. He kept talking, but gestured wildly with one arm, pointing at his truck. What was he doing? He waved me toward the truck again.

In the seat, a huge gray wolf lay asleep, its feet tied together. We weren't sure what might happen when the drugs wore off, so we'd taken to tying up every wolf we caught. I opened the door to get a better look. Fontaine hung up and thrust his hand toward me, grinning.

"Congratulations dude, you had this big boy in a trap this morning."

I pumped his hand. I couldn't believe it. I wanted to hear the whole story.

We took the wolf to the vet clinic where the injured puppies were still in cages. I lifted it and started inside.

"Hang on, man. I wanna take your picture," Fontaine said.

The 98-pound wolf went into a pen with the puppies. He was old, his teeth yellow and broken and worn to the gums. He was probably the alpha male. Two toes on the foot that had been trapped were bleeding, but otherwise he was in good shape. A small crowd was assembling around us while we saw to the old boy. The wolf was identified later by morphologist Ron Nowak as having one of the three largest skull measurements ever recorded in the lower 48 states.

"Looks like we almost didn't get this one," Bangs said. I agreed. I couldn't imagine how the Braun could have snapped only his toes.

Fontaine told me the heroic story of Bangs chasing down the wolf as it bounded over downed logs, bouncing the drag behind it. I felt like a kid and wanted to hear it again and again. I counted it as my first real wolf capture. I just wished I'd been there.

We were capturing the first wolves in the Northern Rockies for the first relocation. It was happening slowly but surely. There was another first for me, too: I darted a wolf from a helicopter. I thought I'd be prepared for it, that I'd have time to plan everything, but I didn't. Circumstances just presented themselves.

An adult wolf and a pup were trotting one minute and out of sight the next, disappearing the way they always do, this time into a waving sea of eight-foot grass at the edge of Dahl Lake on the Lost Trail Ranch near Marion. There were so many places for them to hide in this wild bit of country.

Paul Mangini and I watched the grass with binoculars.

"This would be the perfect spot to bring in a chopper," I said, trying not to move my mouth too much and jar my optics. Behind us, Bangs pulled up and walked over with his hands in his pockets. I told him about the wolves and my idea to use a helicopter.

He was dubious, but left for the ranch house to try and get a pilot on the phone.

An hour passed, but I knew any second I'd hear a chopper. Instead, here came Bangs in his pickup. I eyed the grass again. The wolves still hadn't emerged.

"I couldn't get a hold of anybody," he said. In his estimation that was the end of it.

"What?"

But I could tell he'd given up. "Gimme your truck keys," I demanded.

I mumbled to myself the whole drive back to the ranch house. I dialed, the phone rang once and Ron Gipe answered.

"Ron, its Carter. How'd you like to help catch a wolf today?"

Gipe was a damn good helicopter pilot. I gave him directions and hung up.

When I returned, Bangs and I put darts together for the capture. Gipe would be here in an hour. By the time we'd assembled the last one, the chopper was touching down in the meadow, blowing my hat off and sending papers flying out my truck window. I introduced Gipe and Bangs. I didn't know a thing about shooting aluminum darts at running wolves. Bangs was the one who had all the darting experience in Alaska.

Gipe took the doors off and Bangs got in. I backed my ATV out of my truck and climbed on. I figured I could circle the five or so acres of long grass around the lake where the wolves were hiding and force them into the open.

The helicopter lifted off and began circling. I rode as fast as I dared, whooping and hollering and trying to avoid a head-longer in the deep mud holes.

After 30 minutes, the chopper landed. Bangs stepped out and shrugged.

"I think they ran out of there and you just didn't see them," he said.

"Give it another try Ed," I urged him. "I know they're in there."

"I don't think so, Carter. We gave it our best shot. I think they're out of there." He'd given up, but I saw him reading whatever look had come across my face. "...but if you want to give it a try, the gun is on the seat and there's a dart in the chamber."

"I will." I was pissed. I knew the wolves were still in the grass. I'd been watching and waiting for them to run out and they didn't. Bangs had given up too soon.

I climbed in. I was wearing my jeans and a flannel shirt and had no safety equipment, not even a headset or a helmet. Bangs had done the same. Gipe and I had to yell at each other to communicate. I hooked the seat belt and we took off.

"Fly over to those dead willows. That's where I saw them run go in."

Gipe made a wide circle and was on the way when he yelled and pointed below us.

The rotor wash parted the grass exposing the animal. It crouched, waiting for something to happen. I decided that Bangs should do this and hollered at Gipe to take me back. I didn't know anything about the way darts shot.

As I made that decision, however, I saw Bangs below, riding back toward the ranch house on my ATV.

"It's on the move, Carter," Gipe yelled. He accelerated toward the running wolf.

"OK, let's do it." I yanked on my safety belt and leaned out with the dart gun. I had no idea what I was doing. Gipe closed in as fast as he could on the wolf, which was now running at top speed. I didn't trust the way an aluminum dart might fly. I pulled back the hammer and was ready to fire. Then I hesitated.

"You're going to have to shoot. We've got tall timber coming up fast," Gipe yelled.

I took my eye off the wolf for a second. Sixty-foot trees rushed at us.

"Get closer!" I yelled.

We ranged low until the wolf looked like it was running in place under me. When I had it broadside I pulled the trigger.

The dart flew in a slight arc and passed under the wolf's belly. As I saw this happen, Gipe pulled us straight up, the pointed tips of dark trees passing under us.

Goddammit!" I yelled. Gipe muttered something.

"Maybe we can get another shot," he added.

I chambered another dart and looked around for the wolf. It was still running, its ears back, making toward another canopy of trees. We've lost it, I thought.

Then suddenly, the wolf spun around, like it was chasing its tail.

"Did you see that?" Gipe yelled.

I did, but I didn't know what it meant. Maybe it was thrilled at eluding us and was celebrating.

But then it happened again. And again. Then, the wolf stumbled.

It took a second for me to retrieve the dim hope that the dart and the wolf had connected. When its back end tried to pass its front end, and the animal collapsed for good, I was convinced. I punched my palm and cheered.

"Keep an eye on her and mark the location," I yelled. I made a mental note of the decayed tree that lay next to the wolf. It must have been centuries old when it fell.

"You gotta land, let me out," I blurted. I was afraid the wolf might have only gotten a fraction of the sedative and would jump up and run away.

In the field a mile or so away, Bangs had watched the entire chase. He raced toward us as we landed, jumped off the ATV, nearly tripping, and threw a hug on me, lifting me off the ground.

Gipe took off again and put the chopper in a hover over the wolf while Bangs and I ran towards it, leaping over downed trees and dodging branches. It was a black one, but was turning salt-and-pepper with age. It turned out to be a she and appeared to be a nursing mother, probably the alpha female. Her ears twitched at our sounds, her eyes dilated and staring. There was a bit of blood on the inside of her right hind leg: the dart had skimmed her undersides and hit her leg mid-stride. I almost missed, but I didn't. It was the first wolf to be darted in the lower 48 states.

When I worked for Animal Damage Control, I kept a running tally of livestock that had been killed by wolves or other predators. For my own amusement and maybe for posterity, I kept a copy of every report that I turned over to my boss. Those reports and my diaries came in handy when reporters called. A day didn't go by, once I got involved with wolves, that one side or the other didn't call me up and tell me I was a dirty, stinking liar. But my diaries, when stacked, measure about a foot high, and everything in them tells the way it really happened.

I didn't consider myself a crime-scene investigator until I learned that everyone else did. In their minds, a crime had been committed against their livestock by wild animals and it needed to be answered – preferably with a gunshot. It turned out not to be such a simple job. Without cutting off its hide, I couldn't tell what killed a torn-up sheep or a steer sprawled in the mud. My knife – and my diaries – became my closest allies. I wanted to be thorough, and moreover, I wanted to be honest. I cared what the answer was, even when others in my agency didn't. I did a lot of skinning while the rancher standing over me talked trash about wolves. When I reported right there that disease or weather or something besides a predator was responsible, most of them weren't happy about it.

It was back-breaking, but I skinned every dead animal down to its hooves and combed the area surrounding the attack for clues – every time, and sometimes in the dark. I took photos and videos, and my reports had extra pages of description attached because that's what Defenders of Wildlife needed in order to pay compensation. I'd seen first hand that many of the guys in my outfit – from the highest ranks to the lowest – were yes-men, and I didn't want to be counted among them. It wasn't right. I had confidence that I could tell a rancher what killed his animal – or, more often, what didn't. Some ranchers may not have liked my answer, but most of them appreciated my candor. The extra pages, over time, got me in trouble because my agency didn't want me going the extra mile for a bunch of wolf-lovers, even when it meant that a rancher might not get paid.

Being around dead livestock isn't for weak stomachs. There's stink and maggots and bloating and sometimes a minor explosion of guts, if the animal has been lying in the summer sun for a week. Scavengers run off with body parts, and heat can bring the smell to unbearable levels. The things that happen to an animal when it is dead, the simple biology of decay, often mask the way they were killed – or just died. I had an advantage over most people because of those years when I was a kid who dissected everything looking for answers. Sometimes I shot a bird or a mouse just to cut it open and see how death happened.

Of course, when it came to what killed a steer in its pasture, there was (and still is) no shortage of opinion. The owner phoned his veterinarian and several neighbors and often they were huddled, murmuring theories, by the time I arrived. Sometimes the sheriff and the brand inspector got involved, too. Stir in a little wolf hysteria and I was glad to be so much bigger and taller than most people, and a better shot, generally.

I was amazed that conservative, God-fearing rural folks could conjure such absurd ideas about how a farm animal became dead. I was once called to a ranch north of Great Falls to look at a dead cow that had been reportedly mutilated by people – most likely devil-worshippers – or maybe aliens, according to the sheriff. They'd used scalpels to cut out the tongue, remove the ears and cut out the vulva, teats and udder, he explained, walking me around the cow. He asked what I thought.

I'd known in less than a minute, but I liked his imagination, so I let him go on. Bigfoot and extra-terrestrials were not on my list of suspects. The cow had tipped over at least a week before, so I didn't go much into the initial cause of death, but judging by the tracks, the missing body parts were chewed off by coyotes or skunks, I said. When the sheriff demanded an explanation for the scalpel marks, I showed him how the recent warm weather had caused bloating that stretched the skin so tight that the edges of the bites looked cut rather than chewed. I was dismissed. He didn't call back.

Most trappers I knew did their investigations with the tips of their boots, rolling the animal to one side, never taking their hands from their pockets. Yep, they'd say, looks like a wolf did it, or at least was "possibly" or "probably" responsible. It quickly became the fashion to blame wolves for all things dead. After all, Bangs chuckled, wolves were the spawn of Satan.

I didn't care for the escalating anti-wolf attitude because it caused imprecise reasoning. And imprecise reasoning was quickly followed by actions that didn't solve the problem at hand. When I came to Montana, I willingly took a pathology course with a Western slant from Dr. Bart O'Gara at the University of Montana. I decided on my own that I would find out as often as possible what exactly killed the livestock in my district. That meant I'd be cutting up a lot of dead things, so I started carrying my knife and sharpener everywhere, and driving 500 miles on a Sunday if necessary, just to keep people honest. I wanted the final answer to be right and fair. I *had* to know what happened to the dead stock, if I was going to help the rancher keep it from happening again. If a calf died from disease, I would look pretty stupid setting traps for a predator that didn't exist or trapping an innocent scavenger that came to eat the carcass.

One day, John Bouchard, the trapper in Harlowton, got a call about a dead sheep and I rode with him to take a look. I said nothing for a while, watching Bouchard walk around the bedgrounds, getting his ass chewed by the rancher about black bears. Finally, after the rancher left on an errand, Bouchard concluded that a bear had killed the sheep and planned to set a foot snare. I walked the area where the attack happened, looking at the ground for tracks and evidence of a struggle, then circled back to Bouchard. There were no obvious injuries on the ewe other than a portion of her udder that had been eaten. It hadn't been moved or dragged from the place it died. I asked my trapper what made him think a bear did it.

"Well, don't you think so?" He looked puzzled.

"No, John." I got out my knife and cut back the sheep's hide.

Bears like sheep udders and often eat that part first. Part of the udder had been eaten, but it didn't mean a bear did the killing. I skinned out the entire sheep, removing the dense wool. The animal had no external injuries, but the inside of the sheep's udder was blue and infected.

A truck was bouncing back toward us.

"*You* tell him a bear didn't do it," Bouchard said.

The rancher was all smiles, slamming his door and walking over to us.

"We won't be setting any snares," I said. "A bear didn't do this."

The smile evaporated and the rancher's hackles went up. I kept talking.

"You're a sheepman. You tell *me* what happened, because the only thing I see is an infected bag and no bite marks." I gestured with my knife so he could see what I'd been up to.

It worked. It was simple and the truth and backed by the evidence that lay in front of us. The man stared at his dead ewe.

"Yeah, I had a couple in the band with blue bag. Must have been one of them." After a moment, he straightened.

"You guys want a cup of coffee?"

Later that day, Bouchard was called to a ranch where the rancher said golden eagles were pulling dead lambs apart. Bouchard asked the rancher how he knew eagles were to blame. Simple, the rancher said: The eagles were sitting on the carcasses. Bouchard took out his knife and pulled the hide off one of the lambs. There were coyote bites on its neck. The eagles were just scavengers.

Before it was dark, my two-way radio buzzed with Jim Rost's voice, the trapper south of Bouchard's area. He wanted my help with a dead calf. Its owner was a polite old-timer who was taken aback by our quick response. He was sure he had a bear or eagle problem.

A half-mile away from the man's ranch, near a rock outcropping and down in a draw, lay the 300-pound calf. Its skin was pulled inside out over its legs and head, its insides eaten down to its skeleton. It looked like the feeding pattern of a bear, but the carcass was covered with droppings that indicated magpies, ravens and eagles were feeding, too. So far, the rancher was right. I sharpened my knife and split the hide so I could examine the legs and hooves. No bites or scratches. Then I went the other way, slicing the hide and exposing the calf's head. Its face was swollen. When I made a slice across its nose, fluid poured out. I'd never seen that.

"I think your calf had a serious problem before the varmints got to it," I said. The rancher stood beside me, watching and nodding. I didn't think he'd ever seen this kind of affliction either.

"Gosh," he said, "I'm sure sorry I had you boys drive way out here for this."

All large predators have a way they kill – a signature. Bears often bite over the top of an animal and turn it inside out as they eat it. Lions go for the neck of their prey, breaking it or suffocating it. Sometimes, they leave scratches from their razor sharp claws, and often, they half-bury the prey with dirt or brush or even snow. Lions sometimes lick the hair or fur off their victims before eating them. Coyotes grab by the throat and don't usually kill anything bigger than poultry, sheep, goats or small calves. Dogs (yes, your neighbor's dogs) pull tufts of wool out of a sheep while trying to kill it and are imprecise biters when they kill, often wounding, but seldom eating their prey because they have Alpo waiting for them back home. Wolves are capable of killing alone, but often operate in packs. They prefer their prey to run and attack it from the rear or flank, or grasp the webbing where legs meet the body because it's the easiest place to latch on. Wolves may kill sheep by biting them in the neck, but other wounds are often found on the flanks and rear. Golden eagles leave fine, triangular shaped puncture wounds, the result of their talons. The way predators behave when making a kill is not absolute, but they tend to do it in certain ways. The body speaks, said Dr. Richard Stroud of the National Fish and Wildlife Forensics Laboratory. I learned this even before I met the esteemed Dr. Stroud, and he is right.

My main concern was examining the dead and wounded livestock for any sign of trauma, bruising, and hemorrhage that would indicate a predator might have clawed or bitten them. Once I determined that disease, weather, accidents or other non-predator issues were the cause of death, I'd tell the rancher about it. Dealing with it was up to him.

I don't pretend to know a lot about disease or poisoning or birthing problems in domestic livestock. I tell people to call a vet when I know I'm out of my league. If a fellow is missing 20 head of calves, I tell him to call his brand inspector. But if a predator might be the culprit, I'm the guy who'll know. And if it turns out that predators took advantage because dead stock was left lying around, or because the rancher was neglectful and let his animals wander the range unguarded for too many weeks, well, I can tell about those things, too.

While bears and lions will sometimes drag their kills into the brush or bury their meals in litter and other debris, wolves seldom move their kills very far. Wolf kills are often right out in the open and sometimes can be located by following scavenger birds like ravens, crows, magpies, eagles or vultures. I can understand missing a calf or two. Wolves can be blamed for it. But when large numbers of cattle or sheep go missing on the range, it isn't a wolf problem; it's poor livestock management.

Over time, my field investigations became the cause of murmurings that Animal Damage Control was disloyal to the livestock industry. I wasn't finding that wolves were as evil as everyone thought and I was sure that they weren't to blame for most of the dead livestock in the region. The idea that Animal Damage Control was the "hired gun of the livestock industry," as one of my bosses once put it, was probably news to the U.S. Department of Agriculture, which signed the trappers' paychecks. But the higher-ups at my agency really believed it was their job to go around killing as many wolves as Ed Bangs would allow. Governors and other elected officials gave me all kinds of chances to change my reports – to say that wolves killed livestock. I refused. There came a time when I wondered if critics were dragging carcasses to the back forty, then calling me to come take a look in an attempt to trip me up, but I couldn't quite convince myself of such a conspiracy.

It is a fact that wolves kill so few livestock that the predators barely register on the pie chart of the U.S. Department of Agriculture's National Agriculture Statistics Service. It's respiratory and digestive diseases, birthing problems, old age, poisonous plants and weather that cause most livestock deaths, although coyotes can be hell on sheep. Of course, if your ox is the one getting gored, you'd consider wolves a big problem. I know that ranchers love their animals (until they're loaded on a truck headed for slaughter – then they're just a commodity), and a few really go for expensive breeds, bluebloods and 4-H candidates, but I'm talking about the livestock industry as a whole. I don't know anyone in the ranching business who went out of business specifically because of wolves.

Few ranchers disputed my findings, even when they weren't pleased with them. Then there were others. When trapper Jim Rost wanted me to help him look at seven dead calves at Chuck Weller's ranch near Big Timber, I got there after dark and had to peel away the calves' hides using a spotlight. They'd been baking in the late-summer heat for at least a week. A friend riding her horse had found the calves in various locations on the Weller place. In a newspaper account, she said she'd seen what looked like an antelope or a mountain lion in the distance. When the sandy-colored animal stalked her for a while, she was horrified, decided it must be a wolf, and rode back to tell the Wellers.

I examined each calf, especially the places where wolves would bite if they'd done the killing: behind the front legs, the front of the hind legs, down the rear quarters. Nothing. Even though the telltale hemorrhage from a wolf bite would have long since discolored, it would have been there in some form, tucked away under the putrid skin along with distinct tooth marks. The signs were always the same.

Several of the calves died near water and several had hides so dry they split in my hands. I left my knife in its sheath and peeled these like loose wallpaper. The skin zigzagged as it tore, but nothing had bitten these 500-pound animals, even after they died. The last calf was turned inside out. Maybe there was a bear around here taking advantage of whatever killed these animals, but wolves didn't do this. I thought about where the calves died: near water. When animals are feverish, they head to the water, and that's often where they drop. I'd seen similar signs of dehydration near Choteau, on the land that a rancher leased to graze his cattle: mud caked on cattle's knees. They were dehydrated and had been kneeling in the mud to lap rainwater out of the small puddles formed in their own hoofmarks. Their deaths were blamed on wolves, too.

Rost and I spotlighted the road, searching for wolf tracks or a pile of black wolf shit. We found nothing. I'd made up my mind and we drove back to the ranch. It was late, but the lights were still on.

I didn't ask why they waited so long to call. It had become standard that most people had trouble getting around to it. Mrs. Weller handed us glasses of lemonade and I told the assembled family that no predator had killed their calves. I added that I could tell it even though the carcasses were in terrible shape.

"You might want to call your vet," I said. "I think your calves were sick."

One of the Weller men flung his Stetson across the room. It hit the wall.

"I knew they'd send somebody like you over here," he yelled. "And you!" he flung a hand at Rost, "you've never done us a bit of good either!"

Tomorrow, he'd be calling three veterinarians, several county commissioners and each of Montana's livestock associations, and they could come take a look for themselves, he seethed.

I was thirsty, but never got a chance to sip that lemonade. I set it on the table. Rost did the same and we left. The door slammed behind us.

I called Weller's vet early the next morning and got my side of the story in first. In a day or two, the media jumped on it, a rancher versus big government. However, without a report from me that said wolves killed the calves, the Wellers stood no chance that Defenders of Wildlife would pay for the loss. Suddenly the governor was involved, asking if I didn't want to make a few revisions to my report. No I didn't, I said, adding that I had more experience in this arena than any rancher or veterinarian. I was truly getting fed up with interference from politicos.

The governor of Montana sent a letter to the Wellers saying he was sorry about the dead calves and that he sure hoped their cattle would fare better in the future.

After a second incident at Marion, wolves took over my life.

This time, wolves truly were to blame for several dead calves. The objective was to stop the killing by moving the wolves, so I set traps. But this time, a group of wolf advocates, the Wolf Action Group, got wind of things and went up and down the roads, tromping my trapline, pissing all over it and rendering it useless. Meantime, the wolf kept killing calves. In the end, I went up in a helicopter and shot it. I tried to put a dart in it first, but it ran crazily through the trees, changing direction each time I was upon it. My orders were to do something – anything – to put an end to the dead cattle, so I did.

It was a lone wolf - the yearling female that had escaped death during the first Marion fiasco. It was the first time I'd had to kill a wolf, but it happened because a bunch of naïve people ruined my trapline, which kept me from catching and moving the animal instead.

The newspapers went wild. Ed Bangs took pains to place the wolf's death squarely at the feet of the Wolf Action Group. The incident triggered an unbelievable public backlash, both pro- and anti-wolf, and with it, more reports of wolves killing livestock and environmentalists protesting by chaining themselves to the desks of high-level officials. Defenders of Wildlife paid the Lost Trail Ranch $3,700, and all of us crossed our fingers that a new pack wouldn't show up anytime soon.

With the latest incident at Marion, and wolves taking all of my time anyway, word came that the Fish and Wildlife Service wanted someone working full time on wolf problems in Montana, Idaho and Wyoming. Bangs was willing to put up the money. He was thinking of me.

I didn't intend to change jobs and even scoffed at the idea because change scared the hell out of me, but my state director came back from a big-cheese meeting in Denver and informed me that I'd been nominated. It was decent of them to push me into a new role because I wouldn't have sought it for myself. It came at a time when I was divorced and confused and restless, and when I realized that although I was responsible for a lot of people and a lot of not-so-mundane stuff, I seemed to have no influence at higher levels. I was becoming one of those guys who bitched that nothing ever changed, but refused to hop aboard when change came rolling by.

Bangs pushed the idea, steamrolled it actually. He'd skipped over the small potatoes and lobbied Congress to get the position that would get me working on wolf issues full time. With the Endangered Species Act as leverage, he got his wish. I applied for the job and got it. I'd be taking home slightly more money and no one could say that it was my idea. The federal agency that supported the presence of wolves, the U.S. Fish and Wildlife Service, would pay for it, but I'd remain under the supervision of USDA Animal Damage Control - the federal agency that wanted them gone.

My office ordered new business cards for me. Under my name were three words, *Wolf Management Specialist*. Those words put me outside of my agency's rigid structure – and in time branded me as a traitor. I had the only job like it in the Northern Rockies: I'd been granted permission to be a wolfer just like the old-guard government hunters, but with one huge difference: I was trying to save them instead of kill them.

Everything I'd learned about wolves up to that point, I'd gleaned by accident. I knew how to trap predators though, and how to shoot darts at running wolves from a moving helicopter, and those things gave me an edge. I could use the job to get better traps and develop better methods of dealing with problem wolves. I also liked being in the mountains, or at a ranch. It was where things mattered as far as I was concerned. If I'd thought I would have to sit at a desk to do my job, I would have quit. My place and my calling were to get people talking, keep the wolves out of harm's way, and stay out there doing both until everyone felt like things would be okay.

The trappers I'd supervised felt that I'd taken a demotion and were thrilled that I'd become one of them, all except Ken Wheeler. He thought of me and him as a team and figured that, if I moved on, maybe he would, too.

The trappers saw wolves as an endless pain in the butt. Other than expressing a keen interest in getting to kill one someday, most didn't want anything to do with them. Wolves attracted nuts, they said, bunny-huggers and greenies and people who just didn't understand how destructive a wolf could be. If it was all the same, they'd let me deal with the kinds of people that wolves lured from the woodwork. Their sentiments became action; as soon as I got the new job, they passed every wolf report to me, adding that they'd rather deal with 20 problem coyotes than one complaint about a lobo.

Wolf hysteria was on the rise. It was gradual but steady, like mercury on a hot day. As with any animal that elicits a visceral reaction in people, whether bad or good, there was little basis for it. I felt justified saying so; wolves weren't guilty most of the time.

A few wolves had wandered over the border from Canada, but not many, at least not enough to matter. Without help, wolves couldn't establish themselves as a breeding population. This was the premise for the government's case for reintroducing this native species. A rancher in the Northern Rockies, weather-beaten from eking out a living on a spread his granddaddy started, would put the animal in the crosshairs and pull the trigger every chance he got. He'd bury the wolf on his property, and if he was smart, he'd mention it to no one. Some hunters were no different. These things happened. They still do. It's hard to blame a man for shooting a wolf that's messing with his livestock. Seeing it happen is one thing, but finding a dead sheep or cow or calf does not mean a wolf killed it.

Between 1987 and 2000, I skinned every animal in Montana that wolves were accused of killing. After a while, I wondered about the competence of my supervisors, who parroted ranchers no matter how outlandish the story, and who privately cursed wolves and the "greenies" who loved them. I wondered about the gullibility of some Montanans, too. In some cases, there wasn't a single wolf print in the mud next to the carcass. Had wolves grown wings? The evidence didn't usually match the ranchers' stories. Wolves had been absent from the state for a generation, wiped out by the same federal government that was now considering restoring them. But mention that four-letter word, *w-o-l-f,* and people start seeing the animal everywhere and every dead ranch animal or pet as the wolf's latest eviscerated victim.

A hearing in Helena in 1991 was packed with hundreds of people, most of them wearing Stetsons. They'd come to offer their opinions about reintroducing wolves into Yellowstone National Park and the wilderness of Central Idaho. Similar gatherings had already occurred in Denver, Cheyenne and Boise. A panel of 10 government officials sat at the front of the room, nodding, taking notes, and telling people they'd used up their allotted three minutes of talking.

Hearings are a sign that the government has already made a decision. Taking public testimony is just a way to ease folks into an idea and let them blow off steam about it. The decision was that wolves would be back soon and everybody had better get used to it. Still, people waved cardboard signs and shouted in the hotel lobby outside the hearing room. I sat in the back row, entertained, until someone passed a note to me: the Ninemile pack had killed a calf.

Unlike other places where wolves were accused of crimes they didn't commit, they really did kill cattle in a beautiful Montana valley known as the Ninemile.

There were no tooth punctures in the hides of the dead steers at the Priddy Ranch. It was only when I skinned the animals, folding back the entire hide, that their injuries – and the power of a wolf's jaws – became apparent: massive hemorrhage that looked like grape jelly had reduced each steer's hindquarters to mush – the signature of a wolf attack. The steers had been bitten on the throat and flanks, too. The wolves, known as the Ninemile pack, had eaten neither animal. Perhaps as mere yearlings, and absent the guidance of their parents, they knew how to kill these round, slow animals, but weren't sure what to do next.

The Ninemile pack had come into existence only a year and a half earlier. The black alpha female – the mother of the young wolves that were now killing cattle – had been the lone survivor of the debacle at Marion – and the first wolf I'd darted. She'd been fitted with a radio-collar at Marion and hauled to Glacier National Park, where she was set free. She didn't care much for the park it appeared, because she made her way back south, trotting through Swan Valley, ending her 150-mile journey in the Ninemile when she met a gray male wolf.

By the following spring, the pair was caring for their six puppies, but that summer, the mother was killed, her radio-collar cut with a knife and its transmitter smashed. Whoever did it wasn't caught. The alpha male continued caring for the puppies, now about 40 pounds each, until a car killed him as he crossed Interstate 90 west of Missoula. Then it was Mike Jimenez' turn. Jimenez was a carpenter until he decided to become a biologist. As a graduate student at the University of Montana who was doing research on the Ninemile wolves, he'd been keeping track of them from the day he first heard radio signals coming from the alpha female's collar. He knew the puppies would starve without a parent to bring food to them, so he drove upwards of 50 miles a day looking for road-killed deer, which he left at the den. It worked; he kept the puppies alive through the winter. He also put radio collars on a couple of the half-grown wolves. Newspapers, magazines, TV stations and book authors covered the story from every angle.

Once the puppies were mostly grown, their radio-collars told on them. The wolves had figured out how to kill a steer, but weren't sure what to do afterward. It was typical of youngsters, as I would discover. Trapper Jerry Lewis found the big, oval tracks in the snow near the Priddys' corrals and followed them for three miles until they disappeared up a hill and into thick forest. As Lewis turned back toward the ranch, he saw two wolves, specks in the distance, watching him.

The Ninemile pack was blamed for every dead thing in that part of Montana. One day, a ranch family near Dixon called me about a 400-pound calf they found dead in the middle of their pasture. The rancher and his wife were furious, ranting about the wolves rumored to be in the area. They wanted justice, the couple said.

I put on latex exam gloves, and an hour later, I had the entire hide off the calf. There wasn't a scratch on it, but when I informed the couple, they simply said they figured I'd say that. I was covering for the wolves. They wondered out loud if this was how all ranchers would be treated. But I wasn't finished explaining things. I told them the calf probably died of disease or some kind of illness.

"We don't raise sick cattle," the wife said. She turned her back and began to cry.

I pressed on, asking the man if I could open up the calf. I wanted these people to see that their hysterical reaction to wolves was unfounded.

"I'm no vet, but we could look for something obvious like pneumonia," I suggested.

He agreed and I started cutting.

I was no sooner into the abdominal cavity than I came across an ulcer, which had perforated the calf's rumen and intestines, causing infection and death. I didn't expect either of them to say much. I cleaned my knife and was ready to head out. There was nothing else to discuss. The rancher hesitated, then agreed with me, saying an ulcer that bad probably did the animal in. His wife, however, kept her back turned, even as I said goodbye.

It was my job to go up in a helicopter and dart all of the wolves so they could be moved to Glacier National Park. Managers up the line determined that Glacier was a politically expedient place to send wolves. Technically, it couldn't be considered relocation because wolves already existed here and there in the park. True, the place is majestic, but wolves can't eat mountains. The wolves we moved there always left.

When the weather cleared and we could fly, we found the four Ninemile wolves, strung in a long line, pausing to look at us buzzing toward them before they continued up the ridge. A lush meadow lay on the other side of the mountain. Ron Gipe, my pilot, took his time, edging forward a little at a time, not crowding them. In another quarter of a mile, they would be in the open.

At the crest of an abrupt ridgeline, the wolves trotted under trees. They were hesitant to move with us hovering there, but Gipe waited and soon a black wolf started away. In a moment, others followed.

When the wolves had ventured far enough that they weren't likely to duck back, we zoomed in. I wanted to dart them back to front – perhaps they wouldn't scatter as much. I leaned into my seatbelt, put my dart gun out the door, and waited for Gipe to position me for a shot. A large gray wolf lined out perfectly about 20 feet from me. I aimed at the middle of its shoulders and fired. By the time the aluminum tube traveled the short distance, it had arced slightly and the fat, barbed needle lodged itself in the wolf's left hip.

"We got a hit," I said. I reloaded and Gipe radioed the spotter plane that the wolf would be going down soon. We didn't want drugged wolves getting lost from our view.

The next wolf was also gray and also easy. Two down, two to go.

The plane crew reported that the first wolf was down. The two wolves left were moving fast. Gipe closed in on one, but I missed. By the time I reloaded, we were upon the next one. I hit it and soon it was slowing down.

We chased the wolf I'd missed in wide circles. It kept heading toward the forest and Gipe had to cut short his approach to avoid hitting the treetops. It must have looked like a joke, the wolf leading us to the treeline over and over. It was starting to take too long when we had other wolves lying tranquilized. Then I made a lucky, long shot and hit the wolf as it ducked into low brush on a steep hillside.

Telezol, the drug in the darts, normally takes down a running or struggling wolf in five to 10 minutes. Sometimes, when a wolf is exerting a lot of energy, the drug takes longer to work or wears off quickly because it is metabolized rapidly. It seems to take forever no matter what, like watching water boil.

The final wolf lay down. The action had been fast and furious, but we still had to pick them up. I wondered if maybe I'd bitten off more than I could chew.

"Let's start here and pick them up as we go down the mountain," I told Gipe. After a 40-yard descent, I spotted black fur against greenery.

The wolf had what we call the "Telezol stare," eyes wide open and unfocused, pupils dilated. It was a female and her tongue hung out of her mouth, working in an involuntary licking motion. I knelt down, lifted her onto my shoulders and started back up the hill. I concentrated on putting one foot in front of the other and was running out of breath. Sweat was running in my eyes. I wondered, stumbling over a couple of rocks and branches, whether any of the 5-foot tall graduate students I'd ever talked to about catching wolves would be able to do this. This wolf was about 80 pounds of dead weight. Seemed like everyone who wanted to "do wolves" was tiny.

The next wolf, another female, was waking up. That wasn't supposed to happen yet. I didn't have any Ketamine with me, a drug that would have briefly extended her immobilized state. I thought about shooting her with another dart, but that seemed like it would do too much muscular damage. The charge that propelled the dart could do serious injury at close range and the internal charge that injects the drug could cause even more damage. I was still relatively inexperienced at handling wolves, and this situation illustrated that the only way I could learn was the hard way.

I picked her up, wrestled her onto a tray next to Gipe's door and tied her down.

"Let's hurry and get those other two," I shouted over the chopper's engine. "This one's waking up."

As I feared, the next wolf, a big male, was struggling to his feet. When we landed close by, it startled the animal even more. This was not the way Telezol should work. If he were hit squarely, this wolf would have been down for an hour or more.

I stepped out of the helicopter and walked toward the wolf. It was on its side again, but with its head up, looking at me, rummy but alert. I needed a way to keep him from getting up.

"Take those wolves down to Joe, grab some Ketamine and get back up here as quick as you can." I yelled to Gipe. A moment later, he was airborne, turning the helicopter and rushing down the mountain.

The wolf in front of me was much larger than the two black ones. I had to come up with an idea fast or he would escape. The drug, what little he had in him, was being burned up while I stood there. I started toward him, deciding as I walked that shooting him with another dart wasn't in the cards. As I got closer, he stayed put. Maybe he was too weak to fight me, much less try to jump up. Without really giving it much thought, I lunged at him, grabbing him by the thick scruff on his neck, pinning his head to the ground. He had more fire in him than I figured and struggled under me, even though I'd thrown my full weight on him. I pushed my forearm across his neck.

Minutes ticked by. Here I was, with a huge wolf in a headlock. He was coming out of the Telazol fast, making side glances at me and trying to jerk away. Then he started growling, a deep, pissed-off kind of growl that vibrated through my arm. I was going to lose this one if I didn't do something – right now. I couldn't wait for Gipe and a vial of Ketamine.

As steadily as I could manage, I curled into the fetal position, all the while keeping my weight over the wolf's neck and head. With one hand I pulled the laces out of one of my boots, made a slip-knot in one end and went to tying up the wolf's front feet. Then I carefully shifted my weight and used the rest of the bootlace on his back feet. The wolf didn't like me messing with his back end and let out another long growl. He struggled furiously, lifting me off him momentarily. I kept my balance while keeping his head pinned and avoiding his teeth, which he flashed at me. I got one hind leg close enough to his front feet to throw several more half hitches around it and a few more knots.

He was officially hogtied. If he got away from me, he wasn't going to get far. I kept my weight on him, just in case he tried to get up. I unlaced my other boot and tied his legs even more.

The misadventure seemed like it had taken hours. Where was Gipe? I mumbled to myself that our entire capture was falling apart. A hundred yards in front of me, a platinum-colored wolf, the first one I'd darted that day, was up and wobbling away. The drugs had worn off. I watched it stagger like a drunk for about a quarter of a mile, finally meandering over a hill.

The faint buzzing in the distance was the chopper, coming straight at me like a bee. It was a sound that the big wolf under me, now wide awake, didn't care for. His ears flattened and his eyes darted, showing their whites. Holding him down and keeping him from using his jaws on me was like hanging onto a bucking bronco at a rodeo.

Gipe came toward me with a vial.

"Load the syringe and do it quick," I said. He poked the needle into the wolf's hip.

In a few minutes, the hogtied wolf was out again and I put him in the chopper. We tried a few more tricks to catch the wolf that had wandered away, but it kept to the timber on a steep slope where I couldn't get a close shot. I had to end it. We had the drugged wolves to deal with.

Max Johnson was waiting when we landed. He owned the property and had seen the wolves that morning in a field near his house. Now the animals lay drugged on the side of the road, having just been unloaded from the helicopter.

"You're Niemeyer?" Johnson said as he pumped my hand. "You're fast 'cause I just called your office about these wolves about two hours ago." I didn't tell him I'd put myself up in a nearby motel the night before.

We put the wolves in kennels, getting ready to move them to Glacier National Park. Then we got talking about the screwed up capture and how one got away. Joe Fontaine said he wasn't sure he'd mixed the Telezol correctly. The darts might have been only half-strength, he said. It was the day I realized I needed to always carry a vial of Ketamine, and maybe Telezol, too, in my pocket.

I flew again the next day, trying to locate the Ninemile wolf that had escaped, but never found it.

The story of the Ninemile wolves could have been a great one because it was a story about natural immigration. The wolves had traveled from Canada into Montana without anyone's help. But they just had to start killing livestock. The operation to move them cost about $9,000.

Several weeks later, the one wolf that got away was catching the blame for killing or chasing every cat, dog, sheep, cow or horse in northwest Montana. I started wishing I'd just shot the thing.

The gray Ninemile male that I had hogtied and that later had been collared and taken to Glacier was found floating with a bullet in it in Mud Lake near Bigfork, Montana, during a routine flight to track the pack's whereabouts.

One of the others was killed a week later near Condon, Montana. A man with a few cattle in a pasture next to his house heard a commotion and ran out to see a black canine chasing his cattle. He grabbed a rifle and yelled at the animal as it ran past him for the third time, latching onto a steer's hindquarters. The man leveled his weapon and fired.

Rick Branzell, a special agent with the U.S. Fish and Wildlife Service, asked me to meet him and look at the pasture to see if the evidence matched the man's story. If it didn't, there was a hefty fine in store.

I hopped the fence and systematically walked the muddy pasture. I found tracks in short order and from the looks of them, the wolf had been running. The feet had spread wide and dug deep into the mud. The cattle had been running too, it appeared, tearing up the pasture's scant turf.

But the real indicator that the cattle had been chased was the green diarrhea pasted all over their rear ends all the way to their heels. I checked them for injuries but couldn't see any scratches, bites or blood. Back at the pickup, I examined the dead wolf. No sign that she was pregnant, or that she ever had been, so there was probably no mate around and certainly no puppies.

Branzell didn't say much about the interview he'd just conducted, except that the man was visibly shaken, terrified that he'd be fined and sent to jail for killing an endangered species. Shortly after the incident, a headline in *The Missoulian* read "Wolf Kill Justified, Feds Say." But the editorial departments of several newspapers weren't finished with us on the subject.

Week after week, the sanity of the federal plan to restore wolves to parts of the West was questioned in opinion pieces, editorials and letters to the editor. The use of airplanes and helicopters seemed frivolous, not to mention the number of government employees involved, as well as the cost of the wolf program itself. One person wanted the cost of controlling wolves published in the newspaper to awaken the public to the stupidity of the entire program. Another editorial described how newborn elk and deer would be viciously ripped apart by hungry wolves. I wondered if all the folks who objected to the government spending money to bring back wolves knew about Animal Damage Control's programs and the millions of federal dollars it spent every year killing coyotes, foxes, porcupines, squirrels and starlings for no discernable public benefit.

Wolf fans continued to forecast victory, holding rallies, taking a national vote that showed most Americans wanted wolves back, and raising money to help pay for livestock that wolves killed. They stayed positive even as wolves like the Ninemile pack worked to make optimism difficult.

Just when everyone thought things in the Ninemile were quiet, two more wolves showed up and started causing trouble. One had a collar and was from Glacier National Park. The other was thought to be the Ninemile wolf that got away during the first capture. I met Mike Jimenez, who'd been tracking the pair, at the carcass of a 550-pound steer the wolf pair had supposedly killed. It belonged to Dave Fish, who owned the ranchland as well as a saddle shop in Missoula. Fish was tired of wolves and fired his rifle over the heads of the ones harassing his cattle, trying to scare them off.

It was easy to spot wolf tracks in the mud. The steer had been almost entirely eaten. Only pieces of skull, spine and ribcage remained. I couldn't tell what killed it. I was supposed to set traps and catch the wolves if I found they were at fault. On a fencepost nearby a huge furrow was splintered out, the result of Fish's bullet.

Fish's other steers seemed healthy. The dead one, he said, had been fine, the day before. Jimenez found the wolves' den only a few miles north and was sure the pair had pups. Maybe a spank and release – catching a wolf and putting a collar on it – would do the trick to drive them off.

I set traps on the dirt road that led toward the den that the wolves had been using. The wolves had dropped a couple of big, black turds in the middle of the road. One had calf-hide rolled in it. Masses of butterflies congregated on each big dropping like absurd decorations. Two mornings later, we caught the female wolf. Her condition showed she was nursing puppies so we couldn't hold her long. We weren't going to start starving puppies by killing their parents this early in wolf recovery. Jimenez and I put a catchpole around her neck, gave her a shot of drugs, and shoved her into a kennel in the back of my truck. We had more traps to check.

The dirt on the road was like fine flour, rising into clouds almost before we rolled across it. The faster I drove, the worse it got. Even so, I saw something in my rearview mirror, a little red car. I slowed to let it pass, but it stayed back several hundred yards, stopping when I stopped. It must be the animal rights people, maybe the Wolf Action Group or EarthFirst! I kept driving, slowly, keeping an eye on my mirror.

I needed to check those other traps before somebody else got to them, but I didn't want a confrontation with whoever was in that car.

"What do you think about jumping out around this corner and I'll circle back for you?" I asked Jimenez.

Mike Jimenez was a former gymnast and could do a hell of a bunch of flips on a trampoline. He smiled under his handlebar mustache.

I hit the gas and spun, getting up to around 50 mph and throwing a huge dust cloud into the air. Ahead I spotted a patch of wild roses.

"Get ready," I said. "I'm gonna slow up. See if you can hit that brush ahead."

As soon as Jimenez pushed the door open and rolled out, I hit the gas again, billowing more dust. I sped off, not quite knowing where to go, but hoping the red car kept on me. Jimenez would wait in the bushes until things were clear, then check the rest of the trapline. Maybe I'd just drive to Bob Demins' ranch about a mile further and see if the coffee was on.

Demins was ex-Army special forces. He didn't care much for wolves, but he was always polite to me and interested in the latest news from the wolf-recovery front. As I pulled into the driveway, I saw the red car again in my mirror. It stopped, its occupants watching me stroll to the front door. The trick worked.

Demins was in his bathrobe.

"What are you doing up so early?" he said.

"Well, I was out checking traps and came up with something I thought you might like to see."

I led Demins and his wife to my truck. They gasped and smiled at the big, platinum colored wolf.

"Where did you catch her?" he asked.

"I'll tell you all about it if you make me a pot of coffee," I said.

We stepped into the house. About a half hour later, the coffee was gone and so was the red car. I found Jimenez walking down the road a few hundred yards from the traps.

"You've got the alpha male in a trap," he said casually as he climbed into my truck. He chuckled when I asked if he had any rose thorns in his butt.

Where the wolf had been tangled, it was now gone. I followed on foot the marks made by the trap's drag that snaked down the middle of the road. I hoped I'd soon hear the chain rattling or sticks snapping.

I'd never heard a wolf howl and bark at the same time. Everybody wanted to believe it was the Ninemile wolf that had wandered off as I sat on its hogtied sibling, but I had my doubts. This one seemed different. It was big and cranky and wound around a tangle of shrubs, my trap holding him by one front paw. When he saw me he forgot about the sticks and twigs he'd been chewing to vent his frustration, switching instead to barking and howling, glaring with his yellow eyes and standing his ground. He held his tail high and slowly wagged it back and forth, a sign of aggression. I needed to sedate him but didn't dare step into the eight-foot radius of movement the chain allowed him. Mike tried to distract him while I waited for the right moment to make my move with a syringe pole. When I jabbed him, he jerked his head around and grabbed the pole in his teeth, flinging it end over end into the bushes. But in 10 minutes, he lost his balance and his resolve and crumpled.

The wolf weighed in at 115 pounds, according to my scale, and from now on, he'd wear a radio collar. We turned him and his mate loose because they had puppies to care for. The spank part of spank and release had worked; the pair never bothered Dave Fish's cattle again. When it was over, I filled out a form asking Defenders of Wildlife to pay Fish for his loss, which it did promptly. Defenders also paid for some hay so that Fish could move his cattle away from the wolves.

Not a week after, an ad appeared in *The Missoulian*, which had covered from several angles the latest capture of a Ninemile wolf:

Springtime in Montana and it's time to kill some wolves. Every wolf they've relocated has ended up dead. Fish and Wildlife needs to be reminded of their duty to protect, not ranchers, but the grey wolf, an endangered species.

My name and phone number as well as Joe Fontaine's were at the bottom, along with a sentence or two urging wolf advocates to make our lives miserable.

As some predicted, the three relocated Ninemile wolves had turned right around and left Glacier National Park. Now two of them were dead, but every calf and sheep that tipped over was blamed on the one wolf that remained. The lone Ninemile wolf had traveled east of the Continental Divide, and day after day I checked out dead animals near Bynum, Heart Butte, Dupuyer and Augusta.

John Krause and Don Converse were neighboring ranchers outside of Augusta. Krause reported seeing a black wolf with a radio collar and found wolf tracks in his garden next to his house. I agreed with the tracks. One had come right through his yard. Perhaps the wolf would stay around. Converse reported a calf missing, but I couldn't find any evidence that wolves had been at that ranch.

I told an Augusta newspaper reporter that a "wave of hysteria" was working its way through the area, and was quoted further: "When a wolf appears, the number of reported livestock kills goes up accordingly. We've got no evidence of a pack of wolves in the Augusta area at this time."

It didn't stop the calls.

Two weeks after I checked the tracks in his garden, Krause reported a dead calf to his local trapper, Ken Wheeler. Krause believed that a wolf killed it, but Wheeler was unsure and said so. He hauled the carcass toward Helena and I met him half way, skinning the animal on the tailgate on the side of the road. There were small punctures in the hide that resembled eagle talon wounds, but none of the signature grape-jelly hemorrhage inside. When Wheeler informed Krause of my findings, Krause became furious. My friendship with him ended that day. No more talking to me at rodeos or inviting me to the house.

I was sorry about John Krause. I liked the guy. Because of the situation, I drove the dead calf to Missoula and had it necropsied by Dr Bart O'Gara. I wanted to see if I was missing something. But I wasn't; a golden eagle did it. The tiny punctures were from talons as I had suspected. I remembered this from all those years working with those birds. I relayed this information back to Wheeler and asked him to tell John Krause, but it didn't matter. Krause was done with me.

To the north, in Dupuyer, a wolf did appear at a ranch and started in on sheep. First a 10-pound lamb, then a couple more. Then it moved to the neighbor's place and ate another, this one 30 pounds. All were killed in the same manner, bitten in the throat, their lower jaws smashed and their necks broken. Several people had seen a black wolf with a radio collar, and Wheeler found its tracks in the dirt.

The Fish and Wildlife Service and my agency had come up with an idea: use an airplane to find the wolf and get me in there in a helicopter to dart it. Everyone had had enough of the Ninemile pack and its tendency to kill livestock. Once captured, it would be sent to Wolf Haven, a privately funded wolf sanctuary in Tenino, Washington.

My boss decided to come over from Billings to watch the show. When we caught up with the wolf, it was only a mile west of our helicopter staging area. A herd of black Angus cattle were bunched up in a pasture ahead of us, looking at something. As we got closer, a black wolf bolted from a fencerow and raced across the pasture. The cattle were instantly on their heels, charging, their heads straining forward, noses to the ground.

The view from the air was almost funny. The cattle formed a black V behind the terrified wolf, giving it no room to maneuver. Rick Sanford, the pilot, kept us back a little, trying to keep from scaring the herd through fences. We hoped the cattle would stay focused on the wolf. Eventually it ducked under a barbed wire fence and slid into a scattering of willows along a stream where beaver had remodeled everything into a series of channels and ponds.

Once the cattle ran the wolf off, they stopped their pursuit and we could begin ours. Every time Sanford made a pass over it, the wolf disappeared into thick brush. I held my fire. I was learning how wolves reacted to helicopters and assured Sanford that we'd get her.

"Take your time, man," I said.

It wasn't like shooting to kill. With a dart gun, there's trajectory to consider. Then there's trying to avoid certain body parts like the lung-area, the head, the spine and the belly, any of which could cause injury or eventual death if hit. One hip or the other was my plan, for they were the areas with the largest muscle mass. In my head I figured the helicopter's speed relative to the wolf's speed, the distance between the tip of my dart gun and the panicked wolf below me. How much wind, or rotorwash, was the chopper generating? That would affect how the dart flew. And there was the possibility that, as I aimed, the wolf would change course suddenly, or stop. Before I concentrated on my target, I took one last look for dangerous tree snags, power lines or anything else that could get us killed. Then I leaned forward in my seatbelt and aimed between the wolf's shoulders.

The wolf was getting tired, and shortly it would be down. I'd hit it, as I'd planned, in the hip. Sanford made a sharp turn so we could keep an eye on it. He raced it to the trees, trying to keep the wolf from escaping us in the heavy timber. He herded it from a short distance with the chopper, trying not to panic the animal while the drug did its job, sending the wolf where it would be easy to get to once we landed. The wolf was walking along the creek when the Telezol finally brought it down.

I was worried that the wolf might drown if it fell in the water, but it lay down on the bank. I crossed a beaver dam that was more like a bridge and approached the wolf. Clumps of fur hung from her because she was shedding her winter coat. She weighed 70 pounds.

The entire capture took less than 30 minutes. While we were in the air, a crowd had gathered at our trucks, eager to see a real wolf.

Wolf Haven named her Miss Montana and she lived there with other wolves for 10 more years, dying in 2001. At one point, an independent researcher concluded that she suffered a wolf's version of post traumatic stress syndrome and was afraid of low-flying aircraft, especially helicopters, and therefore aircraft shouldn't be used to capture wild wolves. Maybe he was right, but if the alternative was killing them instead of moving them, I had to disagree.

The U.S. Fish and Wildlife Service sent out a news release in November 1991, announcing that it was gearing up to reintroduce wolves, and that the Department of the Interior had budgeted about $500,000 to pay for the formal documents needed to precede such a momentous act.

Shortly after that announcement, Ed Bangs, who was picked to run the new wolf command post in Helena, Montana, took the idea of reintroduction on the road. He had 18 months to come up with a draft environmental impact statement, a weighty stack of paper full of bureaucratic procedures and explanations about wolf biology that would provide the legal justification for bringing wolves back. The document also needed to include public comments. Bangs asked me to travel with him to meetings and hearings to explain the role of the federal Animal Damage Control and how wolves might affect the agency's predator control campaigns. It sounded like a good excuse, but I suspected he wanted me there because of my size.

With periodic stops back in Helena, we drove to a couple dozen towns and a few good-sized cities in Montana, Wyoming and Idaho. The topic of wolves drew crowds, and a lot of them were anti-fed, anti-wolf and anti-establishment in general. Having a microphone and a court reporter up front let people feel like they could do a little chest-pounding in front of their buddies and blow off some steam.

The Fish and Wildlife Service's public affairs office set things up in the spacious meeting rooms of big hotels. In Riverton, Wyoming, a bull-sized man walked into the hotel lobby with an equally big handgun strapped to his belt. Bangs and I exchanged worried looks before we learned the guy just wanted to drink in the bar.

I was there, ostensibly, to explain to reporters and everyone who asked how M-44 cyanide devices worked, that they were designed to kill coyotes, and how government trappers would be prohibited from using them in occupied wolf range. There was mounting pressure from the livestock industry to stop wasting money on endangered species issues, particularly wolves. But other federal agencies wanted Animal Damage Control around, even if environmentalists didn't. The politics of the situation – wolves killing livestock – dictated that someone at some agency had to deal with the dead livestock and the guilty wolves. Animal Damage Control, as the predator control agency, was the natural candidate.

Part of the money that Congress provided was supposed to help solve this issue, and I ended up being the one who was supposed to make it all happen *out there*. Of course nothing was that simple, and a battle ensued over how I handled my budget. That kind of autonomy was just too much for the brass to swallow. But I was the only person in the agency qualified for such a job. I didn't want it particularly, but once it was foisted on me, I was accused of empire-building. It was to be the beginning of the end of my relationship with the agency that I used to be so eager to work for.

Simply being involved in the wolf issue got me crossways with some of the old-school predator killers in my agency, and with most of the bosses. I had to do things my way though, because I believed my way worked best. If I was going to be in it, I wanted wolves judged fairly. Animal Damage Control at all levels viewed the U.S. Fish and Wildlife Service, and Ed Bangs particularly, as little more than the enemy. Bangs' agency was required by law to recover endangered species, but my agency just saw it as a touchy-feely bunch of bunny-huggers.

Bangs just smiled. He was a bureaucratic bulldozer, tearing down walls that didn't belong there in the first place, but that no one else was brave enough to destroy. He knew he might be beaten back – perhaps permanently – if he wavered for a second. The Fish and Wildlife Service intended to use the Endangered Species Act to make reintroduction happen. A majority of Americans thought this was a great idea. After all, the public lands where wolves were destined belonged to everyone. As one reporter put it, the Fish and Wildlife Service was the white hat in a sea of black Stetsons.

Bangs, who loved to be in charge of public meetings so he could get them over with as fast as possible, went to the front of the room. I donned my only sport coat, put on a name tag and stood in the back where I could keep an eye on everyone. Bangs turned on the microphone and welcomed everyone, doing the speech I'd heard so many times that I could almost recite it. Then someone from the hotel tugged on my sleeve. I had a phone call.

It wasn't my boss, but my boss's boss at the regional office in Denver. He told me to take off my name tag, leave the meeting immediately and go hide in my room so that an ABC news correspondent couldn't find me.

I did what he said, but had no way of telling Bangs. In my room, I dialed up the assistant regional director in Denver for an explanation, and our public affairs chief, too. They didn't want to face the political heat that was sure to come if I talked in public about toxicants like M-44's, they said. The best way to deal with it, according to the upper echelon, was to hide. I got in a hell of an argument with both of them, pointing out that the Fish and Wildlife Service – Bangs – was at that moment representing Animal Damage Control because I wasn't there to do it. Is that what they wanted? And what was this about hiding from reporters?

I didn't win the argument. I changed into my regular clothes and returned to the meeting just as it was ending.

Bangs was incredulous.

"What the hell happened? Where were you?"

As I explained, he shook his head, slowly. "Stupid," he said. "God, what are they thinking?"

We were still talking about it and getting ready to leave when three burley men came into the room, members of a notorious local group, the No Wolf Option committee. It was a cute play on the routine bureaucratic language in environmental impact statements, where various "options" are outlined for consideration.

Everyone else had cleared out, leaving them looking at Bangs and me. They started in, their voices rising, getting mouthy about wolf reintroduction. Bangs, who can somehow diffuse irate people with polite self-deprecation, interrupted them and encouraged them to step to the microphone in the empty room and make public statements for the record. They glared at us. I only took my eyes off of them to look around for a makeshift weapon, maybe one of those folding metal chairs...but it never went that far.

Later that night, Bangs and I stood outside our motel room and smoked cigars, waiting for a drive-by shooting or maybe a homemade bomb to crash through our window.

"Think we're getting paranoid?" I asked.

We'd met a lot of crazy people in the last few years. Between puffs we agreed that there was something about wolves that made people loopy – and most of them cleared their schedules in order to come to the wolf reintroduction meetings.

"Why do you think I bring you with me?" Bangs chuckled.

While I was getting a dose of public opinion at the wolf reintroduction meetings, the dead livestock were piling up in Montana. Most of it was blamed on wolves.

Animal Damage Control managers didn't like my conclusions about what killed most of the dead cows and sheep in Montana, Wyoming and Idaho. In their estimation, the truth about what killed these animals wasn't as important as upholding the opinions and attitudes of ranchers, many of whom were eager to think that, from here on out, wolves surely must be responsible for anything dead. The ranchers could believe whatever they wanted, but I wasn't putting it down on my report. And that got me in a heap of trouble.

The Great Falls Tribune ran a story claiming that four yearling cattle on federal grazing lease land died after being attacked by a wolf or perhaps a grizzly. The reporter must have gotten all of his information from the rancher and run with it because I didn't get a call until the next day – after I'd examined the calves and determined they'd died of dehydration.

"Well? Was it a wolf or a grizzly?" The reporter seemed eager to get more mileage out of this.

"Which one do you want it to be? Sounds to me like you've already hung one of them out to dry."

The reporter got defensive. I cut him off.

"The yearlings died of dehydration."

The reporter was as upset as the rancher had been. I'd ruined a perfectly good story with facts.

Not long after, the same newspaper ran a front-page article about Anna Gail Sabados, whose calf at her ranch near the Rocky Mountain front town of Bynum was killed by wolves. Or so the story said. Trapper Jim Stevens drove me the rest of the way to the Sabados ranch after I'd gotten halfway there only to have a head gasket blow out in my truck.

No wolf killed her calf. No wolf had stepped anywhere in the mudflat where the calf lay. It was tiny, probably less than a week old, and after it died, not even scavengers had bothered it much. The spring snow had melted, beautifully preserving the tracks of mice and small birds, but no wolf had walked there. A small hole, about an inch wide, had been pecked into the calf's soft belly and a long string of intestine pulled out. A raven had done that bit of scavenging. I skinned out the calf and found no other injuries. Stevens and I looked around. Not even a coyote had been by. It might have been a problem at birth, or perhaps scours – a common bacterial disease in calves associated with wet spring weather.

A ranch man came banging up in a truck while Stevens and I searched for signs that a wolf had dared trespass here. He rolled down the window and accused us of trespassing, then began spewing venom about wolves and how he'd shot at the one that killed the calf, chasing it through the mudflats with his truck until he got stuck.

I introduced myself.

"Mrs. Sabados called me about her calf," I said, but he waved me off. A Ruger rifle with a banana clip lay on the seat. I glanced at it, measuring the cost of engaging him.

" A wolf didn't do this," I said anyway.

He snorted, saying he was the one who'd seen the wolf standing over the calf and reported it and, between expletives, that if I didn't kill the wolf, he'd do it himself using neck snares.

"Well, whatever you need to do," I said. "Be careful and don't hurt your cows."

Blowhards like this fellow were everywhere, and continue to be. Their far-out stories don't match the evidence. Sometimes they carry out their threats, but most of the time they lose momentum because a lie is like a boat with a small hole in the bottom; it goes along for a while but eventually sinks and takes its passengers down with it. In the wolf business, there's no changing people's minds, so there's no point in arguing with them or trying to stop them from doing something illegal or just plain stupid. I've never known a wolf hater to become a wolf-lover or vice versa. When questioned, few people have neutral feelings about the subject, and those who are tolerant of wolves are usually afraid to express themselves.

A week or so after looking at Sabados' calf, I drove to Great Falls for an evening public hearing on wolf reintroduction. A swarm of weathered cowboys, most of whom I'd met over the years, clogged the bar and the hearing room. I worked my way through the room, hearing one man that I knew tell another he hoped a few wolf lovers would show up so he could give them a thumping. Wisely, the wolf advocates had boycotted the meeting.

Anna Gail Sabados was there, too, dressed up and beaming with the fame she'd gained over the front page Tribune story. A huge poster had been unrolled in the lobby, showing her standing next to her dead calf. She was the latest example of why wolves and livestock were incompatible.

"Are you Niemeyer?" A cowboy stopped me as we passed in the lobby. He was one I didn't know. He shoved a newspaper at me. "Did you say this?"

It was the front-page story about the dead calf. Next to the story was the same photo of Sabados that was in the lobby. I scanned the quotes.

"Yep." I handed it back to him.

A small crowd that had assembled around us exploded, everyone shouting at once about the feds refusing to admit that wolves kill livestock. This was the theme of their evening protest, that and being upset that I called Sabados a liar in the newspaper, but not in so many words.

I stood my ground. The story was correct in the sense that it reflected what I'd found – and didn't find. When they stopped yelling, the cowboys simply glared at me. I enjoyed getting to glare back.

When I found the tiny, smiling Sabados, she wasn't just cordial to me, she was downright friendly. We talked awhile about nothing in particular, both of us ignoring the news story that should have made us enemies. I decided to bring it up.

"I wasn't calling you a liar. I just couldn't find any evidence that wolves had been on your ranch."

She couldn't be bothered with the details. She was enjoying the limelight.

One by one, ranchers and cowboys stepped to the microphone in protest of the federal government in general and wolves in particular. There wasn't one person who spoke on behalf of wolves. I'd started to think that no one from the opposition had shown up, when a young guy with long hair and sandals walked to the microphone, cleared his throat and waited until everyone was quiet, then proclaimed that he was sick of stepping in cow shit every time he went for a hike on public land in Montana. The crowd hissed and he returned to his seat, smiling.

In my office a month later, I opened a hand scribbled letter postmarked Bynum, Montana:

> *"I know about your wolf guidelines etc., so what the news media says and does won't affect our new friendship. They sure turn things around to suit their fancy."*
>
> *Anna Gail Sabados*

The important thing in ranch country is to do things the way they've always been done, and a person does that by conforming to pressure from neighbors, even if they live five miles down the road. It's a cultural thing, like any other kind of peer pressure, and I'd been encountering it from the first day I stepped foot in Montana. Most of the ranchers who came west to run cattle and sheep supported a heavy-handed predator control program courtesy of the federal government. When the profit margins on sheep plunged and many of those ranchers switched to cattle, they retained their attitudes about predators, insisting that the killing program continue. Coyotes, the predator that does the most damage to the sheep industry, can't do much damage to a calf that isn't small, weak or sick. Full-grown cattle are just too big for them. But the government spends millions of dollars a year killing coyotes anyway because it's what's always been done. It's still true today.

At first, I was as guilty as the next trapper for casually calling every dead animal a "kill." It happened because that's the way it was reported. The rancher telephoned and reported that another animal killed his stock. It was verified simply because the rancher called it a kill. I talked to my trappers about the "kill," and they called the rancher about the "kill," and many times, we went out the next morning to shoot the predator that was assumed to be the culprit. No one questioned the rancher. And until I started doing it and insisting that my trappers do the same, no one skinned dead animals to look for signs that a predator was guilty. This is still a major problem.

When wolves came on the scene, Animal Damage Control had to clean up its act, beginning with me. It once was said that when scratched, I bled type ADC blood. I was a loyal employee, if an undereducated one, despite my degrees. I used to go to stockgrower meetings, and Defenders of Wildlife representative Hank Fischer would turn me inside out during my presentations because I didn't know a thing about why predator advocates felt the way they did. First, I'd get angry, then I'd get flustered, then I'd get tongue-tied. By the time I sat down, I felt like an idiot. I decided then that I needed to know not just my business, but also theirs. I had to get smart enough to defend my world as an Animal Damage Control trapper, but I couldn't do it just using what I learned from my agency and from ranchers. I had to get to know the other side.

Wolves were protected by a powerful federal law – the Endangered Species Act – which even the cavalier Animal Damage Control folks couldn't dodge. When a wolf did kill livestock, it was an ordeal because moving or killing an endangered species, especially one with a big following, involved high-level government decision-making. No matter what the decision was regarding wolves, no one was happy – and that was how I gauged that I was making the right one. Wolves made Animal Damage Control stop and think: How would we catch the wolves? Where do we put them? If we kill them, how will the public react? The public was watching our every move.

Many ranchers told me privately that they didn't object to wolves being around as long as the beasts didn't kill their livestock. But if I repeated this remark to anyone, especially a group of their peers, the ranchers promised to call me a damn liar. It was tricky, but knowing that these attitudes prevailed helped me work more easily with both sides of the wolf recovery issue.

Wolves had become highly controversial as they trickled down from Canada in the years before reintroduction, and though my fellow trappers had been instructed by supervisors not to ask my advice, they called me anyway, wondering what I thought about a certain dead calf or sheep, and telling me not to mention to anyone that they'd called. They didn't want to take the heat from a rancher – or their own agency – for saying that perhaps a wolf didn't do it.

I barely had time to stop and do the paperwork on one dead thing before I was off to look at another. I practically lived in my pickup truck; in one year, I put 30,000 miles on it. I was likened to the county coroner. When I rolled through town, folks who knew me joked that, if I was around, something must have died. By the spring of 1994, I had cut open more than 100 sheep and cattle, four horses, one foal and a mule. All were reportedly killed or injured by wolves. Of that number, I found that only five – four calves and a lamb – were legitimate wolf-kills. My findings weren't popular with my agency, but few ranchers disputed them.

Near Trego, Montana, a log truck driver reported a 1,200-pound cow killed by wolves. Pat and Theresa Shea, the cow's owners, gave me directions and we met at the carcass.

The Sheas had seen wolves on the road near the place where the cow lay and had photographed one. It was local CB radio chatter that started the rumor that a wolf, or maybe several were to blame for the dead cow. I found wolf tracks surrounding the carcass and a hole chewed in its flank, but there was no hemorrhage. I was sure that wolves didn't cause its death, but said nothing. Instead, I took out my knife.

Pulling the skin off of an animal that size is a lot of work. Factor in the hot sun and hundreds of hungry, irritable yellow jackets and it's just plain miserable. By the time I got the hide off, I'd managed to get stung.

The cow had no bite wounds, but it was bruised on one side and a hind leg was out of joint. The Sheas stood next to me, watching all of it. As I cut, I explained what I was seeing. I straightened, and said I was sure it had been hit by a vehicle and hobbled to the side of the road where it died.

I walked a ways down the road looking for broken glass – the kind that would come from a car – and found some. I couldn't prove that this particular glass had anything to do with the cow, but the circumstantial evidence was strong. The Sheas were convinced, going so far as to tell reporters that they exonerated wolves in the death of their animal. It was the kind of thing that needed to happen more often. I think it was because I let them in on what I was doing, which forced them to draw their conclusions from the evidence rather than from the yammerings of others.

Some ranchers did lose animals to wolves, but in the early years, the losses were few.

Wolves were blamed for a horse's death near Stanley, Idaho, even though the animal was found suspended on a barbed wire fence, nearly cut in half by it. Rick Williamson, an Animal Damage Control trapper and expert detail man who is better at small talk and tripping people up than Columbo, examined the horse and acknowledged that wolves were in the area. But he found out a lot more in his own roundabout way: The horse was a new one, just released into a pasture with several others, which took to chasing it to establish a pecking order. The new horse, unfamiliar with the fence boundaries, was driven into the barbed wire. Williamson also discovered that a group of hunters had a bait site nearby meant for black bears. This alone could have implicated bears in the horse's death if anyone but Williamson had done the investigation. Most trappers wouldn't have found out about the bear bait. They would have taken the rancher's word for it and blamed wolves, and then a kill order would have come down – all because a horse wrung its own neck. Wolves just don't go after horses, and rarely do they go after adult cattle. Maybe the risk of getting kicked in the head is too great.

The Defenders of Wildlife compensation program used a carefully crafted protocol – created by Idaho Animal Damage Control director Mark Collinge – that had to be followed in order for the rancher to be paid. There were three possibilities regarding wolves: "confirmed," "probable," and "possible/

unknown." The trapper's conclusion about the livestock death determined how much money would change hands or whether the rancher would be paid at all. A "confirmed" finding meant full compensation at the price the animal would have fetched at auction that fall. Even a "probable" was worth 50 percent of an animal's fall market value. But a "possible/unknown," a term that defined nothing, was worth just that – zero. A UFO could have "possibly" come down and killed the animal. It didn't take long for ranchers to change their terminology. "I've got a wolf kill up here," many said. This planted the seed, which was relayed up the line to supervisors, that wolves did it. By the time the trapper arrived on the scene, he was ready to check the "confirmed" or "probable" box without getting out of the truck.

It fell mostly to the rancher to decide how things were going to be, primarily because many trappers believed that ranchers were their employer. I had a falling out with a good friend because of this idea. He wasn't just a friend, he was a federal trapper whom I'd hired and mentored. But he believed he worked for ranchers, even though his paychecks were signed by the U.S. Department of Agriculture. Such confusion came with the job. Trappers were, and still are, stationed near their work, and in the West, that means they live in rural areas where there are ranches. The trappers' kids attend the same schools as ranchers' kids; everyone shops at the same grocery store. Trappers, understandably, don't want to get crossways with their ranching neighbors, so if the rancher thinks a wolf killed his cow, the trapper isn't going to argue with him. But trappers rarely admit that they're unsure what killed livestock, and when in doubt they often put an X in the "probable" box.

In Idaho, that same rancher could also collect money from his state's predator compensation coffer (which is often federal money channeled to the states) for the other half of "probable" losses, as well as for missing live-stock, which could have disappeared on private and public rangelands in any number of ways, including being rustled – an unexpectedly common thing even now.

In addition to compensating ranchers, the government moved the wolves when there was a legitimate attack. When we ran out of places to move them, we killed them. It was that simple.

I was the only Animal Damage Control trapper who didn't do it right, according to my superiors. Instead of asking the rancher which box he thought I should check, I showed up and walked around the scene, skinned the dead animal to its hooves, and sometimes stapled a couple of extra pages of notes to my official form. For this kind of independent thinking, I was all but kicked out of Montana, and sent to look at dead livestock in Wyoming and Idaho where few wolves had yet migrated. My boss told the newspapers that there was really no need for my services anymore because the wolf controversy had ended. The Animal Damage Control report form barely contained room for a trapper to write comments regarding a livestock death scene. But who needs space to write when the answer to a dead cow is simple: Wolves killed it.

The first wolf to be tracked in Washington state in modern history was captured in 1992, reportedly in an empty swimming pool, and recaptured in a tennis court.

A biologist on contract with the U.S. Fish and Wildlife Service consulted with a veterinarian about the animal, and the two of them decided it must be a wild wolf – except that it was a 30- or 40-pound, shaggy female mutt with short legs and a face like a terrier. The ladies in the subdivision where it hung around had taken to calling it Wolfie, and it followed them on their daily walks. The biologist had continually expressed his desire to see wolves and grizzlies restored to Washington and was in charge of finding out whether the state already had either. When a woman called to say she was sure there was a wolf in her subdivision near the town of Glacier, the biologist showed up and put a collar on it and tags in its small ears. It was only afterward that I was called over to take a look. I called the dog Nooksack, after a nearby river, and I recorded on videotape a good portion of my adventure checking out this rare wolf discovery.

When Jeff Haas, a biologist with the Fish and Wildlife Service, federal trapper Fred Goodman, and I first encountered Nooksack, the small dog was following a lady and her Labrador retriever down an asphalt street in the subdivision.

"Ma'am," Haas drawled in his Texas accent, "would you walk down the street and see if it will follow you?"

She complied, and the dogs followed.

"Ma'am, would you walk to the left?" he asked. She did and both dogs turned with her.

"And now will you turn right?"

He was convinced. The nice lady would have never guessed the kinds of words that Jeff let fly to describe this situation. When she was out of earshot, he muttered to me about how he was going to have to kill the thing to get the collar off of it.

"Hell, why take it out on the poor dog?" I said.

Goodman sat in the backseat. He rode along because he wanted to see a wolf in the wild. He still wondered if this was all a practical joke.

The Fish and Wildlife Service was ultimately responsible for all of this. I wondered how they planned to explain it.

"Let's follow them so I can get some more footage," I told Haas, trying to lighten the mood. The lady took a footpath through the forest, so we followed, looking for any behavior that might have led a biologist to believe this was a wild wolf. The little brown dog frolicked with the lab.

"I'm sure glad I invested in this video camera," I grinned.

Haas asked the woman whether the dog could be approached and subdued.

"She won't let me pet her," she said.

Haas moved toward Nooksack, but the dog ran into the woods, making a wide circle and rejoining the Labrador. We weren't going to get that collar easily, it appeared.

"Well, she's not going anywhere. Anyway you can track her," I snickered.

We drove as far as Seattle, where Haas stopped to call his supervisor. The Fish and Wildlife Service wanted my videotape so that "wolf experts" could review it. I wondered who that could be. Yeah, right. I wasn't giving up my original. They could pay for a copy. The agency decided to take the word of Dr. Steve Fritts. Whatever he concluded the feds would take as the final word on the matter.

I happened to be in Missoula a few days later – with my tape of Nooksack. Fritts and others were meeting for a grizzly bear conference. Ed Bangs and Joe Fontaine showed up, too. We sat in Fritts' motel room and I shoved the tape into the player, explaining how this was the first wildlife film I'd ever produced and directed and that I'd named my creation, "Nooksack: Wild Dog of the North."

Everyone was silent, crowded in a semi-circle around the television. Fritts sat on the bed directly in front of the screen. The first scene showed a coyote that I videotaped prior to encountering Nooksack.

"Well, there it is. What do you think?" I said.

"That's not a wolf, it's a coyote," he said, confident and ready to flip off the VCR. Then a little brown dog appeared.

"What is *that*?" Fritts leaned forward for a better look.

"Oh, I'm sorry Steve, *that's* the wolf," I said, watching his expression.

"Oh, no!" Fritts slapped both hands on his forehead and fell back on the bed.

Several weeks after Fritts informed the Fish and Wildlife Service that Nooksack was not a wolf, Haas drove back to the town and found the woman and her dogs. He asked her to entice them into a fenced tennis court, where he promptly closed the gate. This time the little dog let Haas pick it up. Easy capture for a wolf.

Nooksack wasn't a wolf, but the good people at Wolf Haven, in western Washington, took her in anyway. Once there, Haas unscrewed the radio collar and removed the tags from the dog's drooping ears. If Nooksack was confined there, I was fairly certain that no government biologist would ever try to collar her again.

When Nooksack died in 2005, the Wolf Haven crew revived her brief history as a wolf; they put her engraved headstone among the real wolves buried there.

There weren't many days when I was home. I kept a pile of clothes in my truck and resorted to dealing with domestic needs only when I absolutely had to. I'd been divorced for a while, but I had a new bride, the wolf job, and I spent every weekend nurturing the new relationship. I ate at restaurants and truck stops on my way from one dead animal to the next. It was quite a switch from my naïve life in Iowa where I'd never stepped foot in a real restaurant until I was nearly 20 years old, tooling around the Iowa countryside with Dick Bishop and Ron Andrews. Back then, I was annoyed by a waitress's interrogation: How do you want your steak cooked? What kind of potato? Honey mustard, ranch or blue cheese on your salad? Now I answered those kinds of questions three times a day.

I blew into Helena long enough to see my kids, do laundry and paper-work, and sort slides for presentations, which were getting more numerous. I wasn't sure I liked the limelight, but I found that people hungered for accurate information about wolves and I was apparently the only one who could give them the gory details. I tried not to turn anyone down. Somehow the gap between what people believed and what was real needed bridging, so I drove everywhere, talking to every kind of agriculture and environmental group. Soon academia became interested in how I was balancing the needs of all of the people in the fracas. Though there were few of them before reintroduction, wolves had jumped almost immediately from a biological issue to a social one – a category they've yet to escape.

I'd never mingled with the kinds of people I met because of wolves, and they weren't particularly interested in mingling with a predator killer like me. They were people with names like Shaman Thunder, or who changed from Nancy to Amaroq because it meant something having to do with wolves. These people – and there were a lot of them – were branded as nutcases by my agency and dismissed without much thought. Suddenly, however, these wolf lovers and advocates wanted to hear what I knew about wolves killing livestock and invited me repeatedly to give presentations to their groups. The thing that my agency, the ranching industry, the Farm Bureau and others overlooked was that these people represented a huge interest group that had money, brains or clout, and sometimes all three, and they were planning on using all of it to protect wolves.

My time was split even further when trappers in other states asked me to show them how to conduct a field investigation when the suspect was a wolf. North Dakota, Oregon, Washington, Texas, Nevada, Arizona, New Mexico and Utah hadn't seen wolves in several decades, but were sure that one would show up soon and begin killing everything in sight. I tried to reason the fear out of the trappers at these meetings, but I'm not sure it worked. I emphasized the need for good forensics and necropsy procedures that mirrored police homicide investigations. I reiterated what I'd learned about basic wolf biology and behavior, but my main focus was how to capture, handle and immobilize a wolf, all without killing it accidentally. Keep good records, I encouraged. A few trappers grumbled and shifted in their seats. Take photos and better yet, take videos of supposed wolf kills. A few more snorted and looked at each other. Seek more training with veterinarians on ways to handle wolves in certain situations, I said.

Some of the trappers thought that dealing with wolves sounded exciting and were eager to learn more. They wanted to be ready. They asked a million questions and offered ideas that could improve field procedures. But among the eager trappers were men, supervisors mostly, who stood in the back of the room, their arms folded, missing the point. They were concerned not so much with curbing the reappearance of wolves as they were with stifling me. I was just another trapper. Who was I to try and change things?

I knew many of the supervisors, or at least could spot them in a roomful of trappers. I eyed them as I talked, and they squirmed when I suggested something new or different. They didn't care much for my ideas about conserving wolves. For that reason, I kept talking. Many were defensive of the Animal Damage Control program and felt that the concern for wolves and their welfare was overemphasized and unfounded.

"Wolf traps should be set so that the animal can't unnecessarily injure itself. The wolf's safety and welfare is the primary focus."

I wasn't sure if they needed to be reminded of some things, but trappers are in the business of killing most predators so I went ahead.

"A wolf can easily run with a trap on its foot and drag itself into barbed wire fences, fall off a cliff or drown in a creek, reservoir, river or lake, so if you're at all doubtful, it would be a lot easier on both of you if you just pick somewhere else to set your trap."

Some of the trappers couldn't understand why the U.S. Fish and Wildlife Service didn't want to use bigger traps, forgetting that I'd just talked about trying not to injure the wolf, if possible.

I was the odd man out because, while I appeared to be a turncoat, all I wanted was for the trappers to know how to handle a wolf safely, conduct field investigations above reproach and deal with people fairly. They needed training – and the supervisors needed it worst of all. I sincerely wanted Animal Damage Control field personnel to be the best of the best and outshine all other agencies.

The trappers themselves were a fairly decent bunch. They really wanted to know how to identify a wolf-kill. My advice was simple: Be systematic and first determine if wolves were known to be in the area. Interview people, look for wolf tracks and scats, or listen for howling. Keep an open mind and necropsy the livestock carcass and look for signs of predation like trauma, hemorrhage, and bite wounds. If you want to be the expert, then you have to act like the expert and take things one step at time.

"*You* are the experts, not the ranchers, the biologists, the officers or anyone else. You need to take control of the investigation," I coached.

"Don't let the pressure get to you," I said when a trapper would tell me about getting cussed out by a rancher who blamed wolves for deaths they didn't cause.

"Easy for you to say," the trapper responded. But that was my role now.

In my estimation, the best thing for all of these guys was to spend a week with me. I knew it probably sounded arrogant, but who else knew about this stuff? Getting smart about wolves, however, wasn't something the bosses wanted, and I found myself stepping on toes by suggesting that the trappers and their supervisors not only ride with me, but also get training in how to handle drugs and operate a dart gun and a net gun. Since the supervisors were the only ones who could make this happen, it didn't. A former state director of Animal Damage Control in Montana once informed me that the other trappers could trap and shoot just as well as I could, and that I was making a lot of them resentful. One trapper in the Southwest who would work with wolves later in his career lipped off at a meeting once, "Hell, I've shot thousands of coyotes from a chopper. What's the difference shooting a damn dart gun at wolves?" When he went to do it, he failed. As far as I know, he's never yet hit his target. My agency had a chance to do it right and be the experts at wolf capture, but it chose to fail because it was more concerned about its rough and tough image. There were exceptions: Rick Williamson and Fred Goodman both wanted to know more than they were allowed to, and both rode with me for the express purpose of learning to find, trap and handle wolves.

Williamson worked his way into a niche with Animal Damage Control as the agency's wolf specialist in Idaho. He and I are the only trappers in the Northern Rockies with certificates on our walls from the National Park Service because we took Aerial Capture and Eradication and Tagging of Animals (ACETA) training. Only six trappers in Montana, including me, ever received helicopter net gun training back in the early 1990s. Normal aerial gunner safety training consisted of shooting clay pigeons at a trapper's conference in Montana, but never involved aircraft as long as I worked for the agency.

Just being involved with big predators was a macho thing, and still is. Federal trappers like to think they're good at what they do and most of the time they are – but only when it comes to killing. When it comes to conserving – being careful not to leave a wolf in a trap too long, not letting it drown because the trap was set near water, learning how to mix immobilizing drugs properly, accidentally shooting the wrong ones because they can't tell a pup from an adult – that's where the agency is woefully, willfully sloppy.

The first wolf in Idaho caught by Animal Damage Control ended up drowned in a river. One of the first wolves darted by a trapper in Montana died when a dart was shot through the entire length of its body. Another wolf in Montana was struck in the abdomen with a trapper's dart and had to be taken by airplane to a veterinarian. Other wolves died from hyperthermia (heat stroke) because they languished in a trap while the trapper was busy at camp, making coffee, saddling his horses, talking with people, instead of thinking about the wolf's welfare. In Idaho, a little yellow airplane owned by the agency sported wolf track decals for every wolf its gunners killed.

If aerial hunting – shooting wolves from airplanes and helicopters – were abolished, the government couldn't do any significant harm to wolf populations. The exception would be if poisons were resurrected, which seems impossible, except that more than a few wolves have been killed that way in the past 10 years. In Idaho, one person was convicted in such a case, but so far he is the only one.

If wolves need to be removed from an area, let hunters do it. Fair chase is how it should be. I came to this way of thinking by being the one to have to kill wolves, and believe me, there's nothing macho about it. Nothing at all.

I'd been voted in as the Animal Damage Control's first wolf specialist, but my decisions were questioned every day. I was holding a job that hadn't existed before, and as far as I could tell, my style was giving everyone an ulcer. The guy who took my old job as western district supervisor didn't want me so much as talking to the trappers under his command because I might unduly influence them to find wolves innocent of a kill. My direct supervisor had been on the board of decision-makers that appointed me as the wolf guy, but later disputed my findings that wolves were not to blame for most of the dead livestock in Montana. When I came out of the Gold Nugget in Helena one night after eating supper and found my windshield smashed out, but my guns and gear still on the seat, I started wondering who my enemies really were. After I turned down an assignment in Utah that seemed orchestrated to get rid of me, I received a letter of reprimand over the windshield incident. They put me on probation and spent thousands of dollars flying experts out to interrogate me. I would be fighting my own people from then on. Once or twice, they almost won.

One of the stipulations of my new job was that I had to move to Kalispell, the idea being that I'd be closer to the growing wolf population near Glacier National Park and the North Fork of the Flathead River. It pained me to have to move away from my kids, but the strategy seemed sound. It never happened. The Animal Damage Control leadership in Billings and Denver instead switched gears and decided that I should move to Missoula, closer to the University of Montana and its oblique interest in wolves. Whereas Kalispell seemed logical, moving to Missoula was simply counterproductive. There were hardly any wolves in that part of Montana. Also, I had become part of the wolf team in Helena, alongside the Fish and Wildlife Service where Ed Bangs enjoyed the luxury of having me a phone call or a 10-minute drive away when he needed help or advice. I resisted the move until I got a direct order to go.

There was no room for me at the university or at any other government building, so my bosses rented a warehouse, 150 feet long and 50 feet wide. It had been a Mack truck garage and must have doubled as a fire crew barracks because it had lots of toilets and showerheads. The only convenient way I could get in and out of this place was to yank on the chain and pulley system that attached to a huge overhead door. I felt like a fireman in a cartoon. All I was missing was a pole to slide down. I parked my truck next to the desk and filing cabinet that I'd hauled from Helena, and I slept in a Prowler camp trailer that I'd borrowed from my agency. When the weather turned chilly – it gets well below 30 degrees in the winter in Missoula – I turned on the two gas heaters at each end of the warehouse's 30-foot ceiling. But the heat didn't quite reach me, so I put on my longjohns, my wool pants and my Sorel boots. After a few months, I questioned my sanity for putting up with it and wondered if I would be one of those government employees that was shuffled off and forgotten until I died and stank up the place.

I sat down at my desk one November night, turned on my tiny lamp and put paper in my typewriter. I couldn't remember ever being so depressed. I couldn't sleep, I couldn't get warm, I was living in a warehouse, and I'd just gotten over a case of mono – probably from the stress of everything, including being away from my kids. I started typing a letter to Larry Handegard, the state director, begging him to get me out of here. He'd put me in Missoula, I finally realized, to send me a message: I was getting way too chummy with those wolf huggers at the Fish and Wildlife Service.

Then the phone rang. It was 10 o'clock.

"Carter?" Ed Bangs hesitated. "What are you doing at the office at this time of the night?"

"Why are you calling me this late at night?" I said. It was like divine intervention.

I launched into my tale of woe, which sounded comical I suppose because Bangs broke into chuckles a few times. I ended by telling him about the letter I was typing and that I was dressed in longjohns and winter boots, stuck forever in what amounted to solitary confinement.

Bangs hadn't been to my new "office," nor had anyone else except trapper Jerry Lewis, who couldn't find the door and took to walking the length of the warehouse beating on the metal siding with a piece of rubber hose, yelling for me to open up.

"Carter, this situation is stupid. I need you in Helena. I'll make some calls tomorrow."

There was a God.

I shuffled the few yards to my trailer – my home – and banged my head trying to wedge myself into the tiny bed. My feet hung over the end. I wondered as I flipped off the light whether my superiors would think I was a crybaby. Tough shit, I thought, and fell asleep.

When autumn hit, everyone calmed down, including me. Sheep and cattle were driven out of the mountains and sent to market, trucked to valley pastures or even to another state for winter feeding – a final fattening-up before they go to the slaughterhouse. Every June, the process starts again, and ranchers turn several hundred - or several thousand - animals out on newly greening public lands. When the snow settles in, ranchers can slow down and hold meetings and attend a few conventions. I go, too, if they invite me, because I'm not busy looking at their dead animals.

At the invitation of Stan Boyd, secretary for the Idaho Wool Growers Association, I made a trip to Boise in November 1993 to speak at their convention. I knew a lot of people already, but I met a bunch more with whom I'd be speaking regularly once wolves were back in the state.

I'd been offered a job once in Boise, as the assistant state director for Animal Damage Control back in the 1980s. I turned it down because the backed-up traffic and big city lights scared me. I knew all of the trappers and the supervisors, but I was starting to feel like an old-timer. One of the trappers was Chuck Carpenter, the son of Roy Carpenter, the old boy in Dillon, Montana, who helped me with the golden eagle project in 1975. But it wasn't the trappers who wanted to talk to me at the wool growers convention, it was the high-flyers. Everybody wanted to know what I'd learned with regard to wolves and livestock, what it meant, and how much it might cost in money, time and politics. U.S. Sen. Mike Crapo, Idaho Sen. Laird Noh and the director of the state's Department of Agriculture, John Hatch, as well as some of the state's more connected ranchers wanted my opinion. They had even more questions after I showed a few slides and gave a talk, entitled *The Reality of Wolf Recovery*. I told them the wheels of bureaucracy were moving faster than they probably expected, and that reintroduction was imminent. I gave them my credentials as the only guy out there specifically tasked to investigate the predatory behavior of wolves and unloaded enough statistics to make their heads spin. More than 100 people jammed the room.

I repeated my slideshow two weeks later at Montana's woolgrower meeting, then at the state's stockgrowers convention. There, after a flurry of newspaper and radio interviews, I ran into a ranch couple from Great Falls whom I'd known for years. They turned their backs when I said hello. Our friendship had apparently ended. Wolves had torn a hole in it.

While I was out examining dead things, the bureaucrats had been making things happen. Wolf reintroduction wasn't just an idea anymore. It was going to occur – and soon. I'd been asked to review thick piles of documents to see how much this momentous event would impact Animal Damage Control and its predator-killing routines. It wasn't a popular topic with anyone at my agency, but I thought the whole idea was cool and I wanted to be part of it.

The wolves would come from Alberta, Canada, at first, then British Columbia, and they would be released as two separate groups in two distinct areas: Yellowstone National Park and the steep, rugged mountains of central Idaho called the Frank Church-River of No Return Wilderness. It was going to be a fantastic experiment not so much in biology, but sociology. The fate of wolves in this country has always come down to whether people will allow them to persist.

The Fish and Wildlife Service wanted wolves from areas similar to where they'd be released and ones that had evolved eating elk, deer, and moose, not caribou as they tend to do in Alaska. They were to be free of disease and bad behavior, such as livestock killing.

Wolves that were related – families – were to be moved to Yellowstone and penned first, so they acclimated and were less likely to return to Canada. Idaho would receive the lone wolves, which would be "hard" released, simply let out of metal kennels one at a time to scamper through the snow and into their new home.

Despite the daily threat of lawsuits that could bring reintroduction to a screeching halt, Ed Bangs pressed forward. It was essential that things actually happen, that wolves get caught and readied for transport on airplanes. If there wasn't momentum on such a historic event, government officials might get nervous and hit the eject button. Bangs had it under control, and in November and December 1994, sent a man to launch things. As the wolf specialist for Animal Damage Control, yet on Bangs' payroll, I was hoping I'd get a chance to do something – anything. So I waited.

I wondered how it would go once the animals were released in serious numbers. There were only a few wolves here and there, mostly in Montana, but even that was causing hysterics. Wolves had a bad reputation, but I wondered how many government trappers and ranchers in the old days had ever put a knife to a carcass when they saw wolves slinking away from it. How much livestock did wolves really kill and how much were they just scavenging? In the short time I'd been looking at such situations, I'd found that wolves and coyotes were doing a lot more cleaning up than killing – when it came to cattle, anyway. Sheep were a different story. Everything was waiting to kill one of those.

Animal Damage Control had some serious matters to deal with, primarily money. Who was going to pay for all of the extra problems wolves were sure to create? No one was sure yet, but the politicians were working on it.

I attended a big meeting on reintroduction and afterward called Animal Damage Control's top man in the West, Regional Director Tom Nichols, to tell him that putting wolves back in Idaho and Yellowstone was on the fast track. He seemed stunned by the news. I wondered whether my agency had lulled itself into believing western agricultural lobbies when they puffed up and said the wolf was a scourge that would never again be tolerated.

"So they really plan to do this?" Nichols said after a moment. I could almost hear the gears in his head turning. "Carter, sometimes I guess you just need to shake my tree to get my attention."

The Endangered Species Act, which I had never read until wolves were reintroduced, contained a very specific statement: All federal departments and agencies were required to conserve the species that were on the federal list. It seemed clear that this statement applied to my predator control agency.

I was confused, therefore, at the arguments I heard from my supervisors and even higher up the line. The unofficial policy of Animal Damage Control was to resist wolf recovery. The agency pointed out the complications wolves would cause, specifically that wolves might accidentally get into the traps, snares or poisons meant for coyotes, foxes and other predators that didn't enjoy any kind of legal protection. Agency managers couldn't understand how bringing back wolves was more important than killing the predators that bothered ranchers.

Nevertheless, the wolf move was gearing up and it didn't appear anything could stop it. Every federal agency around did its part, reporting wolf sightings, and rearranging policies in preparation for the big predator that would soon be back.

In all of this, I was the only one who drove around dealing with the problems of wolves taking bites out of sheep and cattle and other animals. Even before reintroduction, wolves were showing up faster than the feds expected, which put me in the hot seat when there were livestock deaths. It was a unique job and a messy one. I realized one day, as I drove to another investigation, that I'd never had to seek a job. The jobs always seemed to come to me. The challenge wasn't the wolves, it was the people.

If things were going to work out with reintroduction, the right people needed to be in the right places. I felt like I could do wolves some good because – though Animal Damage Control didn't like it – I was able to separate the real wolf problems from the manufactured ones. More help came along when Dr. Bob Ream of the University of Montana, while keeping his professorship, won a seat in the Montana state Legislature. From that position, he pushed a proposal through to the federal level to make sure I stayed on the payroll as the wolf specialist. My own agency faltered once or twice, believing that wolf work shouldn't be a priority. Just having created the wolf specialist job got them jabbed by ranchers who accused Animal Damage Control of being wolf-lovers. It was a matter of choosing sides. So they were willing to let the money for the wolf specialist slide.

"Don't let Carter fall through the cracks," said Molly Beattie, the late director of the Fish and Wildlife Service. If my agency wouldn't lift a finger to keep me, she intended to intervene. Defenders of Wildlife also went to bat for me. It was good timing because the money was running out just as wolf hysteria was hitting high gear.

Animal Damage Control managers had nothing good to say about the draft environmental impact statement to reintroduce wolves. Its managers wrung their hands about how to keep killing predators with wolves running around all over the place. Traplines would have to be checked every 24 hours instead of once or twice a week. The livestock industry would go out of business because of wolves and land-use restrictions, and in the end, someone – namely taxpayers – would have to pay for dead livestock when Defenders of Wildlife decided not to pay anymore. These were their arguments.

The more I listened to this, the more I learned about what wolves didn't do. And the more I put up with the narrow-minded ideas of Animal Damage Control, the more I realized that the wolf's worst enemy wasn't the rancher or any other individual here and there with a rifle, it was the "system," and the politics that ruled the various government agencies. I agreed with Ronald M. Nowak, a noted mammalogist and taxonomist who specializes in carnivores. Nowak disagreed with the implication throughout the reintroduction document *that the wolf in Yellowstone or anywhere else in the Northwest can be considered 'recovered' just because some arbitrary number of packs or populations is* established. *The wolf will never come close to true recovery in this region, will always remain highly vulnerable, and will always need coverage by the (Endangered Species) Act."*

Having been a trapper and a hunter, and understanding what I did about wolf behavior, I could kill them without much effort if that kind of order came down. I wondered how many people knew how easy it would be? Just give me wolves wearing radio collars, a helicopter, a shotgun, deep snow and calm winds.

By 1994, the Sawtooth pack had been lurking in the back of my mind for a year. They were wolves that had, like others, been trickling in a few at a time from Canada. Like the Ninemile pack, there was nothing to keep the Sawtooth pack from moving to the U.S.

I'd suspected that the wolves were involved in the deaths of a few cattle, but now I knew for sure. I'd already collared the alpha male so the pack could be monitored as it roved the outskirts of Augusta, Montana.

When they struck, it was at the LF Ranch, killing a two-day-old calf. The mother cow fought them off for a while, but the wolves tore the calf apart anyway. A month later, the wolves did it again. The ranch owner and his foreman, Tim Tew, agreed between them that they'd prefer the incidents remain confidential. The owner would take money from Defenders of Wildlife for the fall market value of his calves, but he didn't want any wolves killed. He didn't need that kind of publicity. But if the wolves started in on his neighbor's stock, he wouldn't care if the whole pack had to be moved or snuffed out.

I showed Tew how to use a telemetry receiver and left one with him so he could keep track of the Sawtooth pack's whereabouts. It was a new thing I'd been doing to gain some trust and tolerance among ranchers. I promised the men that my lips were sealed. Except of course that I had to report the incident to my boss.

"That ranch is harboring wolves," Larry Handegard said when I told him about the two dead calves. He didn't want me out there again.

"They can't get paid for losses if I don't do my job," I countered. But he wasn't listening. Instead Handegard repeated the story at a meeting of the state's livestock associations and word spread. Pretty soon the LF Ranch's phone was ringing and my promise to keep things quiet had been cut to shreds.

Three weeks later, the wolves were back, chasing a herd of cattle on nearby J.T. Weisner's ranch. Two calves had broken legs from being trampled by adult cattle. Weisner said the wolves had been harassing his animals for a couple of weeks and he was fed up.

I liked Weisner. I'd met him initially over the dead bodies of his animals, but he was polite and thoughtful and always willing to work things out and shake hands afterward. In this latest case, I recommended to Ed Bangs that the wolves be moved to our old standby, Glacier National Park, and as always, he gave me all the latitude I needed to do my job.

The capture was difficult from the start because of the timbered terrain and heavy, tall brush along creek bottoms. The airplane crew found the pack just west of the LF Ranch and after 30 minutes of playing cat and mouse in deep snow and shrubby willows, I fired a dart into a yearling wolf that refused to go down. My pilot, Ron Gipe, kept on it for more than 20 minutes before I decided to load another dart and shoot it again. Even after the second dart, it kept running, heading downhill, at one point passing within 50 yards of the ground crew that waited for us at the airstrip.

Finally the Telezol worked and the wolf walked into the willows to hide. But each time we got close, it wandered further off. I didn't want to shoot it again, so Gipe set us down in a pasture above a steep bank about 50 feet away. I carried the loaded dart gun with me just in case, and walked the edge of the willows until I saw the wolf.

It lay there, its head up, watching me. It had enough Telezol coursing through its system to be disoriented, but it shouldn't have been so lucid that it could hold its head up. As I got closer, it jumped up and tried to run.

I don't know why, maybe it was dumb instinct, but I reached out and grabbed the wolf by the tail. I did it without considering what I'd do once I had hold of the animal, or how I'd react if it turned on me. I gambled on what I knew, that wolves don't usually want anything to do with people, and I was right. When I grabbed the fluffy, stiff tail, the wolf lurched forward, digging its feet into the earth, using all of its waning strength to pull away from me. When it realized that it was running in place, it looked back at me and growled. I let go. I should have just shot it with another dart, but I didn't want to overdose it. I stayed behind the wobbly wolf as it headed down a narrow cow path. I grabbed its tail again, and this time when it growled, I flipped it onto its side into the bushes.

In another inexplicable move, I jumped on the wolf and pinned its head to the ground with my dart gun. Ron Gipe had no idea that I was wolf wrestling. I'd descended an embankment that hid me from view. This time, unlike the Ninemile wrestling match, I had Ketamine and a syringe in the chest pocket of my flight suit. But I couldn't reach it because my hands were busy holding down a struggling wolf that was growling and looking at me out of the corners of its eyes.

Forget the drugs, I thought. Time for bootlaces again. I pinned the wolf with one arm and the dart gun, and unlaced a boot with the other. Meanwhile the airplane had been circling overhead, watching this circus and radioing Gipe about it. He came walking to see if he could help, finding me at just the right moment to take the drugs out of my pocket and give the hogtied wolf an injection.

There were only two wolves to catch. The next one went down easily. In short order, both animals were in kennels ready to head to Glacier National Park and Tim Tew was shaking my hand and thanking me for taking care of the problem.

But I was getting tired of having to re-lace my boots all the time.

I felt like Forrest Gump. I seemed to be wherever the major events occurred regarding wolf reintroduction, and where wolves had already wandered over the border into Montana, I was nearly always within shouting distance. I'd never paid much attention to local politics before wolves nabbed me by the scruff of my neck and carried me into their world. Now I couldn't get away from the banter.

Wolf advocates promoted reintroduction. Politicians volleyed back, pointing out the problems wolves would inevitably create for their constituents, especially the livestock industry and sportsmen who were sure wolves would eat their way through all the elk and deer in the West before starting in on people, especially rural kids waiting at bus stops. When it seemed that people couldn't act any crazier, Ed Bangs asked me to pay a visit to Tom Carey Sr., in Boulder, Montana. One of Carey's calves had been killed by wolves.

I usually telephone people who've experienced a livestock loss before I drop in on them. Mostly I want to get acquainted, find out a little more about what they think happened, and ask them to be sure and cover the carcass with a tarp and keep their dogs away from it. I also do it to see if their story jibes with what I see – and if it stays the same from one conversation to the next. A body is a necessity. Without it, I can't tell a thing. Carey called the State and two game wardens arrived, gave the calf a cursory look and left to file their reports. Carey said he buried the carcass immediately after the wardens departed because of the summer heat.

Officers Jim DeBoer and Chad Murphy were acting in earnest by looking at the dead calf and turning in their reports, but they admitted they were operating outside a protocol that had been established between their agency (Montana Fish, Wildlife and Parks) and mine – the one that was in charge of looking at dead livestock. As the wolf specialist, I had to see the carcass to determine whether wolves killed it. If they did, the rancher could be compensated for the loss. DeBoer, as the senior officer, wrote the report that drew no conclusions about what killed the calf. Neither officer was sure what a wolf kill looked like or even how the animal took down its prey, although there were several old wounds on the carcass.

"Are you going to be doing any training sessions soon?" DeBoer asked, adding that he wished he had called me in the first place.

Thirty miles from Carey's ranch, wolves had been reported trotting through fields and hanging around. They could have been the same ones that killed the calf. It would be nothing for a wolf or a pack of them to travel 20 or 30 miles at a stretch. But just because the wolves were present didn't make them guilty. It's a concept that some folks still find difficult to accept. I needed evidence. Without my report, Carey would be lucky to get a dime, and I wasn't budging without a carcass to examine.

Carey was furious. His neighbors had had wolf trouble and were paid for damages. I was willing to give things a fair shot if he was willing to dig up that calf.

"Why isn't the warden's word good enough for you?" he seethed. "I guess you think we're just a bunch of dumb ranchers out here. I guess we have to take a picture of the wolf killing stock for you to believe us." He added a list of things that were making his life miserable, including bighorn sheep reintroductions, deer and elk eating his alfalfa, and now the presence of wolves.

"I tried to call you at your office but you wouldn't answer the phone," he said.

I told him about my answering machine and that maybe he called the Fish and Wildlife Service by mistake. That's where I'd heard about his trouble to begin with.

"Can we start over and talk about this?" I said.

"I'm wasting my money on a long distance call with you," he yelled. Then he slammed down the phone. He forgot that I'd dialed him.

I pulled my chair to my typewriter and wrote a report, even though I hadn't visited the ranch. This one had all the hallmarks of becoming a disaster. By the time I was done, it was five pages long and contained a sentence describing Carey as one of the most unreasonable people I'd ever dealt with.

While I was typing away, Carey got on the phone to the Fish and Wildlife Service and Defenders of Wildlife demanding money for his dead calf. All he needed, he was told, was Carter's report saying wolves killed it. Jim Petersen of the Montana Stockgrowers Association tried to intervene.

"Can you just compensate Tom for his calf?" he asked me.

Peterson was a reasonable guy, but I wasn't sure how many different ways I could explain it.

"Pay him, Jim. Hell, I don't care if you pay him double!" I said. "I just look at the dead stock, I don't write checks."

Carey thought about it for a few days and decided that he didn't want the money. All he wanted was for me to admit that a wolf killed his calf.

"Sorry, Tom."

Carey wrote about his abuse at the hands of the government in an opinion piece printed by a Farm Bureau magazine, then in Agri-News, turning the recent events at his ranch into a rant about government turf wars and crazy environmental groups and their obsession with wolves. Two months later, I thought things had settled down, but instead I received a letter from U.S. Rep. Pat Williams. He was concerned about the way I'd handled the suspected wolf kill at his constituent's ranch and wanted a complete report, including my conclusions on the probable cause of death of the calf. He went on to say that Animal Damage Control should set up a better system of communications within the agency so that messages about suspected wolf kills could be dealt with quickly, even on weekends. And by the way, he added, I also should train other government agents and come up with standards for such field investigations.

The letter made my blood boil. Here was a red-hot example of a politician sticking his nose where it didn't belong. I'd already written a detailed five-page report regarding the bullshit at Tom Carey's place. And any time a politician wanted to sit in on one of my training sessions – and there had been dozens – he was welcome to it.

I complied with the congressman's request for a wordy report because I had to, but I wasn't friendly about it. I knew he was just covering his ass so Carey would stop calling and writing, but I resented the insinuation that I was a lazy fed who never worked on weekends or holidays and who didn't answer his phone until Monday mornings. All I did was work. When it came to wolves, the complaints were relentless.

In the end, the Montana Stockgrowers Association didn't pay Carey; Defenders of Wildlife did. The group didn't have to, but did it to foster better relations with the ranchers. The stockgrowers put a blurb in their newsletter suggesting that ranchers with suspected wolf kills would save themselves a lot of grief by calling Carter Niemeyer first.

Things got livelier in Tom Carey's neighborhood when an Animal Damage Control supervisor, Dave Nelson, caught a 78-pound, adult male wolf six miles north of Cardwell, Montana. Two small calves were reported killed on the Lance Bullock ranch and Animal Damage Control assumed coyotes were the cause. But when a wolf ended up in Nelson's trap, the blame immediately shifted. I didn't have a thing to do with any of this, including the collar that was put on the wolf – until later.

The idea behind collaring the Cardwell wolf was that if there was one, there must be more, and the collared wolf would betray the pack. But it persisted in its lonesome ways, hanging around several ranches over six weeks, eating afterbirth or chewing on carcasses that were left to rot in pastures. Its presence made ranchers tense, and the number of dead and missing calves slowly increased in that area, but I looked at all of them and none showed signs of being killed by a wolf.

After skinning a calf belonging to Morris Ferrat near Toston, I again shook my head. Coyotes and wolves – or a wolf – had been eating at the flanks and hindquarters, but didn't do the killing. I dug my telemetry receiver out of the pile of gear in my front seat and flipped it on. A repeating beep, strong, sounding almost like water dripping into a full bucket, was proof that the Cardwell wolf was very close.

I got in my truck and laid the receiver on the seat, following the signal. It was coming from an adjacent property. When I asked permission to drive through, the owner agreed, but wanted to ride along. We headed through the grazed-off land toward a meager patch of willows in one corner of the spread. The signal nearly jumped out of the receiver and I figured, with nowhere else to hide, the wolf must be in the willow patch. I took my video camera out of its pouch and shut off the truck, getting out quietly, careful not to slam the door.

As soon as I approached, the animal burst into a limping run, its tail between its legs. Its awkward gait was probably the result of a trap injury. It looked all wrong. And when I measured this against its reported behavior, I ruled against the animal being a wild wolf that had wandered down from Canada.

"It might be somebody's pet or something," I told Ed Bangs by phone. "It's just a wimpy thing and doesn't appear to know how to kill anything. It's eating on carcasses."

I called it Wimpy from then on. He was seen a few more times, once curled up asleep in a pasture full of cattle. Wimpy seemed tame and confused, and telemetry indicated he was alone. I convinced Bangs that the wolf should be recaptured and put in captivity or euthanized. I felt sorry for the thing. It was probably just a lost dog that happened to be a wolf-hybrid. My biggest concern was the ranchers and the case of nerves this animal was giving them. Its presence wasn't winning real wolf recovery any brownie points.

In two more days, a plane was up, looking for Wimpy, so that I could have a helicopter take me in to get a shot at it with a dart. But the signal was gone. The plane ascended to 10,000 feet. From that height, and in that open country, a radio collar should have been detectable for 50 miles in any direction. Nothing.

Wimpy couldn't have traveled far enough in two days to get outside of telemetry range. The animal had a lame foot. Maybe its owner found it and took it home. I quizzed Morris Ferrat and his wife about the animal. I was suspicious, but the couple hadn't seen Wimpy in several days.

"Well, call me if you see him, will you?" I said. I sat in my truck and made a journal entry before driving away: *Wolf is probably dead/radio signal gone.*

The saga of Wimpy and his vanishing act had slipped my mind completely by April of the following year when federal law enforcement agents asked casually whether the Fish and Wildlife Service was missing any of its radio-collared wolves. Joe Fontaine thumbed through his files while the agent described a dead, collared canine with ear tags and a collar stamped with "USFWS" sprawled on Highway 10 near downtown El Paso, Texas.

Fontaine had given up when he remembered the Cardwell wolf.

"Oh no," he muttered, "not Wimpy."

The information matched.

"How in the hell did it get to Texas?" Fontaine was incredulous.

"That sucker got a ride," I said. "Probably somebody killed it, froze it and hauled it there as a joke. It sure didn't walk there on its own."

I thought my theory was pretty good, but when Wimpy was examined, he was two pounds heavier than when he was collared. X-rays showed his pelvis was shattered and a femur was broken – injuries consistent with being hit by a car. The only thing in Wimpy's belly was a piece of tin foil. Not even a wild wolf had ever traveled that far.

I thought Morris Ferrat would be interested in this final development.

"You know Carter," he said, "we always figured you and Joe just got rid of that wolf and just didn't tell anybody."

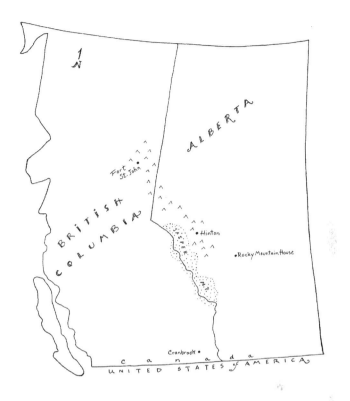

CANADA

When the first field-team meeting came together regarding wolf rein-troduction, I'd already been dealing with wolves in Montana for about seven years. Still, it was exciting in October of 1994 to know that things were on schedule. Alberta, Canada was the place, and the first capture was only three months away.

Maps spread out on tables at Ed Bangs' Helena office showed circles drawn around the timbered, nearly roadless country east of Jasper and Banff national parks. This was the area from which the United States planned on plucking several dozen wolves. Nine Canadian trappers were signed up to do the catching, and would be paid $2,000 for each wolf they caught alive.

Animal Damage Control didn't think much of my involvement in reintroduction, but couldn't stop me from participating in it because Bangs was paying my salary. That had been the inter-agency agreement when I became the wolf specialist. My bosses were probably sorry they had ever maneuvered me into it. Things had sure changed. I'd ended up slitting my own throat by taking the wolf specialist job. I went out and did what I thought was a thorough, honest job and because of it, I was branded a traitor. Every time I said a wolf didn't do it, I got my ass chewed by my supervisor. But I was unflagging in my opinion: Wolves might be a nuisance because they were new, but they were not monsters, and I wasn't letting bureaucrats or congressmen or anyone else change my mind about it. I didn't understand why others around me refused to acknowledge this truth. The few wolves that had wandered into Montana had nearly undetectable effects on ranching and didn't seem to be that interested in livestock. I didn't believe that injecting a sudden, larger population of wolves into America's Northern Rockies would create any sort of burden for most ranchers, except maybe a psychological one. Having wolves around used to be part of the cost of doing business.

There was a general mindset at Animal Damage Control that, as government trappers, we should hate whatever killed livestock. But I didn't hate what I trapped or killed – ever. That kind of thinking never occurred to me. Fox pelts paid my rent and helped me out of debt when my infant daughter was in the hospital. When I trapped an animal, I did it for what I felt was a good reason, not to satisfy an emotion. To me, it was like picking corn or chopping hay. But wolves seemed to trigger a base hatred among some of my co-workers and friends, and it split us apart. There are people who still won't talk to me because of wolves. But in my simple mind, wolves weren't anything but another majestic predator to behold and I believed they belonged back with us.

Animal Damage Control had some serious problems ahead: Although wolves might not actually kill much livestock, they would be perceived to be a huge problem simply because they were wolves. The jolly days of putting out poison for coyotes and not worrying too much about what else might get into it were over. The agency was now going to have to be careful; another endangered species – with a much greater range than grizzlies – would soon be roaming out there. Animal Damage Control would be assigned to deal with problem wolves, among its other duties, but the money for the investigations was uncertain. For all I knew, I'd be out of a job soon. Maybe I'd go back to being a fur trapper.

But not yet. On November 16, 1994, I was headed to Canada. My truck was so loaded down I couldn't see out except through the windshield.

The paper trail, public hearings and other legalities overcome, several other field biologists and I would meet in Alberta to do what seemed surreal: capture wolves for reintroduction into Yellowstone National Park and the wilds of central Idaho.

I'd spent days packing, and wedged everything I might possibly need into my government truck, including lots of cold weather gear because the daytime temperatures would be below freezing most days. I had everything I'd need to attend to captured wolves, too, including a syringe pole, catch pole, weighing scale, surgical gloves, cable cutters, and a tackle box full of first-aid items. The bed of the truck held my ATV, truck chains, a jack and a gas can. Before I left Helena, I met with Bangs, Fontaine and Fritts who gave me a few final orders, a list of people to contact when I got to Alberta and another boxful of wolf-handling supplies and blank data sheets.

"When you get up there, call Jim," Bangs said, writing a phone number on a piece of paper. "He's got it all under control."

Jim Till was a biologist with a master's degree – and a former trapper. He worked for Bangs, roving the northwest Montana countryside, pinpointing wolf activity. I didn't run into him much because, in general, our duties didn't overlap – plus the fact that no one was keen on being where the fur was flying. That was my bailiwick.

As I drove, snow blew and drifted from morning til dark. By the time I arrived at the small Alberta town of Rocky Mountain House, around which reintroduction activities were to center, I was feeling cross-eyed from staring into the monotonous swirl of flakes. Following me in another loaded-down truck was Val Asher, a Fish and Wildlife Service biologist stationed in Idaho. Asher and I had searched the backcountry there a few times looking for signs of wolves, but found none. She took the heat and the cold and never complained. Her brown eyes twinkled every time she shoved a wad of Copenhagen in her mouth.

Jim Till was at the Voyageur Motel, just as Bangs said. Asher and I got rooms and wandered around to find him. Jim was supposed to be the point man. His room looked like a pawn shop full of sporting goods. There was something leaned or stacked in every corner.

"Well, are you ready to get at it?" he said. He rubbed his hands together. All I could think of was taking a hot shower and getting a good night's sleep.

I surmised that Till was shouldering a lot of responsibility for the Fish and Wildlife Service up here. He'd been in Alberta a couple of weeks getting the local biologists and trappers lined out.

"How many wolves do you have so far?" I may have been tired, but I was eager to hear how things were going.

"Well, I haven't really heard from any of the trappers yet," he said.

I'm not sure what kind of look came over my face, but I know my jaw probably dropped. What did he mean he hadn't heard from them?

We talked some more and caught up on things, but it became apparent the more Till talked that a whole lot of nothing was going on where things should have been hopping. Till hadn't heard from anyone in Hinton, a tiny town to the northwest, and the supposed hub of our wolf-trapping activity. He took the silence to mean the trappers hadn't caught any wolves.

I didn't get it. The inertia hit me with such surprise that I lay awake that night, worrying. Everything Bangs had told me led me to think I'd be wading into a hotbed of activity, with teams of biologists and trappers tripping over each other in pursuit of wolves. I heard later that the day his motel phone rang about a captured wolf, Till wasn't around. He'd gone to the store for groceries. It would have been a perfect time for cell phones, but ones that could be easily or reliably operated hadn't been invented yet.

Till thought that I should head for Hinton and find out what was going on. He handed me a list of names and numbers. Start tomorrow with Kirby Smith in Edson, Till suggested, adding that Asher should stay behind and help him organize and inventory equipment.

I got an early start and phoned ahead to Smith, an area wildlife biologist with the Alberta Fish and Wildlife Division. It was Saturday, but he was up. At his home, over a cup of coffee, Smith looked my list up and down, then took a pencil and made a mark next to the name of Wade Berry, a trapper who lived in the woods north of Hinton. Smith made another mark next to the name George Kelly.

"Wade's your guy," he said, "then George. They're both wolf trappers and they've done a lot of it."

Before I drove off, Smith handed me what looked like a small suitcase. A radiophone could be my best friend if I broke down in the middle of nowhere, he said. And when you're in Hinton, he added, stay at the Tara Vista Motel.

A white belch of steam hurled itself into the sky over Hinton, Alberta, expelled by the town's biggest employer, the pulp mill. Hinton and the Tara Vista would be my home for the next three weeks. Hinton, and not Rocky Mountain House, would become the center of activity on the Canadian side of wolf reintroduction.

Founded by railroad man William D. Hinton of the Grand Trunk Pacific Railroad, the exact location of the town had changed 13 times back and forth along a line seven and a half miles long. Before the pulp mill, it was sustained by a railroad stop and a coal mine, both of which folded up and left. Now, it was about to be inhabited by the American wolf team.

I took Kirby's advice and settled into the Tara Vista. After a few phone calls, I was in my truck again, adding to the 753 snowy miles I had already driven since I'd left Helena. Snow began to fall again as I went north on a two-lane highway, and by the time I'd gone 25 miles, its surface was mostly white. It looked like primo wolf country. The roads and ditches were dotted with fresh elk, deer and moose tracks. Probably a wintering area, I thought. I looked at the scrap of paper that I'd written on and slowed, turning onto a dirt road. A young bull moose stepped out of the bushes and stood in the road staring at me, then moved along.

Wade Berry's place looked like a typical trapper's cabin in Montana, but here it was at the edge of a dense forest of lodgepole pines. Smoke curled out of the chimney, fur-stretchers sized for wolves leaned here and there, and an assortment of antlers decorated the siding. A truck in the driveway was full of snares and traps and spare parts, plus a snowmobile to make the job of killing wolves fast and efficient. When I had talked to Berry an hour or so earlier, he was cordial, like he knew I'd be calling. Kirby Smith must have smoothed the way for me.

"Come on in." A man with glasses and a thick wool sweater answered the door and shook my hand. His dog barked at me, then sniffed my boots, working its nose up my pant legs before it was shooed away. "I'm Wade Berry, and this is my wife, Carrie."

Two more men sat, arms crossed, at the dining room table. Wade introduced them as Ken Cowles and George Ostashek, then pointed me to an empty chair.

"So you're with the wolf program in the States?" Wade said. He let me answer, but he had some things he wanted to get off his chest and I cut myself short to let him have his say.

Because of the contracts he'd signed with the Americans to catch wolves and not kill them, Berry had invested a serious chunk of time and effort into negotiating with other trappers to use their traplines and in putting on hold his ordinarily lucrative fur trapping business. He was in it for the money and made no apologies about it. But he hadn't heard one word from the Fish and Wildlife Service or its Canadian counterparts since he put his signature on paper. They were all a bunch of lying s.o.b.'s, he said.

I tried to assure him that the contracts were still good and that I was the guy who would make sure he got paid for live wolves, but Berry and his buddies weren't having any of it. The two men, who were evidently Berry's friends – trappers – but not engaged in the U.S.- Canada wolf project, sputtered in disbelief, then bombarded me.

"Why should we believe you? We've already heard the sales pitch."

Berry chimed in again, interrupting his friends.

"I've spent a lot of time and money and long-distance phone calls *and* I changed my snaring season all around to work with you guys," he was almost yelling. "Why should I believe another government biologist in a government truck with government plates? Why is your word any different?"

"Who'd you talk to about the contracts?" I asked.

"I don't remember," Berry waved away the question.

"Was it Jim Till?" I said. I already knew.

"Yeah, that's him."

Cowles pushed himself back in his chair and pointed at me, then the door. "Hey, why don't you just get in your truck and get outta here."

I'd been at Berry's house for at least an hour. I was hoping to get somewhere, but he and his friends were agitated and pissed off and I didn't blame them. Till had dropped the ball and I realized, sitting in Berry's kitchen, that I was here to pick it up again. Things could go either way now that the trapper told me to take a hike, but I kept my butt in the chair.

"Well, fellas, I ain't leaving 'cause I got a job to do," I said.

"You know, the bigger they come the harder they fall," Ostashek leaned across the table at me.

"And don't let the big ones fall on you," I leaned back at him, and he straightened. I'd had enough of the mouths on these two.

"Wade, why don't you give this project a chance to work?" I said.

Berry got up from the table and went to the refrigerator and, inexplicably, offered me a beer. The two trappers left the house in disgust.

"You wanna stay and eat with us?" Berry asked after his friends were gone. Maybe things were going to be okay after all.

Carrie Berry had stood in the kitchen and listened silently to the discussion at the table. Now she was busy cooking. I changed the subject from wolves to the rustic beauty of their cabin and found out that he had built the whole thing himself. I looked at the heads of all the animals on his walls and told him about learning taxidermy from Charlie Brcka in Iowa when I was a mere kid and that I'd been doing it pretty steady ever since. Berry gestured with his beer at the furniture. He'd built most of that too. The man had talent. At supper, they talked about the wildlife that wandered across their property every day. We were finally connecting as each of us carefully avoided the topic of wolf-catching.

After the meal, a man with a beard came through the front door without knocking.

"You get anything today?" Berry looked up. The man nodded.

"Carter this is Brad Gerlinsky, my trapping partner," Berry said.

He hadn't mentioned that he was running his snare lines despite not hearing from the Fish and Wildlife Service.

"We got two big black ones. They're out in the truck" Gerlinsky said.

"Well bring 'em in here. We'll show you what we do with wolves up here in Hinton," Berry grinned at me.

"So, Wade, you're snaring and killing wolves?" I asked.

"Oh yeah. Counting the two that Brad caught today, we've got nine so far in the past couple of weeks," he said. He was proceeding as a fur trapper, having had no response from the U.S. government. A wolf pelt in good condition was $400 in his pocket.

"I'm offering you $2,000 for a live wolf and you're killing them for $400? That doesn't make sense," I said.

But Berry's reasons were simple: No g-man had come around to pay him for the wolves he snared, so he killed them, skinned them, stretched their hides and would soon sell them to a fur buyer or a taxidermist.

Every trapline in Alberta is registered to its owner, who pays good money for the privilege of killing any fur-bearing animal that gets caught. The traplines can be dozens of miles long and often are owned by the same person for decades. They are jealously guarded moneymakers for those who have the stamina to put up with Canadian winters. Alberta trappers use mostly snares for wolves, which are designed to strangle the animal, leaving its fur untouched. For the wolf project, the Fish and Wildlife Service and Canadian wildlife managers gave trappers with contracts the supplies they needed to snare a wolf without killing it. This involved using 1/8-inch special cable with metal stops that let the snare close tight enough to hold a wolf but not enough to asphyxiate it.

Gerlinsky bumped open the door with his elbow and dragged the first wolf in, flopping it on the floor. It was big, maybe 100 pounds, and had thick black fur. All I could think about was that this magnificent animal had been killed because of a miscommunication between Berry and the U.S. government. A few minutes later Gerlinsky dragged in another wolf, identical to the first one.

"A couple of beauties, eh?" Berry had his own brand of admiration for wolves. He got up and pushed at them with the toe of his boot, then looked at me.

"You ever skinned a wolf, Carter?"

Wade Berry and his buddies were trappers and I was pretty sure they pegged me for a paper shuffler. His condescending tone, and even the question, put me on the defensive.

"Yeah, I've skinned wolves," I sighed, and just when Berry had decided I was probably lying, I launched into a full-scale resume about myself. But he wasn't impressed and instead talked about his partner's talent with a knife.

"You think you can beat Brad in a wolf skinning contest?"

I was frustrated and ready for a tussle. It almost sounded fun. I wasn't gaining anything by keeping my horns pulled in and what better way to earn some respect from these fellows than to play their game.

"Where do you want to do this?" I asked, expecting that we were going outside to some cold shed to freeze our asses for an hour or two.

"Right in here," Berry said, pointing to a corner of the dining room. He was up and rearranging chairs, putting wood in the woodstove. I was dumbfounded. In his house? On the carpet?

Berry stopped in mid-motion, looking up at me. "I suppose I need to get you a knife and sharpener," he said.

Now I was insulted. I held up the tools I never was without. I carried a knife and sharpener like a preacher carries the Good Book.

Berry ignored my questions about whether we could reasonably perform such a grisly task in his home. Gerlinsky and I heaved the limp animals and did as we were told. I needed a sturdy ceiling hook and rope to take the hide off of a wolf. I couldn't see how we were going to rig up those items in his dining room. Gerlinsky sat cross-legged on the floor, pulled a wolf to himself and began cutting. I took a seat along the wall and slung the other wolf over my knee. I looked at Carrie.

"I apologize for doing this in your house."

"We're going to put new carpet in here anyway," Berry interjected.

Carrie was unfazed. "It's okay," she said. She seemed to mean it.

I'd skinned more than 6,000 coyotes in my life, but I'd never attempted to skin anything while holding it on my lap. It was awkward and difficult. I couldn't imagine this being a race. It would be more like an endurance test, going on until one of us decided we'd had enough.

"Hey, do we have any of that chokecherry wine?" Berry asked his wife. Without a word, Carrie went to the kitchen and rattled glasses. Soon I was slurping on a hefty tumbler of potent hooch. It didn't take long for my head to swim.

"So Wade, are you going to work with me or not?" I said, running my knife across the brass sharpener. I wanted to resolve our differences and come to an agreement about catching live wolves. He ignored me.

"If you guys need to piss, go out on the deck," Berry said, adding that the generator that ran the water pump in the house was broken.

The wolf in my lap was still warm and its blood soaked my pants. It had been shot in the head, presumably when Berry's partner came upon it struggling in the neck-snare. An hour or so into the gore, I was drunk and only vaguely noted that the wolf on my lap had evacuated everything in its bowels and bladder and that I'd sliced open my left index finger. My blood and wolf's blood were indistinguishable. I kept on, approaching Berry with questions now and then in an attempt to negotiate wolves for reintroduction. Getting close to being finished with my wolf, I rolled the hide off where I'd removed it from the carcass, like pulling a sock inside-out. I'd left bloody fingerprints on several glasses of wine and was feeling surreal. A few more cuts around the eyes and ears and I was done. Gerlinsky was still working away. He was indeed a skilled skinner and I respected his willingness to engage in such weird sportsmanship, but I'd finished first, so I guess I'd won. After that much wine and the passage of a couple of hours, we'd sort of forgotten why we were doing this.

"What do you want to do with the carcass?" I slurred to Berry.

We carried it together and he opened the back door where we gave the slippery, fur-less body a toss. It skidded to a sudden stop, freezing instantly to the deck boards. I stood in the silent, subzero air for a moment, sucking in deep lungfuls, trying to clear my head. A snowy meadow in the distance glowed a kind of brilliant dark blue. Deer, or perhaps elk lingered at its edge, their silhouettes coming in and out of the shadows.

Later, after Gerlinsky finished his wolf and tossed it outside, everyone forgot the carcasses were there and stumbled over them on their way to take a leak.

"I need to get back to town," I said in a fog. There was no clock that I could see, but I guessed it was late. I just wanted to get rid of my trashed clothes, wash all of the blood and shit off me and go to bed. We could talk in the morning.

"Do you know what the DUI laws are in Alberta?" Wade snorted. "You're not going anywhere tonight. Not in that government truck. You can sleep on the couch."

He and his wife climbed the log stairs to their loft bedroom, followed by their faithful dog. I washed my hands, stripped to my underwear and laid on the couch in a daze.

Sometime later a noise woke me.

Click, click, click, click....

Dog toenails on the loft stairs. The dog pattered into the kitchen and puked on the floor in several loud spasms. Then it went back upstairs. My slumber was disturbed by this a few more times before I had to get up and pee. I looked at the twinkling stars and wondered about Wade Berry, this bullheaded, ornery little trapper. How in the hell would I persuade him to work with me? I negotiated my way back to the couch, hoping the dog only barfed in the kitchen, and fell back to sleep.

It was light. I sat up and rubbed the gunk out of my eyes. I thought about going outside again to get some air, but when I blinked the room into focus, there sat Wade Berry in his longjohns, holding a can of Budweiser.

"Want a beer?" he asked.

"No thanks," I pulled on my blood-crusted pants.

"How do you feel?" he asked.

"Like I been pulled through a knothole backwards."

Wade gestured with his can.

"So you want some wolves alive?"

"Yeah Wade, the dead ones ain't gonna do me much good."

"You want live wolves, we'll get you some live wolves," he said, grinning. "Carrie's going to make us some breakfast and then we'll get going, eh?"

Brad Gerlinsky walked in as we ate and Berry quizzed him between forkfuls.

"The wolves been around Rock Lake?"

"I heard them howling up there yesterday," Gerlinsky said.

"If the wolves are howling at Rock Lake, we have some hung up in snares," Berry said. "We'll take Carter up there today."

Not long into our conversation, the trappers from the day before came through the door, and seeing that I was still there, wondered why Berry hadn't told me to go to hell yet.

"This is my goddamn house," Berry yelled and jumped out of his chair. "Carter's a guest here and if you don't like it, you can get the hell out." Then he added a gem that only the events of the previous night could have clinched. "He's one of us and I'm going to work with him."

The two smart-mouths shuffled back outside without another word.

Before anything else, I needed to clean up and get my wolf handling kit. I drove the half-hour back to the motel, threw my pants and long underwear in the garbage and gathered up my stuff. I called Ed Bangs and Jim Till to tell them about the situation – and that we just might have a couple of wolves today. I made another phone call to Jeff Kneteman, a biologist at the Alberta Fish and Wildlife Division, to let him know we needed kennels for live wolves.

Things had gone from a standoff to furious action. I returned to Berry's and squeezed in his truck with him and Gerlinsky. A raw wind blew snow across the highway until we almost couldn't see.

Rock Lake, near the east boundary of Jasper National Park, was a prolific place to snare and kill wolves. Deep snow was getting deeper. Berry wanted to do a quick check of the snares and would shout if he had a wolf. The two men faded into thick willows poking out of knee-deep drifts. Gusts of wind made the falling snow spiral. What was pretty at first was deteriorating into a blizzard.

They were gone about 15 minutes when I thought I heard something. I put my head out the window and heard a muffled voice in what had become a raging storm. I yelled back, uncertain, and waited a moment. By habit, I grabbed my tackle box and syringe pole and postholed, following Wade's tracks. I could hear now that I was getting closer.

"We got a wolf!" The snow swallowed Berry's voice. I picked up the pace.

A hundred yards in, a silver-colored wolf was curled under the trees, slowly being consumed by snow. Only an animal that could not escape and was giving up its life would lie down like that. It made no attempt to move when we approached it, simply looking at me with big-eyed resignation.

Berry was still using snares to kill wolves because, up until last night, the Americans had given him no proof that he'd be paid for live ones. I wasn't sure he even had the snares with stops that all the trappers were supposed to have been issued. I had to work fast if I was going to save this one.

I estimated that it weighed no more than 80 pounds and measured the Telezol quickly. With the syringe pole I injected the animal and in only a few minutes it lowered its head. The men waded through the snow to check the rest of their snares.

"There's two more over here!" Berry yelled.

I had to finish this one first. The snare cable around its neck was deep into fur and so tight that I couldn't get a finger under it. The wolf wouldn't have lasted another day. I dug through my kit for cable cutters and snipped the wire. I checked the wolf's mouth and throat looking for sticks, grass or other obstructions. The wolf's airway and mouth were clear, but when I opened its jaws, I saw that the corners of its mouth were deeply cut from fighting the cable. Its lips drooped. The wolf was cold, in shock and needed immediate shelter if it was going to live.

Berry and Gerlinsky returned and watched me examine the wolf for other injuries. It was a female with prominent nipples indicating she was probably the alpha female of the pack. Her teeth were worn and discolored, meaning she was perhaps four or five years old. The bluish tint of her pelage was stunning – like no wolf I had seen before.

It was breaking protocol, but I didn't bother to take her rectal temperature. I knew she was cold. I didn't need to know *how* cold. It wasn't like the danger of overheating, but it was serious. The men lifted her onto my shoulders and I headed for the truck. The backseat was crammed full of gear but I leveled off a place and laid her carefully so that her airway stayed open. Berry was alarmed that I put her in the truck with no restraints.

"It's okay, man," I said. "She's so stressed that she's not going anywhere for quite awhile."

Fifty yards beyond the first wolf lay a pup, dead and frozen in the brush. I judged it to be one from that spring, no more than seven months old. Another gray wolf struggled at the end of a snare 50 feet away. The cable was over its shoulder the way a person would wear a sling, probably saving its life. The wolf flipped and splashed in a hard-running creek, flailing in a half circle.

"Be careful, Carter." Berry issued this warning a half dozen times. While I was loading my syringe pole, the wolf bolted toward us and ducked under the creek's steep overhang, which was more like a shallow cave. I could see only the wolf's front legs. She'd wedged herself tightly against the bank and hidden her head. As far as she was concerned, if she couldn't see us, we couldn't see her.

This one appeared to be another pup. If Berry would hold onto my legs, I could hang over the bank and give it a shot. I wouldn't have tried this maneuver if it were an adult.

"You're crazy," he said. "You're gonna get bit."

But I talked him into it. She wouldn't move if we were quiet and moved slowly. Quiet and slow is always the key around wild animals.

Berry and Gerlinsky braced my legs as I reached under the bank and injected the wolf. She flinched, but that was all. They pulled me back and we stood grinning. Our impromptu team had just caught the first two wolves for reintroduction.

I stepped into the creek and peeked under the bank to see how the Telezol was working. She was out. I pulled her from her hiding place. She was soaked to the skin and had a long cut across her shoulder as well as cut lips. I snipped the snare from her and had the men help me lift her onto my shoulders. At the truck, I laid her next to her still semi-conscious mother.

We needed to get to Hinton and get the wolves in kennels fast. Berry used his radiophone to call Jeff Kneteman at the Fish and Wildlife Division. I hoped he had some sort of temporary kennel set-up figured out by now. If the wolves hadn't been injured and traumatized, I would have radio-collared and released them at Rock Lake and gone back to catch them later when we were better prepared.

Berry and Gerlinsky kept looking back at the wolves as we drove. Neither liked the idea of the animals being inside the truck. What if they jump up and bite us, Berry fretted.

"Nah, I won't let 'em get that far," I said, producing a vial of Ketamine from my pocket. "Besides, they'd just be getting back at you for those snares."

The clerk at the Tara Vista handed me a message. U.S. Sen. Conrad Burns of Montana had issued an order to the U.S. Fish and Wildlife Service to halt wolf reintroduction until legal issues could be resolved. Upon hearing this edict, my boss, Larry Handegard, had called the motel assuming it meant I was finished in Canada. But the senator's order meant nothing until I heard it straight from Ed Bangs. I wadded up the message and tossed it in the trash. I was too busy for politics.

Jeff Kneteman had scrounged around and found a culvert trap that was mounted to a trailer. It was parked at his headquarters, ready for the wolves. He'd even spread a bale of straw in the bottom. A culvert trap is exactly that – a big tube made of corrugated metal usually reserved for making road culverts. These kinds of traps are normally used to hold bears, and are sealed with grating on one end and a door on the other. It was perfect for two wolves, with room enough that they could turn around.

The mother and daughter wolf were parked in a heated garage overnight. I needed to hire a vet to attend to the wolves' cuts because they looked pretty serious, but first I needed permission from my government. Everything that had happened since I arrived in Canada was unexpected and I needed authorization from the Fish and Wildlife Service, Bangs specifically, to hire certain people, buy supplies and get the physical act of catching wolves moving forward.

Bangs didn't hesitate. Do whatever you need to, he said, adding that when it came to running interference between the field biologists and the politicos in Washington D.C., it was easier to beg forgiveness than ask permission. "We'll worry about the details later," he said.

The vet I hired in Hinton agreed to draw up a bill that would be paid later by the U.S. government. He sutured the two wolves' lips and the leg on the pup and gave them both a shot of antibiotics. I wanted them to stay in the culvert trap a day or two so I could make sure they healed.

I was alarmed at the lack of preparation for this historic moment in conservation. Wolf reintroduction, in my mind, was a big deal. Everything was so detailed on paper, yet as far as I could tell, the Fish and Wildlife Service had put almost no thought into how we'd actually obtain the wolves. After my skinning contest at Wade Berry's cabin broke the ice, I was on the phone to Bangs several times a day. We had wolves in our possession now. We needed more hands and equipment moving toward Hinton. It was only a matter of time before the media discovered what we were doing. No one had put any thought into that potential circus, either. Bangs gave me carte blanche to make decisions and create contracts with suppliers. He also sent Joe Fontaine north with a load of chain-link kennels.

I told Val Asher to get to Hinton and get herself a room at the Tara Vista. This was to be grand central, not Rocky Mountain House. It was better to be closer to where wolves would be caught. Alice Whitelaw, another Fish and Wildlife Service biologist, was en route to help Asher round up first-aid supplies and mobilize some kind of M*A*S*H unit for the wolves that would soon be in captivity, ready for the trip to their new homes in the United States. Asher found the answer with the William A. Switzer Provincial Park, which had a couple of buildings perfect for wolf processing centers. Dr. Mark Johnson, a veterinarian, would arrive soon, too, as would Bill Paul, the Minnesota Animal Damage Control trapper.

I knew we were unprepared in general. But with the capture of the mother and daughter wolf, I also realized that killer snares were hanging everywhere in the woods around Hinton. It was imperative that the snares be retrofitted with stops immediately to keep more wolves from strangling. I was mostly concerned about convincing Wade Berry of this. He was now my primary source for wolves, but if he didn't get me live wolves, his contract with the U.S. government was no good. I went to his cabin because I wanted him to know how serious this was. The skinning contest continued to buy me favors, and Berry agreed to fix things to my liking.

While we talked, the phone rang. George Kelly was looking for me. I'd left word with the trapper that I was after live wolves. His was the only other name besides Berry's that I'd been steered to.

"Got a live one in a snare if you want it," Kelly said. "Otherwise I'll just kill it."

"Meet me at the Tara Vista," I said.

George Kelly lived on the north edge of Hinton and ran a registered trapline nearby. We met in the parking lot. Like Berry, everything that Kelly said sounded like a question. It was the Canadian accent and it took a bit of getting used to. He wore no coat even though everything around him was frozen solid. A cigarette hung from his mouth. His girlfriend, Nanette, was with him.

George Kelly and Wade Berry, while acquainted, were competitors. From what I'd learned in a few days of asking around, these two men were the main wolf trappers in the Hinton area and bagged the most wolves every year. As far as I was concerned, these were the only two guys we needed. It would certainly make things simpler. Kelly was a big game hunting guide, specializing in bighorn sheep. He'd also earned the nickname Wildhorse Kelly because of the 100 or so wild horses he owned. Actually, maybe it was more. He wasn't sure how many horses he owned, he said, rubbing his chin, but it was pretty much every one running free in that part of the country. He even set rope snares for wild horses so he could break some and brand the others.

"So you're the people who want wolves, eh?" Kelly asked. He fit every stereotype in my head of the Canadian fur-trapper.

"Yes sir, we sure are," I said.

He took a slow drag on his cigarette. I wondered if he caught the beaver that had been made into the hat he was wearing.

"Why?" He looked at me, perplexed and fascinated by this American folly. "You know how those things breed? You got lots of deer and elk?"

"Yeah we have plenty of those."

"Well, you're gonna have a lot of wolves, then," he shook his head and flicked his cigarette into the gravel. "Okay then, I got one a little north of here and I guess maybe you want it."

A little north of here to Kelly meant 60 miles. I hoped the wolf would still be alive. Asher and I followed Kelly and Nanette, ending our journey on a side road in the middle of a huge, active clearcut. We passed trucks carrying logs that dwarfed us. Kelly got out and pointed into the timber. Just up in those trees, he said.

"I can tie it up with baling wire if you want," he said.

"I've got a little fancier setup," I said, digging out my catchpole and syringe pole. I put a vial of Telezol in my pocket. Kelly led the way as the four of us walked single file through a part of the forest left untouched by big saws. Among all the trees, was a 20-foot, whip-like sapling, waving back and forth. A snare anchored to it had a gray wolf by the neck.

Kelly had rigged his neck snares to trees that moved to keep from strangling wolves. The tightening, then loosening of the cable was the only reason this wolf was still standing. The women moved in to distract the animal. When its head was turned, I pushed a needle into its hip. In a few minutes, the wolf leaned into the tree boughs, helpless.

"That's some good stuff you got there," Kelly said. He conceded that my method was better, but his was cheaper. He said once, on a whim, he'd bound a wolf with baling wire and put it on a chain around a tree in his front yard, maybe just to see if he could do it. I believed every word.

I wanted to go with Kelly to check the rest of his snares. I left the wolf on the truck's tailgate and asked Asher to do the exam and paperwork. I looked closely at its mouth. This wolf had cut lips like the ones Wade Berry had caught, but the vet in Hinton could fix that. Kelly was uneasy about leaving the women alone with a wolf, but Nanette seemed thrilled to help and volunteered to write down information on the data sheet.

The rest of the snares hung invisibly in the woods. They were so well concealed that I might have walked into a few if Kelly hadn't directed me to stay behind him. Done with skill, neck snaring is deadly. I talked to one Canadian trapper who told me he once caught a family of 11 wolves using snares. But this time, the rest of Kelly's snares were empty. On the way back, he lit up a cigarette. He'd roamed this part of Alberta for years before the timber companies started clearcuts. So much had been cut, he said, that the landmarks he relied upon were gone, and though an experienced woodsman, he was increasingly disoriented by the rapidly changing landscape.

As had become my practice over the years, I put the wolf on the floorboard of the truck, under my legs, where I could keep an eye on it. The four of us headed back to town, weaving our way through what used to be an endless, dark forest.

Resistance to reintroduction was mounting in places no one expected. Wolf advocates in Canada were opposed to wolves being sent over the border, saying the Americans would just kill them. I found their reasoning ironic. Trappers, ranchers and the Canadian government kill hundreds every year. The capture of the first two wolves on Wade Berry's trapline triggered a firestorm of criticism from Jasper National Park officials who believed the wolves lived mostly in the park and didn't want them tampered with.

In Helena, the Farm Bureau took its case to a federal judge, seeking an injunction against reintroduction of wolves. More members of Congress were jumping into the fight now that it looked like wolves were really going to be shipped down from Canada. Based on the legal brouhaha, Ed Bangs asked me to put radio collars on the three wolves and turn them loose. Our success appeared to be premature. Everybody agreed that even if a court upheld that reintroduction was illegal, Canadian scientists could benefit from having a few wolves radio-collared for the data they might provide.

I complied, and took a newspaper reporter with me when I released the mother and daughter wolves. Joe Fontaine and Alice Whitelaw had arrived in time to weigh, ear tag and radio collar all three of the captive wolves before they were freed. Val Asher took the one from George Kelly's trapline back north where it fled into the woods.

A couple of days had elapsed and Berry had retrofitted his snares so that, if the wolves were caught again, at least they wouldn't die in them. Kelly's style of snaring left more hope for a wolf's survival, but I still wanted him to rebuild them using stops. Contracts and stops on neck snares were only two of the problems I'd uncovered since I arrived in Alberta. The Fish and Wildlife Service had ordered the wrong size cable for the trappers and some wolves were chewing through it and escaping. I had the right kind shipped by bus to Hinton. If we won the legal fights but word got out that we were killing and crippling wolves, the whole project might be shut down for that reason instead.

The principle of using a lot of snares in one location is that once the wolf pack is enticed into an area and one or two are caught, the others panic and run blindly through the brush and trees to escape, getting snared, too. If the adult male and female are caught first, younger pack members may come back to search for them; that's when they get snared.

The snare loops were opened wide, maybe two feet in diameter, with the bottom of the loop about 18 inches above the ground or snow level. The cable was clipped to small shrubs or twigs, with tiny wire that would let the cable jerk free. When the wolf came down the trail or through an opening, the bottom of the loop would touch the wolf near its throat or brisket and drop onto the animal's neck.

December 1, 1994, was a Thursday. I remember it because that day it snowed, then cleared off. Like a typical Animal Damage Control guy, the first thing that came to mind was getting in a helicopter and catching something. There was only one problem: The Fish and Wildlife Service folks hadn't spoken one word to the Canadian outfit that bid and won the aviation contract.

I only discovered this because I wondered if a helicopter crew was ever going to show up in Alberta. So I called Bangs.

He admitted he'd dropped the ball on this one. The contract was with Bighorn Aviation Inc., in Cranbrook, British Columbia, but with all of the recent distractions – snaring wolves and fighting off politicians – he'd sort of forgotten it. But my phone call triggered something else: Seemingly out of nowhere, Bangs asked me to take on the role as project leader in Canada.

"You better talk that one over with the brass," I said. "I can see it now: an Animal Damage Control guy helping bring back wolves – and as the project leader. Won't that go over like a fart in church?"

This kind of thing didn't rattle Bangs. He'd talk them into it, he said.

"Keep doing what you're doing. You're the only one who's getting anything accomplished. My job is to fight off the opposition with a whip and a chair," he said. "It'll be okay, big guy."

With that, I officially took charge, even though that's kind of what I'd been doing anyway. I called Bighorn Aviation using the number Bangs gave me and got its owner, Clay Wilson, on the line. He was pissed and let me know it. Why hadn't he heard from anyone about his contract? It was the same routine I'd gone through with the trappers. I listened to Wilson and agreed with everything he said. When he was through, we got down to business.

The snow was falling in Hinton, I said. Conditions were perfect for finding wolves. Wilson seemed eager, but again there were logistics problems. He had no hangar in that part of Canada and didn't know the area. He needed a fuel source and said that he wished he had been in Hinton weeks ago to make all of the arrangements. All I could do was try to fix things.

My friendship with Wade and Carrie Berry paid dividends beyond measure. Both were employed by the Alberta Forest Technology School in Hinton, she in the administration department and he doing odd jobs and building furniture. Best of all, they knew everyone there.

But Berry stiffened when I told him why I needed his help. He didn't like the idea of helicopters flying over registered traplines and really didn't like the competition. I did my best to explain the reasons for them and told him that his snaring operation still played an important initial-capture role. The helicopters were to find the ones already collared when the higher powers gave us the final green light to fly the wolves to the United States. I had his trust once more.

He walked me around, introducing me to the director and others. I unfolded my list and read it out loud. To my amazement, all of Clay Wilson's requirements fell into one neat little package. The forestry school had a helicopter landing pad marked with an X out on its concrete driveway and a heated hangar large enough for two choppers.

Down the hallway of the administration building, Berry introduced me to an employee who knew every square mile of backcountry airstrips and every fuel depot around Hinton. If the pilots kept track of how much fuel they used, he said, they were welcome to it.

He had one more idea and we backtracked to the director's office and knocked on the door.

"What about the capture teams using the dormitories?" Berry said.

This sounded great. It would sure be cheaper than motel rooms – and closer to the action.

"Sure," the director said, and returned to his paperwork.

Having something work out with ease was almost a shock. I gave Wilson approximate directions. On December 5, he and another pilot came sweeping in with a red and a white chopper, one behind the other. I stood on the helipad and waved them in.

The aircrew was complete when Barry Miner, the fixed-wing pilot, landed at the Hinton airstrip and joined us after breakfast.

Clay Wilson was raring to go and I didn't want to get in his way. He was one of the only gung-ho people on the job. George Kelly was along and offered to fly with Miner. He wanted to look for wild horses, he said, and maybe add a few more to his roster.

Miner, a lean and grinning man, was like a prizefighter and bronc rider rolled into one. He liked his booze, but so did the rest of the aircrew. I sampled some of their favorite white lightning and it tasted the way I imagined jet fuel might. Miner knew himself well enough to know he could easily get into a bar brawl. His strategy was simple: Get chummy with the bouncers whenever you visit a new bar. That way you might come out on top if things get ugly.

Reporter Arthur Veitch from *The Grande Cache Mountaineer* was supposed to call me, so I waited in my motel room for the phone to ring. Several members of the wolf crew dropped in and we talked about how things were going. There was only one person who had a problem with the mess that I'd been attempting to straighten out for the past few weeks.

Dr. Mark Johnson was looking at things with the only perspective he had: a veterinarian's. He didn't like what he saw.

"You have to shut down this capture, Carter," he said, citing poor planning on top of poor-quality facilities and wolves getting cut up in neck snares. I was the only guy who could convince Ed Bangs that we should all pack up and go home and forget the whole thing, he said.

A news report on television a few nights earlier showed a wolf in Alaska caught in a snare while a man attempted to shoot it. It was bad timing and though it hadn't happened yet in Hinton, word could spread that neck snares were injuring wolves that were planned for relocation to America. When it came to that kind of thing, all the explaining in the world couldn't fix it. We'd be spending more time defending ourselves than getting real work done.

For that reason and because Johnson was all about the humane treatment of animals, his primary interest was protocol and procedure. That was fine with me, except when his excessive idealism got in my way. I didn't have the luxury of taking a wolf's pulse and temperature and putting an eyeshade on it when I had moments to get it out of a neck snare and make sure its airway was open. Sure the cut lips were bad, but it was the least of my concerns until I could get the animal out of danger of dying. If Johnson had been a field biologist, he could have related to this.

"I'm just doing what needs to be done, Mark," I felt my blood pressure hitting the roof. "I came up here to help not to be in charge…"

The phone rang. Arthur Veitch was a good guy and had accompanied me when I released the first two wolves with collars near Wade Berry's trapline. He was writing wolf-capture updates almost daily and checked in with me often.

I was telling Veitch what he wanted to know when Johnson began whispering that I should hang up, shut-up. He made slashing motions at his throat.

"Don't talk to reporters!" he said.

"Just a minute Arthur," I said, smothering the receiver in my hand.

"Shut the fuck up and don't interrupt me when I'm on the phone!" I bellowed at Johnson. "I'm trying to talk and I'm trying to listen to Arthur. Now get the hell outta my room!"

I knew I was about to blow up at Johnson and hoped Veitch wouldn't hear it, but I don't think it worked. He offered to call back later, but I just wanted to answer his questions and get it over with.

Once I hung up, I was across the room, grabbing clothes and flinging them into my suitcase. I went in the bathroom and swept everything from the counter into the suitcase, too. Then I started picking up my field equipment and putting it in piles. Trapper Bill Paul, the only person who stayed behind when I ordered everyone out, stood in the corner watching me.

"Where are you going?" he asked.

I didn't even realize what I was doing. I had no idea where I was going, but I couldn't take the bullshit any longer. I'm not sure I even answered him.

"I'll come back later and see how you're doing," he said, slipping out the door.

I banged my suitcase shut, yanked my coat on and slammed the door behind me.

I walked in the dark and the snow for a long time, winding up on the north side of Hinton near the Interstate. I'd been muttering to myself. It wasn't like me to lose my cool. It was even a little frightening. I didn't know where I was going. Maybe I was just trying to wash my hands of this screwed up mess and the people who made it that way.

I'd never been involved in a field operation like the one I'd been trying to salvage in Canada. Wolf reintroduction – the part that mattered most as far as I was concerned – had not been planned in any detail whatsoever. It was essentially a bunch of scribblings on paper back in the States – on a napkin for all I knew. Every element of it had been a crisis; I never knew what new disaster would rear its head from one day to the next. I don't know how long I walked that night, but the stinging wind in my face was better than any belt of whiskey.

In the morning, the aircrew was ready to chase wolves. I shuttled Barry Miner to the airstrip, but I wasn't getting involved. I returned to my motel room, called Ed Bangs and dumped my frustrations on him. I told him about my walk the night before.

"I need people who support my decisions because I have enough problems without fighting the wolf team, too," I said.

Bangs wanted me to stay and keep things on track, but said that he'd support whatever decision I made. After we hung up, and unbeknownst to me, he made a few calls of his own.

For three mornings in a row, the aircrews were out looking for wolves. The plan was always the same: Barry Miner, sometimes with George Kelly along, was in the fixed wing, flying at a higher elevation than the helicopter to look for wolves, while Clay Wilson's chopper, with a netgunner onboard, followed. I assigned myself the mundane task of hauling fuel and taking Miner to the airport every morning to fire up his plane. He'd flown to Hinton and didn't have a car.

It was windy that third morning, but the crews were up anyway. Clay and crew managed to shoot a net and tangle up a large wolf.

The animal was running in the open and was halfway across a frozen lake when the netgunner fired the net over it and rolled it into a ball. Wilson landed and rushed toward the wolf as it fought and chewed at the rope, getting itself loose except for the corner where the projectile weight was attached. When Wilson got closer, the big wolf seemed to get bigger and was now mostly free of the net and standing on a beaver lodge looking down on him. It was as big as a Shetland pony, he told me later. Wilson looked at his drug syringe, which had frozen, then back at the Shetland pony wolf, and decided that this could get hairy. The crew walked back to the helicopter, out of nets, and called it a day.

When the helicopters quit, that meant Miner was out of reasons to be in the air, too. He turned back toward Hinton. The airport there is small and unattended most of the time. It gets little use in the winter because of regular foul weather.

Miner buzzed the Tara Vista to signal that it was time to pick him up. It was our usual routine. But when I got in my truck, I could tell that the gale coming out of the west was causing him trouble. He made a wide turn and headed for the airport. It was only five miles away, but when I caught up with him, the wind was shaking my truck and dirt was blowing across the road. I pulled in and waited, watching Miner negotiate a turn and try to set his plane down into the wind. The airplane hung suspended like a kite. I'd never seen anything like it. The plane went down inches at a time toward the runway, but wasn't moving forward.

Miner was gunning it, the airplane's engine screaming at its highest RPM, as his wheels barely touched the ground. I started to panic for him. I got out of the truck to watch. Something wasn't right. I walked toward him, grit blowing into my eyes. The plane was sitting in place now, wheels on the ground, but he still had the RPM's revved. When I got close enough to see Miner, he motioned frantically with his head, keeping a death grip on the controls.

I tried to figure what he wanted me to do. It dawned on me that the wind was pushing on his plane so hard that he was sort of flying the plane while sitting on the ground. Airplanes are designed to head into the wind at all times. If they're not heavy enough, like a jet, they have to be tied down when not in use or severe winds can send them ass-over-teakettle. If Miner cut the engine now, the gale would flip his plane like a toy. The power of the engine was the only thing giving him purchase on the runway.

I moved behind one wing and started pushing on the strut. Miner nodded approval and gave it some throttle. I kept steady pressure on the plane and moved it toward a set of buildings, then behind them, out of the wind. He let off the throttle and shut it down, the engine roar and the propellers whirring to a stop.

"You just saved my life," his voice was shaking, when he climbed out of the cockpit. "I was running on fumes."

He shook my hand with one hand and held on to me with the other. He'd been thinking about ditching the plane because he wasn't sure he had enough fuel to maintain control in the wind. He didn't want to do that, but on the other hand he couldn't throttle-down his airspeed on the runway to conserve fuel or the wind would have flipped the plane into a pile of twisted metal.

We tied down the plane and headed for town. Miner wanted a shot of white lightning and said he owed me a drink. He still looked rattled. Over the next few days, and in fact every time I've seen him since that day, he repeated the story to anyone within earshot, often getting watery-eyed. Miner's father and brother had been killed in plane crashes and he'd figured that his time had come. But that day, he said, I was his guardian angel.

In the nearly four weeks that had elapsed since I skinned a wolf in Wade Berry's dining room, the wolf crew collared 17 wolves in eight packs and released them back in the wild. Before they were let go in their new homes in America they would be given ridiculously thorough checkups that included X-rays and Droncit, a dewormer. But for now, in Canada is where they'd stay, at least until the legal and political fights died down. The Farm Bureau's injunction hearing was scheduled for December 22, 1994. That would settle everything, one way or another.

"Take some time off, Carter, but I need you in Wyoming right before Christmas," Bangs said over the phone. "You get to be my expert witness at the hearing."

Heading back to Montana sounded like a swell idea. I'd had enough excitement for a while and looked forward to seeing my kids.

I rolled back into town on December 12, but after a couple of days, and after coming off an adrenaline rush like Canada, Helena seemed boring, dreary and depressing. I was catching up on things in my warehouse when my daughter called. My brother, Craig, a basketball star in high school, a planner who looked forward to spending more time with me in the wilds of Montana once he retired, had died. He was only 55, but he was a smoker. Cigarettes and a heart attack got him the same as they had gotten our dad.

I felt nothing. I didn't want to talk to anyone or be around family. I parked myself in front of a keno machine at the Gold Nugget Casino and drank beer all afternoon. A cloud of depression enveloped me. Divorce, a job change, getting sent to live in a warehouse in Missoula, no money, an overwhelming work challenge in Canada, and now my brother was dead. In the past five years I'd become like two different people: one who could accomplish anything when he was at work, and one who couldn't crawl out from under personal disaster. The only thing I could dredge up from within was anger. I was convinced that I was the target of some insidious plot, which meant I was destined to die at 55 too.

Craig's funeral filled the gymnasium of the high school where he'd taught. There wasn't a square inch of space left; people spilled into the hallways. Friends from Garner showed up, as well as my cousin, Bob, who went duck hunting with me the day my dad died.

"How are you?" I asked Bob, who was 57. He'd been in the insurance business and had made some wise investments in the stock market. He'd never felt better, he said. He died of a heart attack five months later.

My work rescued me, as it always had. I escaped, temporarily anyway, from the agony of Craig's death by catching a flight from Iowa directly to Cheyenne, Wyoming, on December 20 to be an expert witness for the defense in U.S. District Judge William Downes' court.

Ed Bangs, Wayne Brewster from the National Park Service, Dr. David Mech and several government attorneys were waiting for me at the hotel. I was unnerved by the prospect that reintroduction might hinge on my testimony about the degree to which wolves would affect the livestock industry. The attorneys lost no time coaching me. They'd already had a crack at the Department of the Interior's three other expert witnesses: Bangs, the Service's lead biologist for the wolf recovery program, Dr. David Mech, the world's foremost wolf expert, and Hank Fischer, who originated the livestock compensation fund for Defenders of Wildlife. I was the expert on control of problem wolves that killed domestic livestock.

On December 22, I sat in the back of the courtroom and listened to testimony all day. It was a good chance to see how the attorneys handled the witnesses. Questions arose about which subspecies of wolf lived in the Northern Rockies historically. One species mentioned was Canis lupus irremotus, among others.

I leaned over to my comrades.

"Canis lupus irregardless is what I'd call them." I'm sort of deaf and when I whispered it to the group, others around me snickered, too. I must have said it louder than I thought.

At five o'clock in the afternoon, I was called to the witness stand.

Attorneys asked that I describe a livestock animal that has been attacked and killed by wolves and compare that to other predator damage. Since 1990, I had investigated 80 incidents reported as wolf damage, involving examinations of 123 dead or wounded livestock. I concluded that 12 individual animals, or 10 percent of the animals I examined, were wounded or killed by wolf attacks.

The court then wanted a brief history of the ways problem wolves had been controlled so far. I described trapping and helicopter darting. And I explained how much we as agencies, and I in particular, had learned, starting in 1987, when we were poorly prepared, to the high success rate of wolf captures and radio collaring by 1994. I also told the court that, overall, I had excellent relationships with ranchers and that it seemed to make all the difference.

When the cross-examination started, I braced myself, waiting for a strike to my jugular.

"Mr. Niemeyer, did you attend college?" the Farm Bureau's attorney began.

"I have bachelor's and master's degrees from Iowa State University."

"From your experience and from your education, do you know how much an adult coyote weighs?"

"Approximately 25 pounds."

"And how much does a wolf in Montana weigh?"

I couldn't figure out where this was going. What kind of dumb questions were these? I told the court that a female wolf weighed around 75 pounds and a male wolf about 100 pounds.

I glanced over the man's shoulder at Bangs, who was barely containing a grin.

"Mr. Niemeyer," the attorney paced around in front of me. "How much are the wolves that they plan to introduce going to weigh?"

This one was right up my line, though, because I just got back from Canada where each wolf had been weighed at some point during its captivity. Even the heaviest wolf ever caught in the West – a 141-pounder I darted in Yellowstone - had never been topped. It was a point of contention that the wolves we were reintroducing were not the same as the ones that used to live in the Northern Rockies.

"They weigh about the same."

Next, the attorney wanted to know if a wolf ate more than a coyote. Yes. Next, how many wolf specialists are employed by Animal Damage Control in the Rocky Mountain region? Uh, one. Me. I presumed he was attempting to show that I couldn't possibly be responsive to a geographic area that included Idaho, Wyoming and Montana, with occasional support to North Dakota and Washington.

"Have you ever seen wolves attack cattle or have you seen a wolf in the act of biting?" he said.

"No."

"Who is responsible for wolf depredation investigations in your absence or when you're out of the office, an example being in court?"

"Any Animal Damage Control personnel in Montana would be checking out any depredation reports that came in during my absence, and those men are qualified to recognize wolf damage because I trained them."

The attorney consulted a notepad on the plaintiff's table and whispered to the small delegation seated there. He zeroed in on a specific case I'd been involved with near Dixon, Montana. He had the details mixed up, but I managed to untangle the story for him. Either he hadn't had time to do much research or he was testing to see if I really investigated things the way I claimed.

He went on about whether Defenders of Wildlife would truly compensate ranchers for confirmed wolf-kills and whether anyone besides me could be the one to make such confirmations.

"I've trained Animal Damage Control personnel in five western states to recognize wolf damage, so any of those individuals should have sufficient knowledge to make that decision."

The last questions were about money. What would happen if the funding for my position were cut off? Well, sir, I'd lose my job. Was the government going to hire any extra help to investigate wolf attacks on livestock? Not to my knowledge.

At 5:32 p.m., Downes used a pause in the questioning to wrap it up for the day.

"Well, Mr. Niemeyer, I hope you didn't give up your hotel room, sir, because we're going to have to call it a day, but I'll be putting you back on the stand at 8:30 tomorrow morning."

Bangs and the attorneys filed calmly into the hall before cutting loose.

"Beautiful!" one Department of Interior lawyer said.

Bangs slapped me on the back.

I wasn't sure what I'd done.

"God, Carter, that was one of the funniest things I've ever seen. I think they had you pegged as some kind of dumbshit."

Downes took over questioning the next morning.

"I'm not deciding this case on the merits during this hearing," he said, adding that he was more interested in the status quo than the technical legalities of wolf reintroduction. He wanted to know what guarantees I could give the court that the current Animal Damage Control program would be effective in the short term if wolves were reintroduced. He also wanted to know how many wolves would be wandering in Yellowstone and Idaho five years down the road and whether my agency had the manpower to handle the problems these animals would cause.

My skills as an investigator and control specialist had evolved parallel to the growing wolf population in northwest Montana, I said. I felt like I'd come up with some pretty good techniques to control problem wolves. There was no way for me to predict with any kind of precision how many wolves certain areas might have in five years, but I'd taught trappers how to investigate potential wolf-kills. On the other hand I was the only person specifically designated to deal with wolves once a problem had been verified.

The West's remote, rugged country, Downes believed, would make it difficult to find dead livestock that had been killed by wolves, and he asked me to elaborate on this point. It was up to the rancher to report losses as soon as possible, I said. Animal Damage Control trappers are on-call day and night, seven days a week, I added. As for finding the wolves, radio collaring the packs was the best way to evaluate the number of wolves involved in livestock deaths, and if need be, we could use the radio collars to find and kill the wolves.

Downes wanted my assessment of the compensation program that had been set up by Defenders of Wildlife, pointing out that privately administered compensation wasn't bound by law and that the organization might decide at any time to stop paying for dead livestock. And what about the argument that not all kills are found?

I believed that Defenders' compensation program was an example of a society putting its money where its mouth was to offset losses to another part of society. The government had no intention of paying compensation so this was the best solution for the time being.

Downes didn't have to ask me anything twice. I took this as a good sign. His last concerns were whether the federal government had safeguards in place to protect stockgrowers from livestock attacks and what the worst-case scenario might be in terms of controlling problem wolves. I was confident that, in the near-term anyway, the feds could handle wolf problems, but I couldn't say what might happen in the future. The larger concept surrounding the Endangered Species Act is to get the species in question off of the list – because that means it's recovered (or extinct). But, I added, the worst-case scenario would be the feds reintroducing wolves without securing the money to deal with problems that would inevitably arise.

At 9 a.m. on December 23, 1994, Judge Downes was done with me. On January 3, 1995, he refused the Farm Bureau's motion for a preliminary injunction. Wolf reintroduction would pick up where it left off. Soon, I was on my way back to Canada.

The necessities had already been taken care of: The wolves we planned on capturing had been collared to mark the packs. Helicopters, planes, pilots and heated hangars were in place. There was even a convenient place for the wolf crew to stay, with good facilities to process captured animals. All of it nearly cost me my sanity, but it was done. Now I could be one of the grunts instead of being in charge.

This time, the reintroduction team was composed of media experts, wildlife veterinarians, wolf experts and wolf capture specialists from the lower 48 states, Alaska and Canada. The group was as experienced and dedicated as they come. Of course, it helped that we had the law on our side for however long that might last. Compared to my first go-around in Hinton, my job now was almost imbecilic: Make sure the darts don't freeze; help run the wolf holding area. I wanted badly to be the first person to go up in a helicopter and dart the first wolf for relocation to America. Clay Wilson, the helicopter pilot, gave me that chance.

Wilson and I hadn't worked together flying and it took a few passes and a fair amount of cursing before I lobbed a Hail Mary dart toward a running black wolf and hit it in the foot. We landed and caught up with it. It was only barely drugged, but enough that I could run and catch up with it as it staggered. I looped the noose of the catchpole over its head. It lurched and pulled me along until I levered the end of the pole around a tree to brace myself. Veterinarian Dave Hunter had the extra drugs and I yelled for him. I wasn't sure how long I could hang on.

Once the wolf was subdued, I could see that he was a male pup – nine months or so. He had a wonderful thick coat. The team took turns hauling him back through the deep snow to the helicopter a quarter-mile away. I named the wolf Carter's Hope – symbolic of my desire to see reintroduction succeed. Biologists usually roll their eyes at naming wild animals, but today seemed different and nobody objected. I decided to keep track of this one.

He weighed 83 pounds and, according to the vets who poked and prodded him, he was in good shape. Carter's Hope was fitted with a collar, and assigned the number R-15. The "R" indicated red ear tags, "15" meant he was the 15th wolf to be turned loose in the park. In Idaho, it would be B numbers and blue eartags. R-15 was a Judas wolf; a week after he was released, he returned to his pack and betrayed its location. The helicopter team caught four wolves and recaptured Carter's Hope, collapsing his lung when the dart accidentally hit near his spine. Luckily he improved after a bit of emergency surgery.

Carter's Hope and his family were named the Soda Butte pack, after the proximity of their acclimation pen to this weird geologic wonder in Yellowstone's Lamar Valley. It was the park's first wolf pack of the modern era. For the next 10 weeks, they were fed road-killed deer, elk, moose and bison meat, and had little if any contact with humans. When Doug Smith, Yellowstone's primary wolf researcher, opened the pen door about two months later on March 27, 1995, he expected them to run out. Instead, they tiptoed only far enough to grab a deer leg they'd been left and drag it back into the pen. Three days later, they'd left the pen and killed an elk – the first one in 60 years taken down by its most natural predator.

I didn't figure I would see Carter's Hope again, but planned to follow his life events from radio tracking data coming out of Yellowstone. On April 22, the pack wandered out of the park, heading toward the towns of Nye and Fishtail, Montana.

A storm had blown into Montana, typical for December. The Soda Butte pack was no longer in the park as far as officials knew, but no plane could go up in the foul weather, so the pack's movements couldn't be monitored. About the time the storm subsided, the wolves made themselves known by killing a dog south of Absarokee. A man was hunting for mountain lions with his hounds when one of them picked up a scent, following it. The 32-pound Walker hound named Smoker was torn apart in seconds. A dog, no matter what size or how mean, is no match for a wolf, much less a pack of them. Wolves are notoriously territorial and other canines in their area aren't tolerated. When the owner heard the commotion, he hurried his other dog to safety.

The dog's owners lived in Fishtail and called their local trapper, who urged his state director to do something. Domestic dogs, however, weren't considered livestock, so Animal Damage Control had no jurisdiction in the case. The supervisor went anyway and found huge wolf tracks all around the kill site. It was the first case of a domestic animal killed by the transplanted wolves. The couple went to the newspapers after the incident, feeling not just irate but betrayed that no one had informed the community about the wolves leaving the confines of the park. Yellowstone, however, is not fenced. Animals routinely wander back and forth across its boundaries. The storms were at fault, preventing telemetry tracking. The Fish and Wildlife Service and Yellowstone park officials promised to do better next time.

After they killed Smoker, Carter's Hope followed other pack members through ranch country and killed an elk east of Cooke City. U.S. Sen. Max Baucus asked the Fish and Wildlife Service to come up with a system to alert private citizens who lived on the outskirts of Yellowstone whenever a wolf pack roamed out of bounds. "I remind you that the Stillwater Valley is cattle country and that calving begins in February... Allowing the wolves to remain in the area is an unacceptable risk...to ranchers' livelihood and wolf viability," Baucus said.

To avoid killing the newly reintroduced, federally protected species, Animal Damage Control trappers scoured their districts, taking down snares and pulling up M-44 cyanide devices designed to kill coyotes. The wolves were supposed to stay in the park and my agency was vocal about it, complaining that wolves were screwing up their practice of killing every coyote on the land. Predator control officials didn't need the kind of publicity a poisoned or strangled wolf would bring.

To the feds in charge of them, the Soda Butte pack was a pain in the butt. To ranchers and fearful dog owners, the wolves were simply dangerous. They had only one strike against them, but that was enough to brew feelings of intolerance. By spring 1996, the pack had four new mouths to feed and had set up housekeeping at a place called Reeves Pond, digging out a den on a private ranch owned by a Yellowstone County commissioner who was running for congress. Ed Bangs decided it was time to move the animals. I'd been busy in corners of Montana dealing with other issues. The Soda Butte wolves hadn't garnered my attention because, so far, they hadn't killed anything defined as livestock.

After a wild chase, Bangs darted two of the wolves. A flimsy seatbelt was all that held him in the helicopter. Then he and National Park Service biologist Mike Phillips pulled three of the pups from the den and trapped the alpha female of the pack the next day. Two yearlings – R-11 and R-12 – escaped capture, as did Carter's Hope. While his siblings were shot illegally some time later, Carter's Hope wandered the land between Fishtail and Nye while managing to avoid the crosshairs. He and another wolf that abandoned Yellowstone, R-27, eventually crossed trails in this area, about 30 miles from Yellowstone's northern border, and right through sheep pastures owned by Vern and Averill Keller.

The Kellers, like their neighbors, were by now fed up with wolves. Bangs called a community meeting to let people blow off steam. We met in the fire hall in Nye on May 30, and about 60 people took turns insulting the feds and cursing wolves. Mike Phillips, a biologist working for Yellowstone, stepped up to reason with the group and was mocked back to his seat. Bangs took over and took the verbal pummeling until the crowd was worn out. My Animal Damage Control boss, Larry Handegard, leaned against a fire engine in the middle of the crowd, his arms folded, and said nothing. Afterward, Bangs decided the wolves should be sent back to Yellowstone and called me in to help.

The wolves were elusive, and so was decent weather. Rain had made it impossible for me to set traps. Although I'd figured out where R-27 was hanging out, I couldn't find her pups. It was the right time of year, and she and Carter's Hope seemed to be paired, so their pups had to be somewhere nearby. Then she or Carter's Hope began killing sheep at the Keller ranch. None of us was sure which wolf was guilty. Maybe it was both. Then a herder saw a gray wolf loping away from a carcass. R-27 was gray. That left Carter's Hope innocent – I hoped. We had to find the pups before we moved the adults or they'd starve. Yellowstone's Doug Smith assigned two summer volunteers to search the hills surrounding the Keller place for signs of the puppies. They hiked dozens of miles, but turned up nothing. Their telemetry indicated the two adult wolves were living separate lives.

I set four traps late one afternoon after finding fresh wolf tracks on a rocky trail several miles west of the Keller ranch. Roger Stradley, a contract pilot with Yellowstone, flew the area in his little airplane and reported back that Carter's Hope was not far from my trapline.

I always find it hard to believe that someone could possibly be traveling on such remote roads as the ones where I set my traps, but they always seem to. Someone ran over two of them, crushing the metal jaws. The third was untouched, but the fourth one was a charm.

Smith and Philips rode with me on an ATV – the only way I could get up the rough road. One sat over the front wheels and one sat behind me. We probably looked like a circus act. When we came upon the fourth trap, I held my breath. It was gone. Smith looked at the receiver in his hand. Carter's Hope was nearby, the signal from his collar booming in.

I turned off the engine. "Be real quiet," I whispered. I was listening for the trap chain jingling.

"There it is," Phillips pointed. He said it without any trace of excitement.

I focused on the shadows in the patch of thin lodgepole pines. Carter's Hope lay motionless, watching us. He looked very different than I remembered him. No longer carrying a coal colored winter coat, he was now a shabby, splotchy lead tone. His head looked enormous without a lot of fur to balance him out. I poked him with some Telazol and he went limp after a few minutes. He hadn't grown much. He still weighed about 85 pounds. I stroked his muzzle and looked at his blank, gold eyes. I wondered what would happen to him. He had a strike against him because domestic sheep had died and he was implicated. I was certain that R-27 was the culprit, probably trying to feed her pups. But Carter's Hope was safe for now. He was on the ragged edge of getting shot if we hadn't caught up with him. Smith pulled the wolf onto his lap and the four of us rode down the bumpy trail. Carter's Hope was on his way back to Yellowstone and I went to give the good news to the Kellers.

Averill Keller fed me every time I dropped by no matter what kind of news I brought – and she had ideas of her own about how to catch the wolves that were eating her sheep.

"Why are you setting traps all the way over there?" she said when I told her about my trapline on the trail. "The wolves are in our pasture. Put your traps over here." Getting after me about where to trap was almost a hobby for her.

"You gotta trust me now, Averill," I'd tell her over and over. She just waved her hand and pushed a plate of cookies toward me.

The day I caught Carter's Hope, I drove in with a big smile on my face. I hoped this would end their current wolf problem. Positioned as their ranch was, however, at the edge of the most famous wildlife park in the world, they were destined to continue feeding sheep to wolves. It happened sooner than I figured. On July 19, R-27 killed two more ewes and a lamb. At least my namesake didn't do it, I told myself.

Carter's Hope was confined to Yellowstone in a pen for nearly two months, until September 17, when Doug Smith turned him loose, hoping he'd stay in the park and out of trouble. The wolf had gained 10 pounds while in captivity. Some of his teeth were chipped, probably from biting on the metal kennel he traveled in between Canada and Yellowstone. It happened to most of the reintroduced wolves. Smith also noted a strange knot on the side of the wolf's face and suspected an impacted tooth might be to blame. No one doctored injuries on wolves unless they were life-threatening. They are better off left alone. Smith phoned me before opening the pen door to let me know that my legendary wolf would soon be on the loose.

Carter's Hope was no longer a member of the Soda Butte Pack. His family had long since taken up residence in another part of the park near

Heart Lake. His father, known to biologists as Old Blue, died near Witch Creek. Only his chewed up radio collar was found. Other members of the Soda Butte pack dispersed. Carter's Hope's mother, R-14, went on to help form the Delta pack until a moose killed her several years later.

When Carter's Hope was released, he had a girlfriend. A wolf from the Nez Perce pack, R-26, had been hanging around his pen and touched noses with him through the fence. The pair ran off together, heading south to the DuNoir Valley near Dubois, Wyoming. Why Carter's Hope refused to stay in the safe confines of Yellowstone mystified everyone. Perhaps he took after me: He'd learned that nothing interesting happens when things are too safe. He and his mate had five puppies and became known as the Washakie pack, the first pack in Wyoming to establish themselves outside the park.

The wolves were living dangerously just by being there. When two calves were killed on a ranch in the Washakies' territory, Animal Damage Control didn't hesitate to blame the wolves. A local biologist called me, saying he was skeptical that the Washakies were guilty. In turn, I called Ed Bangs to see what he planned to do.

"Don't worry, big guy. Even if he did it, it's your wolf's first offense," he said.

But the phone rang again shortly. Bangs' tone was different. The Animal Damage Control supervisor for the Fishtail area, Jim Hoover, had called him, reminding him that Carter's Hope was already considered a sheep-killer because of the incident at Vern Keller's ranch.

"I agreed with him, Carter. I told him we should do some incremental removal."

This meant kill a couple of wolves, or maybe just one. R-26 wasn't yet associated with any dead livestock, plus she was caring for pups. It would look bad to shoot her. Despite the shaky evidence, Carter's Hope had to go, Bangs said.

Though the livestock kill was in Wyoming, Hoover brought in a helicopter from Montana, radio-tracked Carter's Hope through heavy timber in the DuNoir Valley, and shot him. The wolf didn't die quickly and left a blood trail into the woods. Biologists found the carcass draped over a log. I was thoroughly pissed. In hindsight, I had probably put a bulls-eye on that wolf by attaching my name to it. I realized that some folks at Animal Damage Control had probably been salivating to kill it, simply because the animal held importance for me. Nobody called him R-15, they called him Carter's Hope, and his story was well known among biologists. Now he'd been shot in the back by my flunky agency and left to rot in the woods.

A year or so later, I was again acting as an expert witness in federal court. This time, I was testifying against a rancher who wanted all wolves moved or killed for posing a threat to his family and livelihood. I looked at dozens of photos and answered questions. Ed Bangs was there, too, and the day after court, he had business at the U.S. Forest Service in Dubois, Wyoming. I went with him and milled around the waiting room while Bangs talked to the receptionist.

At the far end of the room, was a roped-off area with a plaque. I wandered over to read it. Then I looked up at the stuffed animal the sign described. A brass plate under the animal was nicely engraved: *CARTER'S HOPE*.

I read the sign again. It couldn't be. The animal that stared out at the room looked more like a weasel-lizard thing. It was the worst taxidermy job I'd ever seen, and I've seen a lot of bad mounts. Its face was distorted, its body elongated, its legs stubby. The sign described the wolf's history. Indeed, this was the black wolf I'd named in Canada.

Bangs appeared beside me, but as soon as he did, I had to walk away. If I could have, I would have taken the thing outside and burned it.

Bangs stood and read the plaque.

"You've got to be kidding me. That's Carter's Hope?" Bangs said. "It looks like a lizard or something."

The lady at the reception desk looked over her glasses.

"A lot of people ask for more information about that," she said, pointing with her pencil.

I explained the whole thing to her. As I talked, I noticed a wolf skull on a shelf behind her. When I asked about it, she handed it to me. It belonged to Carter's Hope.

An abscess had left a hole in one of its canine teeth as well as its jaw. It was enormous and must have been terribly painful and debilitating and was probably the reason for the lump that Doug Smith had noted. I told myself that maybe the wolf's death was actually a blessing.

I missed the reintroduction wrap-up party in Hinton, Alberta, because Animal Damage Control supervisors weren't comfortable being in charge of investigating dead livestock. I didn't even have time to say goodbye. I drove 800 miles straight through, pulling into Helena in the wee hours, in time to get a few hours of sleep. When I awoke, it was time to drive again, this time to Rocker, Montana, a tiny town outside Butte, where the supposed wolf problem occurred.

The message was clear, uttered by the Animal Damage Control western district supervisor in Montana: While I was up screwing around in Canada, my wolves were causing problems back home. *My wolves.* This was a new tone, but he didn't stop there. He complained about all the trouble wolves were causing in Montana: A lot of damn airplane time had been burned up searching for the damn wolves, he said, and my damn wolf budget better pay every damn dime of it.

"It's nice of you to pull yourself away from wolf reintroduction to do your job," he added.

I tried to ignore him. Like the rest of the supervisors at Animal Damage Control, he had no interest in what I'd been up to in Canada. Instead, I thought about the wolves in Rocker. I was puzzled. That place was nothing but subdivisions and ranchettes. What would wolves want with it?

Winter had been a good time to be in Canada because there wasn't much else going on in Montana. Cattle and sheep were out of the mountains, kept close and fed hay so that ranchers could keep an eye on them. The few wolves outside of Yellowstone were busy eating deer and elk.

Tracking was going to be easy today. New snow covered the ground. We swung north, then west toward the ranch. About a mile from our destination, two sets of canine tracks were obvious, coming across a field and onto the main road in front of us.

"There's those wolf tracks again in the same place they were the other day," the supervisor said.

I looked at him. He had to be kidding.

"Those are dog tracks," I said.

He challenged me, but I knew I was right. One set of tracks was bigger than the other, but neither set came close to the size of a wolf. Besides, the tracks were rambling from one side of the road to the other, stopping and starting at grass clumps where the dogs peed. Anyone who has ever let a dog out of the house in the morning or out of a car during a road trip has seen this kind of meandering to find a potty stop.

He stopped the truck and backed up. I opened my door and leaned out to look at the tracks. Yep, one big dog and one medium size dog. He told me I was wrong and hit the gas.

We pulled into the ranch yard and met a woman who'd been looking after a bunch of dairy calves in pens near the road. While we talked, I kept an eye on a 300-or-so pound calf that struggled to keep its balance, finally falling onto its side, unable to get up.

"Have you lost any more animals since you called?" the supervisor asked.

"No." She hadn't noticed the calf flailing on the ground behind her.

I decided to interject.

"Do you know if anybody owns any dogs over thataway?" I thumbed south, the direction I believed the tracks on the road had come from.

"Oh yeah, those people in the house over that hill have two dogs," she said.

"Where is the cow that was killed?" I asked. She pointed to a pine-covered hill about a half-mile away and we went there next.

Magpies, ravens and coyotes had done a number on the several hundred-pound carcass, but there was no sign of a struggle. No predator caused this animal to die. But more than that, I was perplexed by its location. What was it doing up here in the trees? It seemed to have been dumped. It didn't die here.

"So, have you seen wolf tracks at this carcass before today?" I asked. The supervisor hadn't. He was focused on the tracks by the road. The whole story was falling apart and all I was thinking about was the big party I was missing in Canada.

We returned to the ranch. I had a couple more questions for that gal.

"Are some of your animals sick?" I nodded at the calf that lay in the corral.

"Yeah, a few of them."

"Can you tell me why your cow is all the way up on that hill?"

It was their boneyard. They hadn't bothered to bury the carcass. When you have dead stuff lying around and scavengers show up, it's only because they were invited.

This boondoggle needed to end. This trip was about finding something that would implicate wolves and I resented it. We went back to the dog tracks and I hopped the fence and the supervisor followed. The tracks went straight toward a homestead nestled between two hills – exactly as the woman had said. A little farther and I found a pile of dog shit, picked it up with a stick and took a whiff. Wolf shit smells sweet compared to Alpo shit. We got closer and a man came out of the house. I waved. We were trespassing and I didn't want to get shot.

"Howdy," I offered a handshake and introduced myself. "I'm following some tracks that are coming from your direction. Do you own a couple of dogs?"

"Yeah," he hesitated. "A Rottweiller and a lab. Why?"

I didn't want to spill the beans just yet. "Oh, we just saw the tracks and wondered if they were made by dogs or not, that's all."

"Are you guys out here about the wolves?"

I said yes and he launched into a tirade about damn wolves and what were we going to do about them?

"Well, we'll decide here pretty quick," I said.

When we got back to the truck, the supervisor put the whole thing together.

"That was the same guy who reported the dead cow and was in the paper complaining about wolves," he said. "They're not even his animals."

"I guess I don't have to tell you this is a bunch of bullshit," I said.

We barely spoke on the way back to Helena. I simply couldn't believe that the guys I worked for were incapable of investigating this stuff without me. Maybe they were capable, but they weren't willing. I was always going to be the guy who told the rancher what he didn't want to hear.

Back home I wondered how things had gone in Hinton and dialed up Alice Whitelaw.

"We had one hell of a party up here, Carter. How did the wolf investigation go?"

At the end of January 1995, wolf B-13 from the recent reintroduction turned up dead south of Challis, Idaho, shot as it chewed on a dead calf at Gene Hussey's ranch.

I'd been in the northern part of the state arguing with a rancher about whether wolves killed his donkey and cow. The former had been dead for several weeks after getting its feet tangled in a fence and the latter died on its back after falling into an irrigation ditch. Another cow walked around with slash marks made by some sharp object, but not the teeth of a wolf. The rancher disagreed with my assessment, but compared to the fit that rancher threw, the Hussey situation went into orbit. When Hussey reported the dead wolf, federal law enforcement agents converged on the ranch, triggering a nasty confrontation with the local sheriff. It almost, but not quite, involved guns coming out of holsters. Everyone was involved, including U.S. senators.

There was bound to be more of this kind of thing because a second reintroduction was scheduled for January 1996. The first round of wolves released into Yellowstone had been a huge success as far as I could see because they managed to stay out of livestock and only two were illegally killed.

But that kind of success didn't change certain things. Politicians and livestock organizations still drummed up a case against the transplant of wolves. But they were unable to sell it to a federal judge. At least with reintroduction, the Fish and Wildlife Service was putting wolves where it wanted them instead of waiting to see where wolves showed up – the way it was happening in Montana. Those wolves were picking ranches a little too often.

This time, I didn't have to go to the backcountry and win a skinning contest to get things off the ground. It was January 1996, and the action centered near Fort St. John, British Columbia, where the daytime temperatures often didn't rise above -32F. When it's that cold, you can hardly sense whether it's getting better or worse. Those with beards and mustaches looked sugar-frosted. Each of us was assigned a particular task. I was to be a mugger – the person who jumps out of the helicopter and goes after the darted wolf.

Moisture had been transformed into tiny diamonds of ice hanging in the air, disguised as fog. The sun hung low, dulled to a mere glow. I was freezing my ass off, but only noticed it occasionally in all the excitement to get my hands on some wolves.

It's a weird feeling to be let out of a helicopter in the Canadian wilderness and watch the chopper fly away. We'd been using two airplanes and two helicopters in close proximity to each other just so we wouldn't accidentally lose someone, like me wandering around, trying to keep warm after I'd found the drugged wolf.

I walked in circles in the knee-deep snow, trying to keep my circulation going and my feet warm. I was wearing Sorel boots but could feel the cold creeping through the liners. I alternately waved my arms in circles and shoved my gloved hands in my pockets. I had so many clothes on, but I couldn't stay warm. There wasn't anything for me to do except wait with the sleeping wolf for the chopper to return. I'd rather have been carrying it, or doing something that forced my body to heat up. The wolf would be fine, its body temperature warmed by the chase through the trees.

The chopper finally touched down near me and I loaded my wolf alongside others inside the ship, but my feet never warmed up for the rest of the day. Sitting in a motel room with the wolf crew that night, we toasted each other on our first day of round two in Canada. I slipped off my boots and socks, tucked my feet under a blanket and sipped on my beer. My feet still felt cold and my right big toe was beginning to burn. In all my years in the outdoors, I had never had that sensation. I finally reached down and rubbed my feet to warm them. I looked at my painful toe.

"Anybody know what a frostbit toe looks like?" I chuckled. A volunteer medical doctor crossed the room, his brow furrowed. He wasn't amused. I brought my foot out so he could see.

"You froze it," he said. "How are the rest of them?" he pulled the blanket back. The chattering and laughter had ceased and everyone was looking at my foot.

"Go put your foot in the sink and run some warm water on it," the doctor said. He rummaged around in his supply kit and came up with a roll of gauze. When I unfolded myself from my weird position at the sink, he gingerly wedged the puff of white between my big and middle toes.

"You're through flying. You need to take care of that or you could lose it," he said.

What? There was no way in hell I was done. I tried to laugh it off, but the doctor chided me. I couldn't believe my Sorel boots failed me. That night I could hardly sleep. My toe throbbed. I popped some ibuprofen, picked up my right boot and looked it over. I was about to give up when I found it, a tiny crack near the toe; it took that little to let the cold in. But I was prepared for day two. I pulled a pair of white moon boots out of my truck. I'd gotten them from Malmstrom Air Force Base a few years back. They were awkward and heavy but had great insulation. If this is what it took, it's what I'd wear. When I modeled them for the doctor the next day, he just shook his head.

With the frostbit toe, I caught wolves the next day in open rolling hills, slopes and thick timber, but the snow was 20 feet deep in places, especially in the forest where it had blown and drifted. I crawled, rolled or dragged myself from tree to tree. The only place a helicopter could land at times was on the frozen rivers or valley floors. I often sunk up to my armpits and prayed I wouldn't end up in snow over my head. And I did it all without hurting my toe any worse.

When we had a load of wolves on board, ready for the kennels, the helicopter pilots radioed Barry Miner, who met us in his airplane at an airstrip near Pink Mountain, alongside the Alaska Highway. I was the flight nurse a few times, helping get the wolves safely to the holding pens 100 miles away. We laid the wolves in the back of the plane and I monitored their temperature, pulse and respiration. It only got unbearable when the wolves, in their drugged state, vomited all over everything, or worse, got a sudden case of diarrhea or farted relentlessly. Miner and I tried to ignore it by remarking on the scenery, holding our breath while we talked. If only we could have rolled down a window.

Back at the holding pens, Jeff Haas and Fred Goodman worked as chefs, cutting up frozen roadkill for the wolves' meals. The men, decked out in coveralls, jauntily chainsawed their way through the bodies, causing a spray of red meat and fat to stick to their pant legs.

Val Asher and Alice Whitelaw asked me to take a look at a wolf that seemed unusually aggressive when it recovered from being drugged. They led me through the maze of kennels, stopping at one and pulling back its canvas tarp. The big gray male had been lying down, but stood quickly and glared at the three of us. He approached the gate of the pen slowly, letting out a low growl. It was the only one I'd seen act this way. He kept eye contact with me. The message was clear: He was fed up with people bothering him. If we released an animal like this into Idaho or Yellowstone and it hurt someone, the politicians would have all the fodder they needed to halt or perhaps reverse reintroduction. I wanted to send this one back to the woods.

I snapped a photo of the wolf, shot some video and tracked down Dr. Steve Fritts about it. But nobody seemed too worried. The day the wolf was put in a metal crate for its trip to America, Asher and Whitelaw made a warning sign and posted it on the wolf's kennel so that handlers on the U.S. side would be forewarned. When the wolf reached Missoula, a biologist was attempting to put ice under the crate's sliding door so the wolf could lick at it when the wolf lunged and bit the man's finger, breaking a couple of bones.

Standard government policy for wolves that bite humans calls for the animal to be destroyed and tested for rabies. Such was the case with this one, but the tests were negative. Like I said, he wasn't a good reintroduction candidate.

We were done in 10 days. Seventeen wolves representing four social units went to Yellowstone National Park and 20 from eight separate packs went to Idaho. We left 14 radio-collared wolves in 12 packs for Canadian biologists to study – to see the after-effects of wolf removal. While our friends and colleagues in the U.S. were releasing the wolves in front of hoards of media, we took down the kennels – all 20-something of them – in one day. We stacked the chainlink fencing, bagged the components and burned the straw that made up each wolf's bed.

After all that cold and effort, we thought we should celebrate. Trapper Fred Goodman went to town and bought a pint of Black Velvet and Whitelaw ordered take-out Chinese food. Soon Goodman and I made the pint disappear. I don't remember the food showing up, but vaguely recall eating chow mein off the carpet of the motel room. The next thing I remember is waking up, face down on a bed, still wearing my flannel shirt, wool pants, moon boots and beaver hat. My glasses were under my nose.

"Where am I?" I croaked.

"On Val's bed," Whitelaw giggled from the other bed where she slouched.

"Where's Val?"

Whitelaw pointed to a pile of blankets and clothes on the floor. Asher's head was barely visible. She was out.

I heard a loud thump and turned my head the other way. Goodman was in a chair, still wearing his cold weather gear. He looked unconscious. Saliva ran down his chin and every minute or so he stomped his foot.

"Fred? You OK?" I said. "Fred? *FRED!*"

He didn't even flinch, but he stomped his foot again.

There had been a big party and once again, I'd missed it.

I traded cold and snow for heat and shorts when I traveled to Zimbabwe a couple of weeks after returning from Canada. At the last minute, Val Asher and Alice Whitelaw decided to go, too.

Dr. Dave Hunter, one of the veterinarians working on wolf capture had been bragging up a trip to learn large animal immobilization. I only had one question: Where do I sign up?

A week of 85 degrees and sunshine can do wonders for cold bones. Even my toe was feeling better. We took a weeklong class in Harare and learned all about the capture drugs most commonly used on wild game in Africa. Afterward, we headed to Fothergill Island where our group of biologists and veterinarians immobilized and then euthanized a sick elephant that had been wandering the savannah, unable to eat because of trunk paralysis. The vets began cutting up the elephant. When it came time to measure its intestines, they asked for my help.

"Here, take this intestine and just start walking." The veterinarian handed me what looked like a fire hose and I obeyed. It was pretty long.

When we were done and could relax and be tourists, I went bird-watching with my video camera. I shot four hours worth of vultures and Marabou storks eating what was left of that elephant. Days later, I celebrated my 49th birthday to the beat of African drums at a lodge on Fothergill Island. My friends sang the birthday song and even arranged for a cake.

I'd been wearing sandals with socks to protect my toe and a couple of nights into my stay at the lodge I carefully removed the sock from my right foot to have a look. The damaged part of my toe had been replaced with bright pink new skin. I'd somehow managed not to bump it or injure it any more. But where was the hard callus that had been there? I turned my sock inside out and there was a petrified piece of flesh in the shape of a "J." I couldn't wait to show everyone and decided that I should drill a hole in one end and make a necklace out of it. At dinner, the group rejected my idea and told me throw it away before I made someone puke. When I got back to my room that night, I tossed the "J" out the window and watched the baseball-sized dung beetles carry it away.

MONTANA, Part 2

O nce the shine of reintroduction had worn off, the troubles between people and wolves resumed, each living up to their worst traits.

After returning from a trip to Albuquerque, where the U.S. Fish and Wildlife Service was wrestling with problems related to Mexican wolves, there was more trouble in the Ninemile: this time on a ranch in Huson, Montana, owned by actress Andie MacDowell.

Everybody in the valley knew the actress as Rose Qualley. She and her husband, Paul, and their three children lived there. Like a lot of celebrities who decide to buy a ranch in a remote part of the West, they were taken aback when wild animals showed up in their yard. I drove to the Qualley place, taking federal wildlife agent Rick Branzell with me.

Paul Qualley answered the door wearing only a towel. He was healing from a groin sprain, an old football injury, he said. He sat on the couch and told us about their calf that was killed right behind the house. The calf had frostbitten feet that were recently wrapped by a veterinarian. It couldn't walk, Paul said, so it was an easy target.

This wasn't the Qualleys' first run-in with wolves. They'd purchased a guard dog to protect their children from the large predators that lurked in that area – mountain lions and wolves in particular. Wolves killed the dog, however, eviscerating it next to the kids' swing set. The wolves' most recent victim, the Qualleys' 300-pound calf, lay covered with a tarp. I walked around the site to figure out what happened. Then I skinned the carcass to determine the cause of death. The wolves, I decided, had attacked the calf as it stood next to a salt block, then dragged it about 50 feet, leaving a distinct blood trail. It had been bitten under its front legs and had a hole ripped open in its flank. Massive hemorrhaging killed it. The calf was full of slashes and bites, but the wolves didn't eat it.

The wolves hadn't gone far. One with a radio collar ran in front of my truck as I was driving away that day. It was close enough that I had to slam on my brakes. I grabbed my camera and snapped a photo when it paused to look at me before trotting into the trees. I'd started developing a pretty good sense of what might turn into a public relations disaster and was trying to think of all the evidence I'd need in order to justify moving or killing wolves – especially on a celebrity's ranch.

Paul Qualley wasn't interested in moving or killing the Ninemile wolves, but Rose Qualley dialed me up soon after my visit and complained that wolves were getting awfully thick around her ranch.

"I think you ought to move them," the actress said.

"We can sure consider that," I told her. "But it's going to be up to the Fish and Wildlife Service."

She didn't push it and I waited for her to call and complain again, but she didn't. It was a time when we were cautious about killing wolves. We didn't know they'd be the prolific, resilient creatures they've turned out to be – even though we'd been warned. They were endangered, and we were trying to conserve every one of them. As much as we dared, we put it on ranchers to remove the things that would tempt a wolf – like a crippled calf standing out in the open or an uncovered boneyard – so that wolves wouldn't get set up. So many times dead livestock – and dead wolves – can be prevented.

But the need fizzled. The Qualleys had a wolf problem, but they weren't eager to do much about it. Defenders paid them for the dead calf, although they probably didn't need the money. It was the last I heard about wolves causing trouble there, although I did learn that the Qualleys moved away not long after the wolf incident. It's rough country out there.

In the mid-1990s, the Wolf Recovery Foundation and Defenders of Wildlife put together the first North American Interagency Wolf Conference. It was well attended, held at Chico Hot Springs in Pray, Montana, a quaint old place at the edge of Yellowstone National Park. It started as an information-sharing conference because everything with wolves was so new and exciting. But it also was an olive branch, extended by wolf advocates, to those who had the most to lose: ranchers. The people who lost livestock were invited to attend and speak. It was the only event like it, and its inclusive nature forged a lot of unlikely friendships. The Chico meetings happened yearly and everyone started looking forward to them because it was the only time all of us made time to get together and cover everything that happened, might happen, or was on the horizon. A lot of good ideas came from those conferences.

The Wolf Recovery Foundation came up with the Alpha Award, given yearly at the Chico conference to the person who had, in the most recent calendar year, made the most significant contribution to wolf recovery. It was an award that required a nomination and a vote by foundation members. Every year in April, as the meeting approached, people in the wolf world wondered who might get the award. A foundation member went around the crowded lecture hall at Chico and discreetly whispered the winner to a select few attendees, asking those folks to say a few words about the winner without actually using the person's name, keeping everyone in the audience guessing until the last minute. I was the winner in 1997. It was the first time I'd been recognized formally for working with wolves, although by then I'd been doing it for 10 years. It was the same year that Animal Damage Control, needing a public image facelift, changed its name to "Wildlife Services," and handed out pencils, rulers and coffee cups emblazoned with the agency's new slogan: "Living With Wildlife." By an act of Congress 11 years earlier, the agency had moved from being a bureau under the conservation-minded Department of the Interior to the sheltering arms of the U.S. Department of Agriculture.

The greatest irony about me receiving the Alpha Award was that the supervisor of Wildlife Services in Idaho, Mark Collinge, was the guy who nominated me, not my outfit in Montana. The three Montana Wildlife Services supervisors who begrudgingly attended the conference skipped the award ceremony in order to sit in the hot springs. But the lecture hall was jammed with people I never thought I'd intentionally befriend.

I walked to the front of the room deafened by the applause. Everyone was standing and clapping and smiling at me, the guy they'd always cussed for being a killer.

While I was being revered with the Alpha Award from the bunny huggers, as my cronies called them, my relationship with Wildlife Services slipped another notch. Larry Handegard appeared to be on a crusade to get me to quit and routinely read a laundry list of complaints about me to the regional director. The latest was that my warehouse was an eyesore, and in short order Handegard canceled the lease, telling me – and the two trappers I shared space with – that we had to share a new warehouse to save money.

I'd sort of been expecting something like this. In place of my trusty warehouse in the Helena valley, Handegard found a new place for me in the federal building in downtown Helena. The office where I was to do my paper shuffling was about the size of a closet. I jammed my file cabinet, storage cabinet, copy machine, fax, phone, chair and desk into the room. Once in, I couldn't turn around, and almost couldn't get out again. The warehouse portion of my new workplace was on the bottom floor near the loading dock. At one time, it held the trash and recycling bins. It had one light bulb, no heat, no electrical outlets and no running water. Through it, ran all of the plumbing, air and electrical gadgetry for the entire building.

"You've got to be kidding," I mumbled.

A few trappers drove to town and helped me move all the stuff I'd accumulated in 23 years since Bill Summers and I built the old warehouse. They were dumbfounded.

"What did they move you here for?" they asked. At least at my old location, a guy could fire a shotgun or skin a varmint. They decided they could go somewhere else for the supplies they used to get from me.

"Man, somebody don't like you, Carter," one said.

I'd decided that I wasn't going to change my style just because of my new digs. I brought my wolf bait containers into the warehouse. Two days went by before I was met at the front door by security guards, whom I was getting to know by their first names.

"We think there might be something rotten in your storage room," one said.

The other chimed in. "Hey, don't you realize the federal judge's parking place is right next to that room?"

No I didn't. But frankly, I looked forward to the day the judge pulled in and was confronted with a bloated calf carcass.

"That's probably my bait that you smell," I told the guards. I thought about the hundred or so people who worked in the building, in their nice suits and dresses, getting a good whiff of anal glands, skunk essence and rotting meat as it circulated freely through the ventilation system.

The guards told me to get that stuff out of there. I told them to take it up with my supervisors in Denver. Handegard intervened again, saying to leave everything right where it was. I did, and, since it was summer and a heat wave was conveniently settling in, I locked the warehouse doors and took six days of vacation.

A few weeks later, the regional director called with a great idea. How about if I got transferred to Wyoming?

"Hell, no I don't want to move to Wyoming," I said, adding that I appeared to be the cause of a serious personnel problem and that we should fix it right here in Montana.

My new warehouse in the federal building got its real initiation on Christmas Eve 1998. A trapper had hauled a frozen calf into town and wondered what to do with it. He suspected that wolves might have killed it.

"Bring it on over," I said, grinning as I hung up the phone.

The trapper backed into the loading dock normally reserved for UPS and Fed-Ex deliveries. He shot me a worried look, but I just smiled. We slid the several hundred pound calf onto the dock, propped the doors open and dragged the carcass into the building, leaving a bloody smear on the concrete along with tufts of hair and cow shit. I jury-rigged a drop cord using the hallway plug and switched on a fan that I'd brought from home, pointing it toward the carcass. It would take several days to thaw.

One of the security guards met me in the hallway after Christmas.

"What the hell is stinking in there?" he demanded, adding that people upstairs were ready to puke.

"That's a good sign because that means it's ready to cut open." I thought he might arrest me, but I just didn't care anymore.

"I want you to get that thing outta here. Now," he pointed toward my warehouse room.

"I'm just doing my job, man. If you want to raise hell, be my guest." I smiled and went past him.

"This shit is going to stop," he called after me.

"And you're the guy to do it!" I waved and kept walking, meeting a fat blue bottlefly patrolling the hall.

The calf stinking up the federal building belonged to Ed Cummins, a retired NFL player who had taken up ranching near Stevensville along Bass Creek. Once I got the hide off, I decided it was indeed a wolf kill. I visited Cummins' ranch and was ready to set a few traps when I learned about a private trapper nearby who'd caught a wolf in one of his coyote sets. It weighed

108 pounds and had nearly mangled the trap. I called Joe Fontaine and asked him to bring me a radio collar. Cummins and his neighbor, Tom Ruffato, had reluctantly agreed that the wolf should be turned loose so it could give up the location of others in its pack.

Cummins invited Fontaine and me to stay for supper that night, and in the middle of the meal, he came up with an interesting idea: Why we didn't develop some kind of system where a wolf's radio collar could activate noises that would scare the wolves away? Fontaine and I passed on the idea to predator research specialists at the Wildlife Services National Wildlife Research Center. Soon, they developed what became known as a RAG box – Radio Activated Guard – and it did just what Cummins imagined it should: use the radio signals from wolves' collars to activate prerecorded noises like screeching tires and gunshots in order to scare the wolves away from live-stock. We tested the box around the Cummins and Ruffato ranches for a couple of months with limited success. Later, a better version proved that RAG boxes, combined with other deterrents like multiple guard dogs, worked – and resulted in fewer dead animals all the way around.

Near Butte, Montana, a woman looked out her window and saw five wolves frolicking in her pasture. She spilled her coffee. Her heart raced and she got butterflies in her stomach. The wolves were only a few yards from her family's 60 cattle. She knew they were wolves because they looked just like the one on her living room wall that her husband killed in Alaska in 1975 – 250 pounds – the biggest wolf ever taken there...

This was the gist of a wild newspaper story about a bunch of wolves terrorizing people near Butte. Because of it my phone rang relentlessly. The tales grew until at least three cows were reported killed, and the state game warden and a Montana Stockgrowers Association representative wanted to know what I was going to do about it.

I hadn't heard about any of this, so I bought a copy of the paper. A Butte animal control officer responded to the woman's call and the two of them watched five wolves leaping into the air, catching field mice. A Montana Fish, Wildlife and Parks biologist surmised that it was an entirely new wolf pack. I sighed and plopped the white pages on my desk to look up the woman's phone number.

I took Joe Fontaine with me. When we pulled into the ranch yard, a television reporter was waiting. I was never one to turn down the media and this didn't seem like a good time to start.

"Sure, come on," I said. The newsman picked up his pile of gear and followed me to the door.

I wanted to talk to the woman before taking a look outside, asking her to point to the exact location where she saw the wolves – which side of the haystack, how far from the fence. It had snowed since her sighting, so I needed a few fixed reference points to help locate the wolf tracks.

Fontaine, the newsman and I trekked to the spot the woman pointed to. The reporter looked at the tracks in the snow.

"Those aren't wolf tracks," he said. "Aren't those coyote tracks?"

I'd gotten in the habit of carrying a plaster wolf track with me just for this reason. I pulled it out of my coat pocket and put it next to one of the dozens of coyote tracks.

"Good eye," I said. "Take all the pictures you want because this is sure gonna let the air out of everybody."

I followed the tracks across the field, under a fence, across a road and into an adjacent field, where the animal control officer had witnessed the five wolves. The reporter wondered how people would mistake a coyote for a wolf.

"In the summer, a coyote is a spindly, scrawny, boney-legged, long-eared critter," I said. "But in winter, their fur doubles in length, and they get a lot of scruff around the neck and face, making them look twice as big as they are and a lot like a wolf." I showed the reporter where the coyotes had done their business in the snow, further proving their identity.

The woman was disappointed and defended her belief that wolves were around because her neighbors had heard howling. Nevertheless, she was happy to give an interview.

"What that trapper said makes sense," she said into the television camera, "but I'm going to keep a close eye on my livestock anyway."

At the end of the year, I wrote my usual wrap-up report. In it, I recorded the number of visitors I'd had at my new location: two. My complaints about the federal building went unheeded.

"We're not moving you just *because*," said Jeff Green, the regional director.

I tried to stay on the road even though I was pretty much prevented from working in Montana anymore. But that was okay, because Montana wasn't the only place in my jurisdiction where wolves were causing trouble.

John Aldous, a rancher in tiny Carmen, Idaho, was suddenly under siege, losing three calves to wolves. The Wildlife Services trapper for that region, Rick Williamson, had confirmed two wolf kills, but was unsure about the third because it had decomposed badly before it was discovered.

Aldous once had the dubious distinction of losing more cattle to wolves than any rancher in Idaho. He belonged – still belongs – to a grazing association with federal forest allotments. Cattle in the association are intermingled, all of them belonging to different people. But sometimes the animals belonging to one rancher get off by themselves and run into trouble. That's what happened to Aldous's cattle.

Williamson had set five traps, but waited for me to arrive before deciding to do anything else. I'd met Williamson the year before at a trappers conference, but this was the first reason we'd had to work together. Wolves were still a novelty and no one was quite sure how to deal with the investigations.

"Howdy," John Aldous grunted at me from under his bushy black beard. He wore an equally black Stetson. I could understand why Williamson called him Fuzzy.

Aldous spit from the wad of brown tobacco in his mouth. His hands were rough from work, and most of the time he kept them in his pockets and didn't say much. When he walked, he limped a little, and though it was morning, he offered me a Busch Lite out of his truck's cooler.

We traveled a dusty road in the Salmon-Challis National Forest and visited one of the remaining calf carcasses. Wolves had consumed the other, except for a few ribs.

"I think that's gotta be what's left of one of those calves because the mother cow keeps sniffing at them and won't leave,' Williamson said.

The suspects in these deaths were the Jureano wolves. I'd put collars on four of them the previous summer and they were still calling this area home. Williamson's five traps were in various locations in the meadow.

We fanned out and I saw fresh – really fresh – wolf tracks on the main dirt road. When we reconvened at the meadow, I said that I'd be heading for the road with my traps.

"I've got orders to trap in this meadow," Williamson said. "My boss says we're not gonna catch the right wolves, if we're not trapping right at the carcass."

"Yeah, but Rick, the only wolves in this area are the Jureanos," I said. "We're missing the boat if we don't trap where they travel."

"Well, I don't know how you can just *do* that." He was amazed at the idea.

"You just *do it*, man. Forget all that red tape crap. You're the trapper. You're here, they're not."

The Forest Service road was where we caught the Jureano wolves, just like I predicted. Williamson's skill as a trapper was tremendous, but it got better that day.

John Aldous had been standing there, listening to Williamson and me discuss what the bureaucrats wanted. He finally spoke up.

"Wherever you go, I'm goin' too," he said. He didn't intend to have a discussion about it.

I explained why I needed to work alone: Too many people on a trapline leaves too much scent, then the wolves leave and then where are we? I tried to be diplomatic. He just looked at me.

"I don't know about all that, but I know I'm goin' with you up there," he grunted. He was pissed about his dead calves and wanted to see what we were doing about it. "These reintroduced wolves are a bunch of bullshit," he added.

"Okay, John. But if you go, I don't want no spittin,' pissin,' or shittin,' and I can't allow no sunflower seeds or peanut shells or beer cans." I was hoping he'd think it sounded miserable. He'd spit tobacco at least 16 times since I'd been standing there, and I'd noticed Busch Lite cans smashed up and down the road. "*And* I'm using an ATV, so if you ride with me, you don't get off unless I tell you." I figured he would tell me to go to hell, or hit me, or maybe get in his truck and leave.

"I can do that," he murmured.

It was a tight squeeze, but Aldous spent the next day and the next on the ATV with me. We checked Williamson's traps first, then went to the road where I'd set five. Aldous's anger about the wolves seemed to diminish as long as he could be a close observer. I figured he'd eventually lose interest and go back to haying. Before we mounted up the second day, he produced a camera.

"By God, I want to see one of them damn wolves. Everybody else hears 'em and sees 'em running across the road except me." As far as Aldous was concerned, they were just ghosts out there, killing his livestock.

Biologists from the Nez Perce tribe's wolf program arrived, in case we needed help. The tribe had stepped up to monitor wolves after reintroduction because Idaho lawmakers refused to let their fish and game agency do it.

Our convoy of ATV's bumped and jostled down a side road, through a small marshy area and into a shaded meadow full of mosquitoes. Aldous was ready with his camera. A gray pup lunged from its hiding place in tall grass a mere 10 feet in front us, tumbling as it hit the end of the chain. My trap had it by the right front foot.

"Goddamn, look at the size of that wolf!" Aldous hollered, snapping photos but staying put. The procession behind me came to a halt. I told everybody to stay where they were so we could use a catchpole without too much more struggle on the puppy's part. I put the cable around its neck and Williamson moved in to pin it down so I could remove the trap. It was only a 45-pound male pup, too small to risk using drugs. The other biologists helped put ear tags and a collar on him and take a blood sample for DNA assessment. While they worked, I watched Aldous. It was the first time he'd seen a wolf and he kept talking about how huge it was.

"Where are you taking him?" he asked.

"Well, he's really too young to be taken from his parents, so how's about if we let him go right here?" I balked, thinking he'd cuss me for letting it go, but Aldous didn't seem to notice.

"I'm namin' that wolf after me then," he said, fixing his eyes on the pup. "I'm callin' him Little John."

I couldn't argue with that. Williamson just smiled and shook his head. The biologists finished up and turned Little John loose. He scampered through the brush, tail between his legs, and disappeared.

"Hey, save some film. We've still got four more traps to check," I said. I was hoping for an adult. I rode ahead to check. When I saw a coal-black wolf standing calmly in the last trap a mile away, I turned around and hurried back. Black wolves are my favorite. They look mysterious.

"John, my man, I'm gonna show you a real wolf," I said, churning up dust as I came to a stop. Aldous grinned. The man had three dead calves and these wolves were costing him money, but I could see that he was enjoying this new experience. Like the rest of us, he was lapping up an outdoor adventure.

When we pulled into sight of the big black wolf, I heard Aldous behind me, gasping for the right word, mumbling a few expletives about the size of *this* one.

"Can I get up closer?" he whispered.

"Let's get him under control first," I said.

Williamson and I went to work with the catch pole, but the wolf wasn't going down without a fight. He eventually got the trap chain wrapped around a tangle of trees and brush until he couldn't move anymore, but he still chewed the hell out of the circle of cable on the catchpole and jerked us around. We finally got the wolf's head in the loop and cinched it so one of us could move in and inject it in the hip. Soon it was drugged and oblivious.

This male wolf weighed 112 pounds, but unlike Little John, he was going for a ride deep into the backcountry away from cattle. The next time he stepped foot on Idaho soil, it was in the state's northern panhandle several hundred miles away. The pups were self-sufficient enough that they didn't need this big fella to survive. He may very well have been the one initiating the cattle killing. But Aldous had one request before we loaded the wolf on an ATV.

"I want my picture taken with that one," he beamed.

The excitement was over and we hoped the cattle killing was as well. Williamson, Aldous and I dropped in to the Shady Nook, the saloon in Salmon where all of the locals hang out. A group of dusty, worn out cowboys turned our way. It seemed everyone knew John Aldous.

"Whattaya been up to?" one hollered.

Aldous grinned under his huge beard, puffed out his chest and strolled over to the group.

"I'm a wolf trappin' son-of-a-bitch!"

While Wildlife Services and its cronies in Montana were busy finding ways to jam a monkey wrench in the gears of Northern Rockies wolf recovery, U.S. Fish and Wildlife Service Director Jamie Rappaport Clark called an impromptu meeting to discuss the high-profile wolf issues in Idaho, Montana and Wyoming. Clark wanted four people back east as soon as possible: Ed Bangs, Doug Smith, Mike Phillips and me.

There must be some mistake, said Larry Handegard and Wildlife Services officials at higher levels. Why would the director of the federal Fish and Wildlife Service want to talk to Carter Niemeyer? The predator control folks scurried around deciding which stuffed shirt should go instead.

But Clark phoned Bangs personally to clear up any misunderstandings.

"Buy Carter a plane ticket, Ed. I want him there."

Meanwhile, I was called to look at a dead colt, which had plainly not been killed by a predator. Wolves were blamed, but after disagreeing with the owner, I insisted on hauling it to a vet clinic for a second opinion. In Helena, Dr. Keith Stav followed me into the parking lot, still gloved from surgery, and pronounced with barely a glance that the colt had been kicked dead by a stud horse. He pointed at the crescent shaped wound on its flank, the partial shape of a horseshoe. It was pretty common, he said.

"What about the scratches?" I asked, echoing the colt's owner who stood with his arms folded.

"Bites," Stav said, "made by an adult horse. When you confine a stud and a new colt in the same pasture, you can almost count on it."

Trapper Jim Stevens, who had taken the call on the colt before asking me to look at it, called me that evening at home. As part of his usual routine, he'd reported the colt incident to his supervisors. They told him bluntly to stop asking my opinion about whether wolves were to blame. I got a similar call the next morning from Ted North, the trapper from Arlee, Montana. He, along with the other trappers in Montana, had been given the same order. No more talking to Carter Niemeyer.

"I don't know what's going on with you and all those guys," North said, "but I want to stay out of it. I need my job."

I wasn't supposed to talk to trappers and they weren't supposed to talk to me. What a way to run a business, I thought. Though I had been sidelined, Defenders of Wildlife still required my signature on reports in order to pay compensation to ranchers. There was no one else they could trust, they said. Wildlife Services had put everyone in a real predicament by trying to go around me.

In the summer of 1999, the yearly trappers conference came and went. I was not invited. It was the first one I'd missed since I went to work for the agency in 1975. Steve Thompson of the Missoula Independent was aware of my turbulent relationship with my employer and picked the day of the conference to interview me for a profile piece. He used recent wolf "control actions" and the resultant dead wolves as a vehicle to segue into the squabbles I'd had. The full-page story ran a couple of weeks later and caused considerable buzz in the office and among Montana trappers. The story's timing seemed to be an omen: I knew I wouldn't be working there too much longer. I didn't understand it all, but I'd outgrown them.

IDAHO

A fledgling wolf working group had adjourned in Bend, Oregon, and Suzanne Laverty of Defenders of Wildlife and Roy Heberger of the U.S. Fish and Wildlife Service carpooled back to Boise, Idaho. Oregon didn't have wolves yet, but officials were braced for it to happen any day. After all, they'd been running around just over the border in Idaho for the last several years. A small female wolf, B-45, had recently swum the Snake River and wandered around eastern Oregon, causing panic among livestock producers who predicted death and destruction because of her. The wolf never killed any livestock, but the Fish and Wildlife Service, prodded by Wildlife Services and ranchers, agreed to bring in a helicopter and move her back to Idaho. When biologists tried dumping wolf B-45 out of her kennel, she cowered and refused to move. The media frenzy lasted a week.

Heberger was planning to retire in July 2000, and have some fun for a change, fishing and building wooden boats. He'd already started looking for someone to take the hefty reins of the federal wolf recovery job in Idaho.

Heberger was a fish guy, more properly an aquatics specialist. He'd only inherited the wolf job because wolves fell into the endangered species "listing and recovery" category, which is nearly the sole purpose of the Fish and Wildlife Service's Snake River Basin office. Heberger was in charge of that section of the office and also was second in command for the Fish and Wildlife Service in Idaho.

"Who in their right mind would want to do this?" Heberger said, steering east on Interstate 84. Laverty was quiet for a moment.

"I can think of someone," she said, grinning. "How about Carter?"

Heberger shot her a look. "Niemeyer? You think he'd do it?"

Suzanne Laverty phoned me almost the second she was home and said that as far as she was concerned, it was settled. She wanted me to say yes and start packing. All that did was make me dig my heels in.

I'd been helping Doug Smith in Yellowstone to dart and collar wolves in new packs, more as a coach than anything. He was on his way and didn't need much guidance anymore. I was driving home when my new-fangled cell phone rang. It was Heberger. I feigned surprise.

I pulled over because taking a new job and moving away from Helena wasn't something I could talk about while I was driving. The whole situation reminded me of my Iowa State days and how Dr. Peterson wanted me for his rabies project. It sounded just a little too overwhelming.

"There's a lot of support for you to do this," Heberger said. I was flattered, but I needed to think about it. I may have hated my working situation with Wildlife Services, but I hated the idea of change even more. I'd lived in Helena longer than anywhere else. My kids were there as well as my friends and, well, my identity.

A couple of weeks later, I was sitting in Ed Bangs' office talking about dead livestock or, more likely, my nasty opinion of my supervisor. I wasn't going to bring it up, but the subject of Heberger's retirement eventually came around.

"I think you ought to do it, Carter," Bangs said, leaning back in his swivel chair. He was always frank with me, even though the relationship between our agencies had made us cautious around each other at first. Bangs would be my supervisor of sorts, Idaho being one of three wolf recovery outposts. "If you think about it, it's what you've been waiting for."

I sought more opinions, grinning at myself one day when I had a flashback that it was what I'd done before heading off to graduate school. Mark Collinge, the state director of Wildlife Services in Idaho, told me straight out that having a wolf expert in his state would be ideal and encouraged me to say yes. I wondered if he knew that Defenders of Wildlife was equally enthused about me taking the job. People have more in common than they think.

But the more I thought about changing my life around, the more panicked I felt. Maybe I'd just put it off for a while. Maybe they'd just forget the whole idea. Besides, there were enough new things happening. I'd squeezed into the tiny office at the federal building one morning to find a computer in the middle of my desk. A little device next to it had a sticky note attached:

Carter, this is your mouse. Do not kill it.

I crashed the computer five times that day, but my finest hour was when I lost my cursor. It took a computer expert some time to find it. I recorded the mishaps in my journal: *Computers are a pain in the ass.*

Shortly afterward, on my 53rd birthday, I sent my first e-mail. I was intimidated and tense trying to make the machine behave, but when responses trickled in, they made my day. I may have fumbled doing it, but I'd joined the 21st century.

Nobody was planning on letting me forget about the wolf job in Boise, however, so when I met Bob Ruesink and Roy Heberger, I decided to be prepared. We met halfway between our offices, sitting down for lunch in Ketchum, Idaho. I pulled a folded scrap of paper from my pocket. I had filled it with questions so I wouldn't forget. By this point in my career, I felt like I should be able to make a few demands. Then we could negotiate.

Ruesink, with his upright posture and shaved head, was like a good-natured drill sergeant. He was the field supervisor for the U.S. Fish and Wildlife Service in Idaho, and with a smile, told me that this wolf job was going to mean I was a bureaucrat, pure and simple. The wolf thing in Idaho was just starting to heat up, he said, and he wanted a butt in the chair taking the bullets and keeping the peace.

I swallowed hard. No more field work? I wasn't sure I could do it, sitting behind a desk all the time. I wondered if I could maneuver things to my liking and laid out some conditions, spreading out the list on the table. I didn't want to forget anything. Most importantly, I wanted a clear line of authority to make decisions, and I wanted better communication. I also wanted more money. Ruesink and Heberger nodded. "We can do that," they said, looking at each other.

Heberger wrote the job description based on my background and abilities. There was another person who he knew was planning to apply for the vacancy, but he wanted my resume and the job description to match so that I would be selected. It's no small trick to get a position description that's obviously been written with a certain person in mind through the humorless folks at the federal personnel office. The position being a brand new one, Heberger gambled that the personnel office would have no idea what a wolf recovery job entailed. Between his daring and their cluelessness, it worked. Jeanne Swick, Larry Handegard's secretary for many years, helped me type my resume and fill out the forms for the job. She wanted to help me out almost as badly as I wanted to leave. Again a job had sought me. Several weeks later, the paper shuffling settled, Bob Ruesink telephoned me. I was in the middle of looking at a dead goat that was blamed on wolves. I'd been hired.

Shortly after I made the leap from Wildlife Services to the U.S. Fish and Wildlife Service, wolf recovery coordinator, Rick Williamson was realigned within Wildlife Services to work solely on wolf issues in Idaho. He'd be doing exactly what I had done in Montana. I marveled at this because it was a necessity that the state supervisor, Mark Collinge, recognized – and was progressive in addressing. I packed boxes and made out lists of federal property that I'd take with me (because the Fish and Wildlife Service had paid for it) and lists of property I'd leave behind. It was weird to think that once I left Montana, no one would be doing my job. I wouldn't be replaced. I left Wildlife Services after 26 years, but no one at my agency threw me a party and only a few trappers called to say goodbye. For someone who loves parties, that's not easy, but my friends were elsewhere now. Ed Bangs threw a going-away bash for me at his house and afterward all of us danced at Bullwinkle's bar until last call.

My office and warehouse had thousands of dollars worth of equipment just sitting around, but nobody at Wildlife Services seemed too concerned. I locked the doors one last time and put my federal identification card, truck keys and everything else on the counter at the General Services Administration office in that same building. Everything that seemed like a security risk, I stuck in an envelope and mailed to my boss in Billings – my government MasterCard, gas credit card, government passport that I'd needed in Canada, and my cell phone. At least if something happened to the package while it was in transit, it would be on the U.S. Post Office. I walked down the hallway for the last time and out into the sunshine, finally free of that nearly window-less building that had so often reminded me of a penitentiary.

For a few days in 1999, I lived nowhere. I put everything I owned in the back of my pickup truck and left Montana for Wyoming where I was sched-uled to give a presentation to the National Cattlemen's Beef Association. During a question and answer session, I was asked where I lived. I told them the truth – in my truck until further notice. After that, I headed to Twin Falls, Idaho, where reporter Nels Nokkentved with the local Times-News wrote a profile story to introduce me to Idahoans. "Relating to Beast and People" appeared in the Sunday, September 3 issue. Most sources Nokkentved inter-viewed were glad to see me come to Idaho, including Sen. Laird Noh, the Idaho Conservation League, and the Idaho Department of Fish and Game. But Nokkentved poked around and found someone who didn't agree. Ralph Weller, the rancher in Big Timber, Montana, called me a "dirty son of a bitch." He was still steamed that years earlier I'd exonerated wolves of killing his calves. "He's all for the wolf and not for the rancher," Weller popped off.

One of the first weekends that I was officially an Idaho resident, I headed back to Montana for a party at Ted Turner's ranch. My friends Alice Whitelaw and Val Asher were now employed at the mogul's huge property under the umbrella of the Ted Turner Endangered Species Fund. A live band in Turner's huge and beautiful barn and a watering tank full of booze made for a great party. I ran into several old friends, including Mike Phillips, who had become the executive director of the Turner fund. Dr. Dave Hunter, the former state veterinarian for Idaho and a pal from reintroduction days, was there too, now working for Turner.

"So, have you talked to the president yet?" Phillips said, tipping a beer.

"No." I looked at him. "The president of what? You mean Ted Turner?"

Phillips gestured. I looked behind me to see where he was pointing. Five feet from me, Asher, Whitelaw and others were talking to a bald man with a big red spot on his head.

"Is that…Gorbachev?" I mouthed.

I turned around and joined the conversation behind me. The President of Russia and his daughter were a delight. I talked to both of them for quite a while, but I never did figure out why they were at the party.

There's no one who can twist the guts of a fed like Jon Marvel. He is the founder of Western Watersheds Project, and in that capacity his mission is to see that public lands grazing in the West is not only halted, but vaporized in an appropriately Captain Marvel kind of way. I met him before I was even on the U.S. Fish and Wildlife payroll. I happened to be in my new Boise office and he called the main switchboard. Everyone in the upper ranks was shuffling out the door to a meeting.

No one ever wanted to talk to Marvel. He was abrasive and insulting, and though he rarely raised his voice, he could without warning latch onto a person's backside like a vicious little dog. When Western Watersheds Project sues the federal government, it usually wins. Marvel seems to understand the law and its intent better than the teams of federal lawyers who claw back at him. For this, the government hates him – or perhaps just fears him – to the point that many federal and state employees are directed to hang up on him immediately. He is as pro-wolf as they come, and believes that public lands should not be fed to privately-owned sheep and bovines.

The office receptionist held the receiver in one hand. The other lines rang impatiently while she waited for someone in charge to decide whether talking to Jon Marvel was worth ruining their day. It was about wolves, the receptionist said.

I was eventually going to have to deal with him anyway. I settled into a chair in my new cubicle.

"So Carter," Marvel said coolly, "why would the Service hire a killer like you, anyway? I guess you have to talk to me because no one else who's in charge will."

Marvel spent a good portion of the next five minutes insulting me for killing everything in sight and for my previous life working for the collection of dunces that comprised Wildlife Services. He said he was trying to guess the fate of wolves in Idaho with a nut like me at the helm.

"So what's your point, Jon?" I asked repeatedly, throwing my question over the top of him. The conversation devolved to a series of one-liners. Biologists typing away in their cubicles stopped what they were doing and rolled their chairs into the aisle to listen to my side of the sparring match. I don't think Marvel and I usually said goodbye; we just hung up on each other after we'd both had enough.

Not much in the way of good, ass-kicking excitement happened in Boise's U.S. Fish and Wildlife Service office. For that reason, my loud phone conversations became a major source of entertainment for bored biologists stuck in a stuffy building interpreting the Endangered Species Act and writing permits for parties whose sole purpose in life seemed to be trying to get around the law. It didn't take long for my booming voice to cause me to suddenly get my own office, but then I noticed that there was an awful lot of loitering around my door, upon which I'd taped Gary Larson cartoons and anti-wolf bumper stickers created by some of the West's most atrophied minds. My favorite read: *If Only Closed Minds Came With Closed Mouths.*

At first, the office folks seemed to enjoy the commotion, but after about a year, the honeymoon was over. A few even went to yanking my door shut with a bang. Entertainment of the sort I brought was only so entertaining.

I had better things to do anyway than argue with Jon Marvel. I was busy learning my way around the office and getting used to life in Boise. I seemed to be constantly needed at a bewildering array of meetings that went on and on and accomplished nothing except a plan for more meetings. I was forced to learn how to use a computer for the second time in my life and was pleased to discover that e-mail could be my friend. I only needed to be rebooted three or four times a day by office technicians. I had their number memorized because I had to dial it so often. One woman started answering her phone, "What did you do to it this time, Carter?" She knew that visits to my office would take a chunk out of her day, and I could see that I drove her nuts. She wasn't the only one.

I was exempt from budget cutbacks and travel restrictions because the money for my job was line-itemed by Congress, courtesy of prodding by state livestock interests. They wanted someone dealing with the problems wolves were bound to cause, and didn't want to hear a bunch of piddly-assed budget excuses from the feds who were responsible for dumping wolves in Idaho to begin with. A select group of humorless office mates gave me the stink-eye when budget shortfalls were announced at staff meetings, followed by "… of course this doesn't mean Carter." I was further maligned for insisting on a truck that I didn't have to share with anyone else. Who'd want to ride in my truck with its dust and filth and assortment of horrible smells? I didn't want to load and unload everything once a week so that someone could use it to visit a fish hatchery or pick up a fellow bureaucrat from the airport. Bob Ruesink, the supervisor, agreed that I should have what I wanted. It wasn't much, but I insisted. You can't have a wolf program and run it from behind a desk – a concept I was hoping to gently impress upon him.

I sort of suspected it before I moved there in 2000, but compared to Idaho, Montana's wolf politics were a Sunday picnic. Idaho, with the exception of its few fiery environmentalists lodged mostly in Ada County where Boise is, and Blaine County where the rich and famous of Sun Valley live, was as redneck as they come – from the Legislature to the people on the land. The state's official position on wolves from the beginning was simple: The animals weren't welcome. When the first load of wolves was released in 1995 at Corn Creek in Idaho's Frank Church-River of No Return Wilderness, the Legislature unanimously passed a law prohibiting the Idaho Department of Fish and Game from having anything to do with them. Much later, the Legislature also passed a meaningless but symbolic bill calling for the immediate removal of all wolves in the state by whatever means necessary. Instead, the Nez Perce Tribe, whose ancestral relationship with the animals was fraternal rather than adversarial, stepped up with a plan to monitor the new predators. Curt Mack ran the program and Jim Holyan trapped and collared wolves and ran the numbers, keeping from day one the most accurate and comprehensive account of wolf activity in Idaho. A slew of biologists came and went every summer, some staying on for several years. I'm sure none of them had any idea what they were in for.

The few of us involved in day-to-day operations were frustrated that wolf recovery seemed to be floundering or perhaps going backwards. Since reintroduction, the feds had taken an increasingly heavy-handed approach to wolves that killed livestock. Although it was part of the promise at the beginning – that livestock-killing wolves wouldn't be tolerated – it seemed that almost every pack in the state was in trouble that way. It wasn't doing a thing for either side of the debate.

I wasn't alone in my resentment toward environmentalists who lashed out at ranchers. People who raise animals for a living are understandably frustrated with having them killed by wolves. Right before I arrived in Idaho, the Fish and Wildlife Service ordered the killing or moving of four wolves in the Twin Peaks pack and five more in the White Cloud because they kept killing livestock. The end result was that the wolves were dead, everybody had spent a wad of money, and nobody was happy. How could wolf recovery progress when ranchers refused to co-exist with wolves, the wolf-lovers wanted to shoot the ranchers, and the wolves kept doing things to make us kill them?

I began my days in Boise by staying in the office late. I got to know the janitor pretty well and I was usually still working after she finished vacuuming, often around 10 p.m. Sometimes she accidentally turned out all the lights in my area, leaving me in the glow of my computer screen.

Others noticed my hours, too.

"I saw your truck in the parking lot last night when I was at WalMart," one of the administrative gals would chastise me. "You can't do that. You have to go home after eight hours."

"Oh, okay," I answered.

Yeah, sure.

My old agency, Wildlife Services, was on paper as an official partner of the Fish and Wildlife Service, helping with livestock investigations and killing or moving wolves when the wolves killed livestock. The Wildlife Services director in Idaho had encouraged me to take this new job and seemed like a reasonable guy, unlike my director in Montana. Though he was under continual pressure from ranchers, I hoped we could find common ground when it came to decisions about killing wolves. If not, I was willing to override him. I now had the authority to do it.

It was my job to oversee the official relationships among all the agencies and governments with a stake in the wolf game, but every time I turned around, there was a new set of people who had taken it upon themselves to be involved with wolves. I became the fence-mender. It wasn't animals that got people wrapped around their own axles, it was other people – ones that weren't as easily dismissed as a pack of naughty wolves. My principal goal in Idaho was wolf recovery, but I was having the most trouble with people. At least with wolves I could predict their behavior. I repeated myself until even I was sick of hearing it. But I wasn't sure anyone was truly listening: Nothing was ever going to work unless everybody tried to get along. The ranchers aren't your worst enemy, I told wolf-lovers. And to the ranchers I broke the news that wolves weren't ever going away, so everybody needed to find a way to live with them. When it came down to it, everybody in the wolf fight had a lot more in common than they'd ever believe.

When I arrived in Idaho in 2000, the Legislative Wolf Oversight Committee had recently drafted its 14th version of a state plan to manage wolves once they were removed from the federal Endangered Species list. No one on the committee could agree on a number of points, including how many wolves would be enough and under what circumstances they should be killed.

I flipped through the plan. It struck me as nothing more than a long-winded permission slip to kill as many wolves as possible. I suggested to the higher-ups at the Fish and Wildlife Service that I give the committee a hand. It was unconventional, but I got the nod, and shortly afterward, with only a few snarky remarks on the side from certain small-minded legislators, the plan was finished. It only took two more drafts before Ed Bangs rubber-stamped it and the Idaho Wolf Conservation and Management Plan went to the Legislature where it was approved. The plan contained little conservation and lots of management. Though many asked every way they could think of, the state adamantly refused to consider creating wolf-viewing areas, never mind that such places could bring a heap of money into certain beleaguered counties.

Wolf advocates weren't happy with the plan because, even after all of the revisions, it didn't adequately protect wolves. I agreed. But on the other hand, I told them, it's Idaho; this was as good as it was going to get. With all of its faults, the plan is still the only shield the state has against the feds taking back control of wolves. Unfortunately, what's agreed to on paper, rather than what happens in the hills, is the only thing that counts.

It was my nature to stonewall people who boiled over with hatred toward wolves for reasons that were vague at best. In my new job, it was even permissible. I didn't mind their opinions except when they did things like stop me on a back road to tell me which way the sun comes up, or scream at me on the phone. But they were fun to toy with. After so many years in the wolf business, there wasn't a thing anyone could lay at my feet that I hadn't already seen or heard. Folks could think whatever they wanted about wolves and mouth off about it, too, but I wanted evidence of a real, insurmountable problem before I'd agree that even one wolf needed to die.

From the second I arrived in Idaho, I felt like I was in a war zone. My phone rang all the time about wolves killing livestock, Wildlife Services wanting permission to kill wolves, and everyone fighting with each other. It was what I was familiar with, even if it wasn't fun. The only good thing about it now was that I was where the buck stopped. Having some level of control also kept me from focusing for long on the fact that I'd left Helena and was living on the federal dime for the time being, in a big city, in a hotel with a popcorn machine in the lobby.

I actually liked the AmeriSuites. The maids fixed up my room every day and there was cable TV and no limit on popcorn or on hot water in the shower. It was a relief to go there after so much time in the office where the e-mail and phone calls were incessant. I took long walks around the mall area of Boise and passed not a soul on the sidewalks. Six months into my stay, the office secretaries told me I had to move out of the hotel or start paying for it. My allowance was up. I lived in another hotel for a while, but I could see daylight through the cracks in the wall and there was no popcorn at night. I bought a house only because my friend, Suzanne Laverty, made me.

It felt strange to sit in an office day after day and talk to others about what was happening at a ranch somewhere far away. It didn't seem right not being where the fur was flying, so after a while, I started avoiding the office altogether. I didn't mind the issues or talking on the phone; it was being cooped up in that building. Other than folks directly involved with the wolf wars, I didn't know anybody. Biologist Ben Matibag and I were in the same boat. We were hired on the same day in September 2000, and once placed in an office, we didn't know what to do with ourselves. At noon, neither of us wanted to sit in the windowless lunchroom, watching people eat tofu lasagna out of Tupperware and wordlessly work the daily crossword puzzle. We discovered our mutual dread of offices, and cities in general, after repeatedly seeing each other sitting next to a fence in the sun, eating a burger, watching cows graze in the pasture next door. The old farm they belonged to looked a lot like my parents' place in Garner with its rusted farm machinery and board piles. I knew from experience that it was junk that someone loved, and that given time, the whole place would be turned into a parking lot.

After a year or two, I felt my soul leaving my body every time I climbed the stairs to my office. I hated that place, and it didn't take long for me to get lathered up about it. Thankfully, no one but me wanted anything to do with wolves. Too controversial. But the controversy was the only thing that got me out of the office. Mostly I was spending my time in Clayton, Idaho, population 30 or so. It was because of a guy named Curt Hurless.

I remembered reading about Hurless in the newspapers in Helena. He attracted wolves like nobody I'd ever seen, which I thought should raise a big, red flag. I was just thrilled that I didn't have to deal with him or anybody else in Custer County, Idaho. Then, shortly before I was offered the job in Idaho, Bangs called me.

"How'd you like to drive over and check on a situation at the Hurless ranch?"

"Uh, what exactly do you want me to do?"

"Maybe just show him how to use a radio receiver," Bangs said. He made it sound like I'd be showing the man how to build a sandcastle.

A Nez Perce tribe biologist had loaned Hurless a receiver to monitor wolves in his area, more to get the guy off everybody's back than anything. Hurless commandeered most of trapper Rick Williamson's time, too, wanting Williamson to look at tracks in the dirt, or old scabs on a colt. He badgered Williamson endlessly to set traps, and when Williamson told him that the order had to come from me, Hurless called me about it – daily. He phoned every elected official in the state to claim that wolves were eating his calves, or running them around the pastures, which kept the bulls from getting the job done with the cows. In the end, Defenders of Wildlife paid him a grand total of $2,900 for the deaths of two calves and one adult cow.

Hurless had been a statistician in college and armed with that training, took to carrying charts filled with numbers showing how the presence of wolves affected cattle breeding. Soon he wore out the paper they were printed on. But the noise he made about wolves got the ear of politicians, livestock groups, Wildlife Services and the anti-wolf crowd. He was probably the first person to bring all of these people together, merging them into one giant organism until no one could tell one end from the other. It takes a certain amount of talent to do that, and to get important people with hectic schedules to travel half the day on a winding, narrow highway just to spend an afternoon in tiny Clayton, Idaho. But Hurless did it, and with style. He toured folks from the governor's office around the ranch he leased – the Broken Wing – and showed slides and videos of me capturing wolves and peeling the hides off of his dead calves. He fired up the barbeques, got the press there, and generally put on a show that would impress the biggest of public relations firms. His complaints about wolves made him a pseudo-celebrity statewide.

It was Ed Bangs' habit to send me to deal with the biggest pains in his ass. Naturally, once I took the federal wolf job in Idaho, he was thrilled that he didn't have to deal with Hurless anymore.

"He's all yours, Carter," Bangs said, believing that somehow, with me involved, everything would be fine. When I got through with ranchers, he told a reporter once, they were baking me pies, trying to adopt me, or wanting me to marry their daughters.

I showed up for Hurless's field day – and at all of the good ol' boy gatherings – to get to know these folks myself. I knew a few already because of my ties in Montana. In the sheep and cattle business in the West, there aren't so many players that you don't know them all sooner or later. I shook hands with everybody, but the ranchers weren't the folks I was there to see. A growing number of self-appointed wolf experts – anti-wolfers – had started popping up here and there in the newspapers and on websites. They'd been getting pretty long-winded about how wolves were going to ruin life as we knew it. I'd been in the wolf business for the better part of a dozen years and I'd never heard of these guys. But here they were, clinging to politicians' shirt tails.

Idaho wolf hysteria also triggered the birth of the Central Idaho Anti-Wolf Coalition, and a few of its members began worming their way into political events like the one at Hurless's ranch. Its founder, Ron Gillett, gained a surprising number of followers with his tedious, fire-and-brimstone style. Because the group managed to find friends in all of the cob-webby corners of the state, it dropped the "Central" from its name and became the Idaho Anti-Wolf Coalition. Gillett took his brand of evangelism around the state holding rallies and fundraisers, trying to convince people that the behemoth wolves we brought down from Canada were altogether different from the small, meek ones that used to live in Idaho's hills. Gillett coined a catchy phrase to describe the wolf's insatiable desire to kill everything in sight: "sport reflex killing." Saying he was sick of hearing about science and biology, Gillett claimed at a meeting once that wolves are terrorists on the order of Osama bin Laden.

Gillett and his disciples vowed to force the state to get rid of wolves once and for all by trying to gather enough signatures to put the issue on a statewide ballot and let Idahoans decide. The effort fell apart after the group discovered that many who signed the petition weren't registered voters. I thought it was a great idea. I'm always eager to give those who want to hang themselves as much rope as possible.

The biggest difference between folks like this and me was that I actually knew what I was talking about. I may not have been able to tell a rancher what killed his animal, but I sure as hell could tell him what didn't. So I waded into the field days and other meetings like them to hear these guys for myself – and make sure they knew who was running the show in Idaho.

I was usually invited to give everybody a rundown on the wolves as a way to introduce myself to those I hadn't met. At one event at Clayton's American Legion Hall, several rows of dirty, sunburned men frowned at me from under their sweat-stained hats. Freshly pressed politicians lined the walls. As long as I had their attention, I read them my pedigree: I was a government trapper and supervisor for 26 years as well as a wolf specialist. I was involved with wolves one way or another 10 years before they were reintroduced, and I've looked at more dead stock than you fellas can shake a stick at....

After that, I added my degrees and the fact that I was raised in a small rural town and worked on plenty of farms, just in case they thought I didn't know what hard work was. They shifted in their metal chairs. The ones that were leaning forward, ready to jump me, didn't quite know what to do. They were expecting a tie-dyed, pony-tailed hippie, I suppose.

Witnessing politicians visit the Broken Wing Ranch and tell each other how life in the great outdoors had gone down the toilet because of wolves was more than a little incredible. It made me wonder about their general intelligence. They repeated themselves over and over at town hall meetings all over Central Idaho. It wasn't the wolves that made me more inclined to be on the wolf's side, it was the macho swagger of people like this. They claimed that their anti-wolf stance was simply representative of Idahoans. But as far as I could tell, they represented very few.

Ed Bangs was right from the very beginning. Wolves have nothing to do with reality.

Generally, when I went to Clayton, so did Rick Williamson. We met on a highway pull-off away from town to talk about the latest happenings and strategize before we continued to the Broken Wing. During one trip to look at wolf tracks and listen to Hurless's wild ideas, we ended up in downtown Clayton for lunch. As we passed the general store on our way to a sandwich, Williamson pointed at a handmade sign in the window:

Kill all the Goddamn Wolves
and the People who Put Them Here

Having wolves around seemed to give everyone who was previously bored with life in tiny, isolated towns something new and spicy to complain about. It was a force more unifying than high school football games, church or the local watering hole. Being against wolves brought a certain solidarity even among lifelong enemies, and the reintroduction of wolves reaffirmed a collective neurosis among residents that the federal government was out to get them.

A man who raised rabbits up the highway from Clayton, near Challis, Idaho, phoned me because he was convinced that a wolf killed all of them. I went and looked, seeing six dogs running loose on the road leading to his house. The tracks around the torn-up rabbit pens were undoubtedly dog: round and small compared to huge, oval wolf tracks.

"I'm gonna sit out here and kill every wolf I see," he spluttered. "They come around my yard light at night! I seen 'em through the windows!"

"Just be careful shooting toward your neighbors' place," I said, tacking on a couple of remarks about all of the laws that protected wolves these days. I got in my truck and left. I didn't have time for this. Besides, the only thing he was going to put a hole in was his neighbor's wall.

It wasn't that Hurless didn't have occasional wolf trouble, but I told him that if he'd kept the dead stuff cleaned up the way his neighbors did, he might have had fewer predators paying regular visits. While I scouted around his ranch searching for potential travel corridors made by wolves, Hurless discovered a dead deer in his pasture. He wanted me to do a necropsy to see if wolves killed it. I examined it and concluded that it died from complications of a hunting arrow embedded in its hind leg. Not long afterward, he discovered another of his calves lying dead and he was mad as hell. He was sure I'd deny that wolves killed it. There were no tracks, he said, but he knew wolves were to blame.

The calf lay against a rock outcropping on a two-lane dirt trail near the ranch house. The ground was hard-packed.

"Stay behind me," I motioned to Hurless. I wanted to get a good look at things before the scene was disturbed.

It was still early enough that the sun was at a steep angle. I squatted down to see if I could make out any depressions in the dirt. Hurless asked what I was doing.

There it was. A wolf track. Any later in the day and people would have trampled the mostly invisible clue while looking at the most obvious feature at the scene, the bloody calf. It was enough to put the wolves at the carcass, for there had been obvious signs of feeding, but I needed to find out whether the wolves did the killing. I took out my knife and removed what was left of the calf's hide. What was underneath was what counted. There were two or three bloody tooth punctures on the sternum and on one shoulder. If Hurless hadn't noticed his dead calf immediately, or if the wolves had eaten this final remnant, there wouldn't have been enough evidence to say exactly what happened. At least for me, there wouldn't have been enough.

That was the moment that I earned Hurless's respect. He insisted I stay for lunch. Later, he talked about me finding that track to anyone who would listen.

Based on this latest skirmish, I got permission from the U.S. Fish and Wildlife Service and ordered a helicopter so I could dart the wolves for relocation. I believed the guilty party was the Twin Peaks pack, a lone pair of alphas that roamed the area close by. I found and darted both in a half hour. The female was pregnant and was an easy target, but the male, though dazed from a dose of drugs, managed to stay on his wobbly legs and try to escape. My pilot, Steve Prescott, let me out in the steep, jagged rocks and sagebrush, and I walked close behind the wolf, coaxing him as he staggered downhill to a place where the helicopter could more easily land. The wolf kept a drunken eye on me and even managed to growl, but at least I didn't have to carry him. When we got close enough to a clearing, I sneaked another shot of drugs into his hip and loaded him onto the chopper.

We landed in Hurless's pasture where he stood videotaping the whole thing, grinning hugely. Biologists and volunteers would tend to the animals, put them in metal crates, and truck them to their next home, more than 100 miles away – and far from livestock.

As long as I had access to a helicopter and a pilot, I wanted to catch two black, sibling wolves in the Jureano pack, and flew out the next day to find them. They hadn't bothered Hurless – yet – but were staring just a little too long at the cows at a profitable dairy 80 highway miles away in Salmon. It took me two days to get them, both of which I had collared only the year before. When the pilot brought me in on the second one, B-81, the wolf used power lines to avoid capture. I wasn't sure the wolf did it on purpose, but I had to smile at what seemed like animal ingenuity. He took us on a wild chase through trees, and along treacherous, steep hillsides and narrow canyons. At one point, he hid in thick brush where I had to get out and walk along the canyon rim, throwing rocks to flush him out. When he fled his hiding place, I ran back to the helicopter and the chase was on again. I eventually got a clear shot and the dart sailed right into his hip. He kept running, finding a forest road where he poured on the steam trying to get away from the helicopter. The wolf was closing fast on a parked Suburban where two men were taking a quiet pee. The men zipped up, got back in, and drove away. The wolf was right behind them, but out of their view because of a bend in the road. He slowed and staggered, eventually falling over exactly where the men had been. If those guys had only dillydallied another minute, they could have had something to talk about for the rest of their lives.

Idaho Cattle Association president Dave Nelson, whom everyone called "Big Dave," pushed me to hand out permits under the Endangered Species Act so that ranchers could kill wolves that attacked livestock on private property. I pushed back. We didn't agree philosophically on the presence of wolves, or on what constituted a real problem. Wolves walking around did not a problem make. I didn't want folks thinking I was handing out permits like they were candy.

"We've gotta get on this wolf thing, Carter, or you and me are gonna go toe to toe." This was Big Dave's favorite tune and he used it on me regularly, but fortunately it didn't come to that. He and I treated each other like big, ornery horses that refuse to get in their trailer without a fight. We walked each other in circles and tried again. We never really convinced each other of anything; we just wore each other down. Big Dave pulled all the strings in Washington that he could get his bear paw-sized hands on to make sure the means were there when I needed to kill or move wolves.

Many wolf issues happened on public land. The argument – and a good one – was that losing livestock to predators in these areas should be an accepted cost of doing business. It shouldn't be the government's place to intervene. It makes sense, but it's an argument that has never gained much traction. Maybe there are too many other things in life that need attention, or maybe livestock interests are just too powerful. Or maybe most people are just unaware that the system still operates as though the West is still being settled.

All I knew was that, even with the wolf population growing fast, I could count on one hand the number of folks with real wolf trouble. They were quiet and shunned publicity, and they were too busy with ranch life to join anti-wolf groups.

In the mountains around the East Fork of the Salmon River, several miles from the Broken Wing Ranch, small disasters were unfolding daily. The Whitehawk pack, with its snow-white matriarch that wolf fans named Alabaster, had been on a killing spree for several years – taking down cattle, sheep and guard dogs. It happened on public land, but also on a private cattle ranch that belonged to Dick and Betty Baker.

The feds had been picking off the Whitehawks one at a time for their offenses, though no one really wanted to pull the trigger on Alabaster. Getting rid of them a few at a time didn't make much difference. Alabaster added puppies each spring, and each spring, when there were new mouths to feed and when a sheep rancher drove his bellowing animals right into the Whitehawks' territory on national forest land – the cycle of killing started again.

The Bakers were several families of fine people who had raised cattle along the East Fork for generations and whose ranches dotted the steep country. They used federal grazing allotments, too, and did their spring calving on their own property. But the wolves didn't know the difference. A few wolves, older ones usually, visited the dark pastures early in the morning, choosing their victim and chasing it around a few times, making sure they could take it down. Then they closed their powerful jaws around the calf's back end, and under the webbing of its front legs. They pulled it down and began their meal before the calf was dead.

Dick and Betty's ranch was surrounded by public land – the kind that's perfect for big, wild carnivores. They gave me permission to try everything I could think of to keep any more of their cattle from falling victim to the Whitehawks. They didn't have to be so conciliatory; I'd given the families written permission to kill wolves that were killing their cattle. Dick could have sat up nights waiting for the next attack and simply shot whichever wolf he got in his crosshairs. His brother, Eddie, had done it once already, and he'd been justified, according to federal agents. Still, the Bakers were patient, agreeing to let me try and put more collars in the pack so that we could try and scare them away using Radio Activated Guard boxes. They agreed to my plan because they wanted to be good citizens about it. The Bakers' biggest worry, next to losing valuable cattle, was their name hitting the papers.

The Whitehawks had been wearing collars since last spring – all but one elusive yearling – and after they were collared, they started getting into regular trouble with the Bakers' cattle, first at Eddie's, then at Dick's. I was sure my plan would work, but I needed Rick Williamson's help and he was being hijacked by the commotion at the Hurless ranch. Something had to give.

I found myself wearing a path between Boise and Clayton. I liked Curt Hurless in spite of myself, but I'd gradually recognized that he was running my business. He fancied himself a liaison between the people in his neck of the woods and the government wolf program and even called me with suggestions about how I should spend the money that Big Dave Nelson scored for wolf control. He also thought I should get the Secretary of the Interior over to Clayton for a show-and-tell wolf capture, and even offered to use the compensation money given to him by Defenders of Wildlife to buy more radio collars. If it wasn't Hurless calling, it was someone complaining about the man. The whole situation was grating on my nerves.

When the tribe wanted its radio receiver back, Hurless refused. Pretty soon wolf supporters wanted receivers, too, because they believed Hurless was tracking and killing radio-collared wolves. I was hearing about it from up in the ranks, too. I asked Hurless to return the receiver but he refused to give it to anyone except me. I spent half the day driving to Clayton to get it, but by the time I arrived, I'd made a decision: Instead of taking it away from him, I'd exchange the tribe's receiver for one belonging to the Fish and Wildlife Service. I didn't know why Hurless felt like he had to have a receiver or what he was up to exactly, but I knew he wasn't killing wolves. A receiver was a small price to pay to keep him on my side. I'd seen the kind of mess he could stir up. I decided to let him have his fun. My managers didn't like it.

"Just trust me on this," I told them.

A group of wolves started hanging out at the Challis landfill, eating garbage and roaming as far as the Broken Wing Ranch. The dump was more than a dozen miles from Clayton, but Hurless called me about it daily, just to tell me the latest. Williamson set up Radio Activated Guard boxes inside the open garbage pit and rigged them so they wouldn't go off until the wolves were standing at its rim. When one of the wolves triggered the box, the sounds of explosions and gunfire sent it running at a full gallop. The following week, when biologists from the tribe flew to do routine surveys, the wolf was near McCall, almost 100 miles from the dump.

But when Hurless complained again, not just about wolves getting into his cattle but about wolves hanging around Clayton and leaving prints and scaring people, I called Williamson and told him to load his rifle. He ended up shooting an uncollared wolf that was running around with a collared female known as B-104. These wolves were unrelated to the Twin Peaks wolves that I'd darted and sent away. It was a whole new development.

I hoped shooting one wolf would end things, but B-104 kept hanging around Hurless's cattle. I finally told Williamson to shoot her, too, even though she hadn't committed any crimes. B-104 had an old leg injury that must have made daily life painful, so perhaps he put her out of her misery.

With this latest dead wolf, I realized that Hurless was running the show and I was jumping just like everyone else.

When Wildlife Services trapper Chuck Carpenter – the son of Roy Carpenter from my eagle days – decided that a few scratches on the neck of one of Hurless's newborn colts might have been made by yet more wolves, I scoffed. Hurless wanted me to issue him a permit to do his own wolf control, but he'd pushed my last button. This time I said no. A half hour later, Williamson called to say he'd set several traps in Hurless's pasture just to keep him happy. I told him to pull them up.

He did it, but when he explained things to Hurless, Williamson said, the man cursed me and picked up several boulders, one after another, some of them weighing maybe 30 pounds. He heaved them over his head and into the river.

"Then he stomped over to his haying machine and pounded a dent in it," Williamson reported breathlessly. "And *then* he pulverized one of his fence posts with a rock!"

But there was more.

"Then he said 'I'm gonna throw a lariat out in this field and me and Niemeyer are gonna get in that circle and decide this thing.'" Williamson was beside himself as he neared the end of his tale.

"I just got in my truck and got outta there. I don't think I'd go anywhere near Clayton for a while if I was you."

Hurless called me several weeks later.

"Hey, big guy, I haven't heard from you in a while. What's the deal?"

"Well, Curt," I took a deep breath and propped my boots on the desk. This could turn into a long conversation. "I heard you were madder than hell and beat a fence post into the ground because of me, so I kinda figured you weren't in the mood to talk."

"Aw, shit. I'm sorry, Carter. I was just having a bad day."

There weren't many people who could explain away something like that, but I believed him. We talked for quite a while, ending with me agreeing to stop by soon for a hamburger.

"I still think we should have tossed a loop out in my pasture that day," Hurless added. "If I kicked your ass, we'd put those wolf traps back in the ground, and if you kicked my ass, we'd leave 'em out."

"Curt, you probably could've kicked my ass, but the outcome would've been the same. I ain't letting Rick set any more traps at your place."

It seemed that of all the public land in central Idaho, the Whitehawks should have been able to find refuge in a place like the rugged Sawtooth National Recreation Area. But they couldn't. That area, like so many other national forests, was full of livestock in the summer – precisely when a wolf pack is searching for meat to feed its growing pups.

Eight or so years after reintroduction, all of the places where wolves could live were full to the brim with packs. Like people, wolves are mostly intolerant of newcomers, and for that reason alone, I stopped moving them when they got in trouble with livestock. Instead, I killed them. It was a relief to some and outrageous to others, particularly because a lot of wolves died while roaming public land. But wolves that kill livestock, once they start doing it, rarely stop. And moving a wolf into another pack's territory might make certain people feel better, but it's a death sentence for the wolf. In my estimation, there was little choice and we were getting there with the Whitehawks.

Jon Marvel and others were determined to stop the death of even a single Whitehawk wolf. They spread themselves out in the Sawtooth valley where the aerial gunning would take place. He and I had heated exchanges about the situation and I finally agreed that if he told everybody to get out of the area, I'd see if I could find someplace to move the wolves, even though I knew that was a long shot. But filmmaker Vanessa Shulz and her crew, who'd put together a bit of propaganda about how badly federal biologists treat wolves, followed Rick Williamson trying to determine where he'd set traps for the Whitehawks, hoping to interfere with the capture. They shot video of the piles of equipment in his truck bed and even hired an airplane to follow him.

When I heard about it, I called Marvel and told him the deal was off. Marvel said he couldn't control everyone, and that the film crew wasn't affiliated with his folks. It didn't matter. No one seemed to understand the mechanics of the situation. We had to catch the wolves in order to move them and we had no chance of getting our hands on the Whitehawks, if people were out there screwing around with our traplines. It was another case of wolf advocates being the wolf's worst enemy. I made a personal vow that day of being purposely vague about my plans.

It didn't take long for word of all this to get out. Big Dave Nelson tore me a new one for making any kind of pact with Jon Marvel. Get on with killing the damn wolves, he said.

Curt Hurless, despite the fit he'd thrown, had become my biggest advocate. He stood up at a local meeting and endorsed me. If I can work with Carter, anybody can, he told the crowd. I grinned and gave him a thumbs-up.

A couple of years had passed and I'd gotten to know pretty much everybody in Clayton. At yet another meeting, I brought Bob Ruesink, the Boise Fish and Wildlife Service supervisor, with me. A small but significant showing of brass and about 40 ranchers settled onto folding chairs in the community hall. I was impressed that everyone was so well-behaved. Tempers only flared occasionally. Things were going pretty well until a man in a red cap stood and began hurling insults at the government officials. The crowd tried to silence him, but without much heart. Once the meeting ended, the brass made a beeline for their cars, leaving me, Rick Williamson and others facing several dozen Claytonites, and the bar next door that had just opened its doors for the evening.

On a hunch, I'd brought along a few hundred dollars worth of government-issue 12 gauge non-lethal munitions, including rubber bullets, beanbag rounds and cracker shells. Nobody ever passes up a chance to shoot a few of these off. Someone found a brand new aluminum trash can and dragged it around back of the community hall. Williamson and I showed everybody how all of it worked and the crowd took turns pulverizing the garbage can and reveling in getting a few taxes back by burning up government ammo. People had gotten used to the idea that they couldn't just shoot a wolf without a federal permit, so shooting rubber bullets and bean-bags and cracker shells at them was the next best thing.

It didn't seem like training to them, but it was. Those who pulled the trigger could see that rubber bullets traveled a long way while beanbag rounds only launched about 30 yards. Cracker shells exploded with a terrific boom that echoed through the valley, revealing what they really were: firecrackers. Everybody was proud of hitting the garbage can consistently. When we were finished, it was a shiny, flattened mess. Somebody put it back and our small crowd slinked away to the bar.

I don't know what the regulation book says about federal employees and alcohol, but I am a firm believer in mingling with the locals and there's no better way to do it than to tip a beer with them. I settled onto a bar stool and had three bottles greet me, courtesy of my Clayton friends. That was probably against regulations, too. I got a few refreshing swigs down before the man in the red cap got in my face, literally. He was the guy from the community hall meeting who'd shouted down speakers, interrupted everyone, and been, generally, an ass. If it weren't for him, the meeting would have seemed more civil. Now, his nose was about six inches from mine as he cursed and bellowed about the goddamn government and wolves. Spit flew with every word. I just stared at him. Then, taking off on another anti-fed tangent, he mentioned something about once working for the U.S. Forest Service.

"Whoa, whoa, wait a second," I yelled over him. 'You worked for the Forest Service?"

He blinked. He looked genuinely puzzled. But I wasn't finished.

"Hell, you're a bro!" I slapped him on the shoulder, then offered him a handshake. "You're an old government man just like me."

I'd rendered the windbag speechless. Several guys at the bar heard the exchange and smiled.

The man in the red cap turned toward me. I tensed, ready for a punch.

"You sonofabitch," he said, fighting a grin.

The Whitehawks didn't always choose livestock for their meals. In fact, the group sometimes disappeared for an entire winter, following deer and elk into other valleys and eating them instead. But they always showed up again in the spring – right when sheep were turned out to graze and calving time had arrived, and right about the time that wolf pups are born.

During one week in the spring of 2002, I took 22 phone calls about the Whitehawk wolves. That week, three incidents were attributed to the pack. Jon Marvel called me the most, warning me that he would shortly be suing several federal agencies over shooting wolves on public land. I couldn't worry about that. My biggest concern was changing the Whitehawks' behavior. If I could do that, I could save the livestock *and* the wolves.

When the Whitehawks established themselves as livestock killers, I asked Rick Williamson to kill a couple of them, hoping it would make them stop. Williamson had picked them off one at a time until he'd taken five of the pack's 10 members. For a while, they stopped killing the Bakers' cattle. After that, environmental websites and the media went into overdrive, and the Whitehawks gained a massive following worldwide, partly because of a program launched by Defenders of Wildlife.

Suzanne Laverty hatched the idea – the guardian program – during one of the Whitehawks' killing sprees in 2000, and for a while it worked. By the next grazing season, Defenders of Wildlife volunteers were poised to camp with rancher Bill Brailsford's sheep on his Sawtooth National Recreation Area grazing allotment.

But Brailsford turned his sheep loose in 2001 without mentioning to anyone exactly what day he'd be doing it. Suddenly, there were nearly 2,000 sheep wandering around in the middle of the Whitehawks' territory.

Ranchers with federal leases usually turn their animals out in the mountains in June. Although news of recent killings by the Whitehawk pack had spread far and wide, it didn't occur to Forest Service officials that the pack might be lurking right where Brailsford's sheep were headed. I wondered later if Brailsford might have considered moving his sheep to avoid the wolves. It wouldn't have mattered. There wasn't another site available.

Not too many nights into their summer encampment, Brailsford's herder jerked awake, his four Pyrenees guard dogs barking furiously. The sheep stampeded through an aspen thicket near his wagon. Dust choked him. He jumped out to see what was happening. In the dim light, he could make out the bloody remains of eight sheep strewn across the sagebrush, and the oldest of the guard dogs sprawled out, dead. The younger dogs cowered under the sheep wagon.

When it was light, the herder walked off the mountain to the closest pay phone and called Brailsford first, then Rick Williamson.

"Lobos," he told Williamson in excited Spanish. "Come quick."

When Williamson relayed the incident to me, my first thought was that pups had to be close by. Killing the guard dog seemed like an overly aggressive act unless the wolves had youngsters to protect.

The day after the attack, a Nez Perce biologist, Isaac Babcock, unaware of what had happened, sat on a hillside and counted the Whitehawks' pups playing in a meadow. He wrote the number "9" in his field journal. Cheered by this unusually large litter, he packed up and descended the ridge, reaching his truck as the sun was setting. At the road, Babcock encountered Williamson and eagerly told him about the pups. By the time Williamson finished telling him about the dead sheep, Babcock's smile was gone.

Maybe it would have happened anyway, simply because wolves were around, but the constant circus in Clayton caused the media to take notice. I was giving at least one news interview a day. I made a lot of friends at newspapers and television outlets. I think it was because I wasn't sophisticated enough to make things mysterious. I just laid it on the line, whatever the issue. I tried to give everyone as much information as I could because I figured they were going to hear more rumors than truth anyway. I wanted to train reporters to call me first. It must have been a good strategy because I didn't get in trouble with the U.S. Fish and Wildlife Service's public affairs gurus in Washington D.C., or at the regional level in Portland, Oregon. In fact, I sometimes got brief notes from busy federal flacks telling me I gave a good, even thoughtful interview. But I couldn't in good conscience pawn a reporter off to someone else. Most of the stuff happening with wolves involved several layers of detail that no one knew except me.

ABC News anchorman Peter Jennings decided to include the topic of wolf reintroduction in his series, *In Search of America*. He traveled to Idaho to interview a few folks, me included. I didn't fully appreciate the gravity of what he was doing until later when I could see the entire program. He was attempting to show how the founding fathers' principles worked on the land and in everyday life. Everyone in my Boise office was atwitter at the presence of this media mega-star. Right before the cameras rolled, a public affairs officer grabbed my glasses off my face, polished the lenses, then placed them on me again. They were a mess, she said. The interview was short and unsatisfying, but then again, it was a blip on a huge topic that would be televised nationally. I'd learned not to expect much when it came to big media outlets.

The only thing that saved the day was that Jennings said he'd like to have dinner with me and a few others. His staff picked a quiet, intimate place on Boise's Basque block. Jennings, I discovered, was a thoughtful, interesting man and seemed genuinely interested in the issues that wolves brought to the land. I told him to come back soon and I'd take him and his wife on a wolf-watching tour. He readily agreed and promised to be in touch. We finished up our meal and talked about what the rest of the Friday evening might have in store. It was dark but still early.

"What's a guy like you do in town?" he asked, signing the bill for all of us.

"I thought I'd head across the street for some dancing at Humpin' Hannah's," I said. "You wanna come?"

Jennings chuckled.

"You're not going to wear that shirt, are you?" he said.

He grinned when I asked him what was wrong with my Southwestern-pattern polo shirt. It was my favorite. His assistant turned red and apologized profusely for her boss even as he kept up a mild chuckle. The next day, I was in the office, as had become my habit on weekends, and I opened an e-mail from her. She was still distraught.

I can't believe he said that. I am so sorry, Carter. I thought your shirt was nice...

Around the time Peter Jennings came to town and insulted my wardrobe, a guy from Hollywood called and left a message at my office.

"You're sure a hard guy to track down," Tom Mickel said, explaining that he was a movie producer. I admitted that I didn't have a phone at my house.

He wanted to get together and talk about doing a movie based on my life. I didn't quite believe what I was hearing. What about my life? I hadn't gone over Niagara Falls in a barrel or been shot up in a war or taken massive amounts of recreational drugs. I'd always thought such things were prerequisites. But Mickel and a cohort had already written the screenplay. I sort of wanted to see it, but they didn't offer me a copy. Instead, Mickel handed me a check for nearly $7,000. He wanted me to be a technical advisor.

"I guess I'm kinda confused about why you fellas are doing this," I said, looking at the check. It was a lot of money, but I wasn't sure how I felt about it.

"Well, I'll tell you why," Mickel leaned forward, lacing his fingers. "When I look on the Internet to get the story on wolves in the U.S., the name I see over and over is Carter Niemeyer."

I hired a Los Angeles lawyer that Mickel recommended. I needed one, he said. But I didn't cash the check in case it secretly tied me to something I didn't understand. It would be just like me to get catapulted into some crazy scheme. Several weeks went by. Then several more. I didn't hear from Mickel. I looked him up and left a couple of messages, which went unreturned. One day, I got an e-mail. Funding for the deal had fallen apart, he said, but didn't elaborate. After Mickel and company disappeared. I consulted my attorney who told me the check appeared to be legit, despite the producer's disappearing act.

"Go ahead and cash it," he said.

I did. It wasn't rubber.

More important than my Hollywood future was the announcement from Curt Hurless that he was getting out of the cattle business. He did it willingly, and as far as I know, he didn't blame his business decision entirely on wolves. He planned on ditching the headaches of ranching to take a job at a combination store/restaurant/gas pump that his parents were constructing on the outskirts of Clayton. Lynne Stone, one of Idaho's most outspoken wolf advocates, didn't like Hurless and was glad to hear he'd be choosing a profession that didn't include wolves as collateral damage. I'd met Stone within days of taking the Idaho job when we practically crashed head-on on a dusty road near Stanley. She could out-hike anybody and almost outdistance a wolf. She knew the central Idaho wilderness well enough to write books about it. On the day I met her, however, she rolled down her window.

"And who are *you*?" she asked in a cutting tone that told me she might already know.

She did, she said, and she also knew my rap sheet as a wolf killer. No matter how few wolves I'd ever had to kill personally, I couldn't escape the reputation I'd somehow earned as a mass murderer of lobos.

It wasn't easy, but over time, Stone and I came to respect each other and even became friends. I grin every time I think about it, because that day in Stanley, I was public enemy number one.

Stone complained about Hurless and other ranchers along the Salmon River's wild and scenic East Fork, and about the horrors of public land grazing in general. She repeated a story – a lot – about Hurless leaving a dead cow in the river the year before I came to Idaho. She couldn't understand why some ranchers couldn't clean up their acts.

"I don't know, Lynne," I told her after hearing the cow-in-the-river story the umpteenth time. "I think Curt is a new man now that he's gotten rid of his cattle. He just seems more relaxed."

"Oh, really?" she snorted.

"Why don't you just forget all that stuff about the cow? It ain't doin you or anybody any good to keep harping on it. You gotta take him for what he is now."

She reluctantly agreed to give this outlook a try, but she was loath to give up bitching about folks in Custer County and their attitudes toward wolves. And she didn't like Hurless having that radio receiver. That was fine. She didn't need to like it, and neither did anyone else. But it gave Hurless something to do and still feel like he was involved somehow. If federal property was all it took to keep him quiet, he could have the damn thing forever.

Defenders of Wildlife offered to replace Bill Brailsford's guard dog, but it was too little too late. The battle cries had begun. Politicians had gotten wind of things and, as a result, wanted me to start killing the Whitehawk wolves. Now. The Forest Service supervisor was, for the time being, on my side. He told Brailsford that there would be no wolf shooting in this national forest – at least not on his watch – and if that didn't set well, Brailsford was welcome to move his sheep somewhere else.

I spent the better part of a day on the phone trying to calm everyone down. It seemed to be what I was always doing. The bickering was fraying my nerves. While everybody was quarreling, the sheep were roaming in the Whitehawks' territory too early, unescorted by anything more than a herder and one less guard dog.

The Buffalo Ridge pack formed in 2002, near Clayton and very near the Sawmill Station, the store run by the Hurless family. Curt and his brother, Dana, could sometimes see all of the wolves out the store's windows.

Occasionally the wolves visited a nearby steelhead pond that belongs to the Idaho Department of Fish and Game. The water got very low once, and the wolves waded in and gorged themselves.

Curt Hurless took a keen interest in the Buffalo Ridge wolves, mostly because they were around his place a lot. He kept track of them using his receiver, and muttered to himself when they killed one of the many elk that also frequented his family's property. Dana Hurless was no fan of wolves, but he grinned as he shot video of the pack having a case of diarrhea after eating all those fish, or as the wolves crossed the road and up the steep cliffs behind the gas station. In the evenings, the brothers would sometimes venture out to hear the pack howl. The only way they got wolves in their crosshairs was with a camera.

The wolves left deep, perfect tracks – hundreds of them – in the mud at the holding pond. People started hearing about it; a few visited the pond to make plaster casts. Soon, however, the water level was restored and the tracks were submerged. The last time I ate a burger at the Sawmill Station, Hurless was selling plaster Buffalo Ridge tracks for $40 each and had already sold quite a few to tourists.

In 2003, I found one of the wolves dead, its face pulled back into a grimace, its legs straight, the pads of its feet torn and bloody. It had tumbled down a huge rock slope, landing akimbo at the bottom. Wolves just don't die like that. It had been poisoned.

Sodium fluoroacetate, or 1080, will kill just about anything, and getting dead with 1080 isn't pleasant. Wildlife Services still uses it in collars on sheep to kill coyotes in some western states. It is also a common ingredient in rodent poison, so it's no mystery how someone had a sack or two sitting around. Federal agents never found out what the wolf ate that contained 1080. In fact, they didn't look very hard. They just folded the wolf up and put it in a giant picnic cooler and drove away. The case was never solved.

A wolf that eats meat poisoned with 1080 engages in uncontrollable running, then cardiac arrhythmia and convulsions before falling over dead. It appeared that's what happened to this Buffalo Ridge wolf. The same thing would happen to a pet dog. It also can kill most everything else that takes a bite of the meat: bears, lions, eagles, ravens, and smaller, less sexy animals like weasels, skunks and raccoons.

When I called the Hurless brothers with the news, they were ready to settle things their own way.

"If I ever find out who did it, *I'll* deal with 'em," Dana said. "And the feds can have the leftovers." Dana had trained his dog to retrieve shed elk antlers and the two regularly roamed the hills where the poison had been tossed.

But that was only the beginning of the end for the Buffalo Ridge wolves. Five years later, the pack killed cattle on national forest land. The Idaho Department of Fish and Game – the new guardians of wolves in the state – ordered all of them shot, putting an end to a favorite photography subject for Hurless, and rendering his plaster paw prints historical souvenirs.

Saving the Whitehawks depended on having a sufficient number of radio collars in the pack; without them, Radio Activated Guard boxes and telemetry were useless. At one point, Rick Williamson and I took Gina Patton on our trapline. She worked for the tribe as a wolf biologist, but also was training the Defenders of Wildlife volunteers who had set up camp with Brailsford's sheep.

We didn't mean to, but we caught a Whitehawk puppy. Defenders volunteer Cheri Beno was along, too, giddy at the chance to hold the pup. It was too small for a regular radio collar, and we dithered about what to do. It's never good to catch a pup. They're often too small to collar safely and it puts the rest of the pack on high alert. But this might be our only chance.

Williamson wondered if we could take apart a regular radio collar and affix the transmitter to something small enough to fit around the puppy's neck, yet break away once it became too snug. It was a great idea, but we couldn't find something of the correct stretchiness. We dug around in Williamson's camp trailer. Rubber bands? Not strong enough. Cloth? Too restrictive.

"What about my bra?" asked Patton.

Williamson and I stopped digging.

"I think the elastic would be perfect, don't you?" she beamed.

Patton turned over the item and Williamson went to work with a pair of scissors. Soon, using a can of pork and beans as a size model, he fashioned a miniature, stretchy collar. I assured Patton that the government would reimburse her for her donation. And in a burst of cheer, which was rare given the Whitehawk mess, I named the tiny wolf T-Cup.

Patton took the pup in her arms and sneaked through the brush with it just as the sun went down. She got as close as she could to the rest of the pack, then put the pup down. It bounded happily back to its pack. We found the collar later, a gnarled mess. The others had taken one sniff of the odd object and chewed it off the youngster.

The collars that were already in the pack would have to do.

Brailsford was ambivalent about an experiment to see if the Whitehawk wolves could be run off. He was anxious about strangers being around his animals and disrupting their routine.

It was better than more dead sheep, Suzanne Laverty pointed out.

When Brailsford finally gave the green light, volunteers set up camp and installed fladry on the sheep bed grounds. Fladry is a simple, nearly ancient tool comprised of a long piece of twine with flapping ribbons sewn to it. It was used in Europe to funnel wolves into a designated area during a hunt because, for some reason, wolves are afraid of the moving ribbons. In the case of livestock protection, it keeps the wolves from approaching their intended prey.

Several times, the volunteers, armed with telemetry so they could pinpoint the pack's location, ran the wolves off in early morning darkness by screaming and banging pots and pans. The herders were sleeping lightly, too, and fired their guns into the air.

The guardian concept seemed to be working. I sent e-mail to everyone I could think of to showcase not just the successful experiment, but to demonstrate that people who fought a lot were also capable of working together. All it took was a collective will to fix the problem.

The bliss didn't last, however. The following spring, the Whitehawks were back in the East Fork killing calves at Dick and Betty Baker's ranch.

I was out of options. I knew that Rick Williamson, who had examined the Bakers' dead calves and confirmed that the wolves did it, was now standing in their living room waiting for me to call and tell him what I'd decided.

Everything I'd tried had failed, and it churned my stomach. I'd *promised* everybody that we could fix this thing and I was wrong. I dialed the Bakers' number as slowly as I could.

I put my shotgun in my truck, alongside boxes of shells and an overnight bag. I had barely exited Boise, heading east on the freeway, when my phone rang. Suzanne Laverty asked if I was on the road yet. It was barely light.

"Are you going to kill them?" she asked.

"Yeah." I didn't need to explain. She'd been in on all of it.

She sounded like she was sobbing. For years, her entire life had revolved around trying to save wolves.

"I'm sorry, Suzanne."

She took a moment. It was awkward. She was one of a hundred or more people who followed this pack not just with interest, but fondness.

"I'm not crying because of the wolves," she said, finally. "I'm crying for you."

Shooting Alabaster was going to be like killing a pet dog that belonged to the whole country. I jerked forward in my harness to test its holding power. Under the doorless helicopter, Idaho's delicately greening backcountry rushed by.

I heard my pilot's voice before I was ready. "There's that white one, Carter. She's coming up on our right."

She looked like something out of a fairy tale. I could see why people were enamored of her. She stood watching us in a patch of low, scrubby pine as though she was noticing a hawk drifting by. I lifted the shotgun, pointed it out the helicopter and chambered a shell.

Before we'd seen her, I imagined something happening to turn this whole thing on its head. Maybe someone would radio us and say that lawyers had succeeded with an injunction. The weather might turn us back, or the wolves might escape into thick timber. Perhaps the telemetry in the plane would suddenly fail. Instead, Jack Fulton skillfully brought the helicopter lower and angled my side toward Alabaster. She put her ears back and turned away, laboring up the ridge. Her belly was low-slung, full of near-term pups. She wasn't afraid of this giant, noisy intruder and only trotted a little faster as we closed the distance.

Thirty years of predator control under my belt and suddenly I was choking. It made no sense. I'd had to kill wolves before and though I didn't like it, I didn't have much of a reaction to it. I'd never handled Alabaster, only her pack mates. Maybe it was her notoriety I was feeling, everyone else's love for her – the white wolf, Alabaster. Other than her name and her color, she was just another wolf, I told myself.

I tried to focus. My plan was to kill the adult wolves first so that they couldn't lead the yearlings into the trees and disappear. Youngsters were always followers. It was easy to use that behavior against them. Bob Danner piloted the little plane that was making tight circles above us. He and Rick Williamson were keeping an eye on the pack, but staying out of the helicopter's way.

Alabaster was 30 yards out my door, vanishing, then reappearing in the brush. An open meadow lay ahead of her. I clicked off the safety and waited for her to appear in a clearing. As she did, I squeezed the trigger. I fired again in case she was suffering.

Fulton said nothing, circling over the white wolf, now dotted red, for one last look before we leveled out and followed the airplane to her mate, B-47. He dashed downhill into thick timber. We circled for 10 minutes near an old log cabin with a broken down door. His collar signal was strong, but he'd disappeared from sight. I thought maybe he'd run into the cabin to hide. The only other cover was a slim stand of willows. Fulton set us down in a meadow near the cabin. I unhitched my safety gear, removed my helmet and stepped out with my shotgun. I looked in the cabin door. Nothing. Danner made a low pass over us and radioed that the wolf had to be close, according to the beeping telemetry signal. I poked around in the brush and bent down to look in a culvert under the road. Nothing. I climbed back in and we went back up, hovering only a few feet above the willows. The rush of wind from the helicopter beat down the wispy branches. It was a way to bump the wolf if he was hiding there.

"You just flew over him," Danner radioed. "He ran out of the willows behind you. Turn around."

Fulton pivoted the helicopter and again came up to the willows, laying them flat with rotorwash. The wolf was holding tight, invisible in the limited cover. But then he made the mistake of panicking and dashed into another thin clump of brush, stealing quick, wild-eyed looks and shrinking from the helicopter.

I pointed my shotgun into the feeble stems that shielded B-47 and fired. When Fulton set us down, I made my way to the crumpled, bloodied wolf and took him by his hind legs, slinging him onto the chopper.

Everyone was always focused on Alabaster, but the plain, gray male with no name except B-47 is the one that is stuck forever in my head. He was the wolf I collared years earlier in Carmen Creek, north of Salmon, Idaho, the day that a backwoods redneck threatened to kill me because of wolves. Now B-47 stood no chance of escaping, all because of that radio collar. If he hadn't been wearing it, no one could have known his hiding place. Seeing him cower like that, his tail between his legs, like he was just waiting to die, made me sick. In that moment, I began thinking differently about helicopters, too.

Betty Baker's words had started creeping into my mind of late: "If you're just going to kill them, why on earth did you bring them back?"

The alphas were dead, so killing the others would be simpler even though it was no less disgusting. We flew back to where Alabaster lay and Fulton helped me hoist her lifeless body into the helicopter next to her mate. I would skin them later and save their pelts.

Three wolves remained, two with radio collars and one without. It would have mattered little if the uncollared wolf escaped, but because things always seemed to go from bad to worse with the Whitehawks, the uncollared wolf was the next one in my sights. I killed it as it ran along a long stretch of open meadow where a few wildflowers were starting to bloom. Its sibling, B-121, met a similar, quick death, but B-123 made it hard on himself. He raced along a steep, rocky slope above Deer Creek, nearly tripping over boulders in his attempt to outrun us. The downdrafts and squirrelly winds made pursuing him into the V of the canyon dangerous. When Fulton got me as close as he dared, I aimed far ahead of the gray yearling as it tore down a steep slope. I fired every shell in the shotgun as fast as I could. The buckshot followed the wolf as it dashed into a mass of trees at the creek's edge. I couldn't tell if I'd hit it, but I feared that I couldn't have missed. The wolf appeared to tumble as it was swallowed by deep shadows. Bob Danner circled above us while we flew back and forth trying to see into the trees. After 20 minutes, Danner's voice came over my headset. According to the telemetry, the collar and the wolf wearing it were no longer moving.

While Bob Danner and Rick Williamson returned to the Challis airport, Fulton and I flew down the East Fork to Junior Baker's ranch. Junior was Eddie's son, and he and his parents emerged from the house as we landed in their pasture. They watched us in silence as we unloaded Alabaster and B-47 and flopped them on the grass. I'd left the three dead yearling wolves where they fell on the mountain. Their pelts were no good, as young as they were. The ravens and magpies would take care of their bodies, and I, along with others, retrieved their collars later.

More dead wolves in the East Fork; it had happened before with the Stanley, the White Cloud, and other packs – all killed by the government for sins against livestock. The East Fork was a great place for wolves, and because of it, those packs were eventually replaced by the group that had been known as the Whitehawks. The only reason this one was different was because I'd tried everything I could think of to keep from killing them.

I waited for Williamson to make the drive back from the airstrip before starting the skinning and necropsy. When he arrived, we tossed ropes over roof braces in Junior Baker's old barn and hoisted the wolves up, each by a hind leg.

"I wonder what people would say if they saw us doing this part," Williamson said. He adjusted the cap he always wore and put his knife expertly into Alabaster.

Her nine pups were about two weeks away from birth. When we finished our gruesome task, Junior Baker dug a hole with his backhoe and we buried the unborn puppies and the carcasses of their parents. The only thing in the stomachs of Alabaster and B-47 was the remains of a deer.

Dr. Ralph Maughan, a professor of political science at Idaho State University, and normally a soft-spoken, thoughtful man, yelled in my ear on Monday morning, then slammed down the phone before I could even open my mouth.

"I can't believe you wiped out the entire Whitehawk pack because they killed two calves and a fuckin sheep!"

He'd probably spend all day burning up the phone lines telling the world what a rotten s.o.b. I was. After that, he'd probably crucify me on his wolf website. But I believed I'd bent the rules until I broke them.

In the midst of the unending heap of questions and accusations thrown at me on e-mail and over the phone, I realized that the rumor mill that had been churning day and night since the Whitehawk mess began was now totally out of control. I was getting a crash course in human psychology and the old adage that perception is reality. Everyone had a value system by which they judged the Whitehawk wolves. I called Rick Williamson and asked him to put together notes about every Whitehawk situation he'd ever dealt with and I would do the same. Within several days, in between interviews, meetings and being cursed at on the phone, we completed the task. Combined, our accounts revealed a stunning outpouring of money, time and energy directed toward saving this pack. When we were done with the chronological list of Whitehawk offenses, it was half a dozen pages long and outlined the pack's behavior between 1998 and 2002. In total, they killed one cow, 13 calves, three yearling cattle, 17 sheep and a guard dog. The chronology also showed that we had tried everything we could think of to stop them. The Fish and Wildlife Service offices in Boise and Portland added the chronology to a news release so that at least the media would get it right. I hoped Ralph Maughan would take notice.

By late Monday, I was frazzled. The criticism was getting to be more like harassment and I was starting to take it personally. The ones that got to me said something like, "Do you know how hard I (or "we") worked to get wolves back in the West and now look what you've done!" Or ones that went on at length: "You are a murderer. Your act of killing the wolf pack is heinous, despicable and thoroughly disgusting. You are sick and depraved and I condemn you. How can you sleep at night? How do you look at yourself in the mirror? Where does the government find mental midgets like you? Do you guys do coke?" Again I wondered what these people knew about wolf recovery. With few exceptions, there weren't many who had the faintest clue about the federal rules that governed what we were trying to accomplish: a viable population of wolves in the Northern Rockies. Some said the rules stank. Well, I didn't write them, but I sure as hell was bound by them. If I didn't follow the rules, it was possible that my little corner of things in Idaho could trigger the landslide that caused the entire wolf experiment in the West to be rescinded. No, these people had no clue.

I sat there seething. It was past five o'clock and most everybody in the office was gone. Then Bob Ruesink poked his head in. As the guy in charge of federal endangered species work in Idaho, he often kept hours like mine.

"How're you doing?"

"I'm OK," I said, but I felt a lump rising in my throat. I really wasn't doing very well at all. He was the only one to ask.

Ruesink motioned to me and I followed him down the corridor to his office. I was relieved to get away from that computer screen.

"I don't want you to deal with this alone," he said, closing his door. We sat and talked for an hour. He called home and told his wife he'd be late for supper, then we burned up another hour. By the time I left, it was dark and raining, but I didn't mind. With help from Ruesink, I felt like a great weight had been lifted off of me.

My e-mail inbox had amassed more than 400 messages by the end of the week, many of them with capitalized expletives and exclamation points in the subject line. I scrolled down, but only recognized a few names. All of the messages were about the Whitehawks. I answered each one and attached two documents that I believed everyone should read: the Federal Register's final rule on reintroduction, where the elimination of livestock-killing wolves is specifically discussed, and the chronology that Williamson and I put together.

Many people were angry not just about the deaths of the wolves on the private Baker ranch, but about public grazing practices that had made other wolf executions permissible. Letters appeared in my mailbox raising the same questions over and over, and I started a stack on my desk that towered until it very nearly fell over. Prodded by remarks such as "I know you won't read this," or "I don't expect an answer from you," I decided that every person who wanted an answer was going to get one. I returned every one of the phone calls, too. I interrupted a few suppers, but no matter. People seemed shocked to hear from me and though they were extraordinarily pissed off about the reason I shot the Whitehawk wolves, they thanked me for bothering to explain.

In the mail, I also received separate letters from 11 county commissions in Idaho saying they knew that shooting the Whitehawk pack was a difficult decision and thanked me for upholding the rules. A letter from the Idaho Anti-Wolf Coalition encouraged me to keep up the killing.

A lot of people accused me of killing the Whitehawks to appease the other side. There was no way, I'd discovered, to make everyone happy, or anyone for that matter. Ten years from now most people won't remember a thing about any of this, nor about what it took to get wolves here in the first place, I thought. And I was right.

These days, in a remote canyon of Idaho's East Fork of the Salmon River, not far from where Alabaster took her last breath, a new wolf pack is roaming. And last I heard, they were in trouble at the Baker ranch.

EPILOGUE

My job ended in January 2006. Wolves were handed over to the state of Idaho, oddly on the same day that I threw in the towel. This was a big affair in the eyes of Idaho because it meant gaining the upper hand. Soon, if the legal battles over de-listing went its way, the state would be free to kill wolves at the least offense and a hunting season could bring the wolf population down to the very minimum the feds would find acceptable, and no more. In a small ceremony on January 2, in the governor's private chambers, television cameramen crowded each other while the rest of us sat shoulder to shoulder in folding chairs. Gale Norton, then Secretary of the Interior, did the honors and nodded my way, thanking me for getting Idaho's wolf population into such good shape. Gov. Dirk Kempthorne did the same and so did the U.S. Fish and Wildlife Service's regional director. The whole thing was surreal. Had we really arrived at this day?

Afterward we mingled, and rancher Phil Soulen and I compared ties. I'd chosen one that morning with a wolf on it. His had dozens of little white sheep. Gale Norton's handler from Washington D.C. waded through the crowd to tell me the Secretary wanted to meet me, so could I hang around? The Secretary finally worked her way over, but was quickly whooshed away by the governor. Still, I had enough time to invite her to my retirement party that night.

My kids, and two of my late brother's kids came to town for the party that my new wife, Jenny, had spent weeks organizing. She and I were married the previous December. We'd met several years earlier at a wolf hearing, of all things. I'd never intended to tie the knot again, but she was the kind of person who made me change my mind. I had no idea what she had planned the night of my retirement, but I'd made one request: minimum talking, maximum dancing. She arranged for Roy Heberger, who ran the wolf program before I came along, to bring his blues band with him. The party was at the Basque Center, which had a full bar, a big parquet floor for lots of spinning and two-stepping, and a stage for the band. By seven o'clock, despite winter driving conditions, post New Year's interruptions, and the fact that it was a weeknight, the place was packed. The buffet included lamb stew, which I thought the wolves would appreciate.

Gale Norton never showed, but I didn't really expect her to. There were a lot of politicians and high rollers in town because of the Secretary's announcement earlier in the day. It was almost overwhelming – so many huge things happening in a 12-hour period. State Sen. Brad Little bought me a belt of tequila, which I realized I needed, and shook my hand. He was with a slew of others who couldn't stay for the party, but by the time everyone who had RSVP'd wedged themselves into the bar room, it was quite a mix. In fact, until the night of my retirement party, I'd never been in the same room with that much political diversity – ranchers, hardcore environmentalists, bureaucrats, and my family. It was something that everyone noticed. I had somehow managed not to burn every bridge I'd ever crossed.

Despite the request against speeches, there were a few:

Curt Mack, who headed the wolf program for the Nez Perce tribe, described the usual scene after a particularly trying situation or meeting. I'd suggest we go eat, and then we'd sit and drink a beer or two. Pretty soon, we'd solved all of the world's problems.

"But it's not until the next day," he said, "when you start thinking, 'Did Carter take me to the woodshed last night?' Getting an ass-kicking from Carter is like getting a massage from a Swiss masseuse."

Ed Bangs said that I don't convince people of things as much as I simply suck all the oxygen out of the room, thereby making everyone surrender.

I think I've repeated myself in my career because I wasn't sure I was getting through to folks. The wolf issue has brought out such hatefulness in people. I want them to see that it doesn't have to be all one way. It can't be.

Sheep rancher Margaret Soulen walked to the lectern and adjusted the microphone. She looked at me as she spoke, and pointed out that many people who now clinked dessert dishes at the many candlelit tables would normally avoid each other. That's what wolves have done to people, or rather what people have done because of wolves. But here they were tonight, she said. She wanted me to think about that, and she wanted everyone else to think about it, too.

"Even though you were recently quoted as having 'spent a career presenting facts on deaf ears,' I want you to know that there are many of us – very many – who have heard you both loud and clear," she finished.

An hour and a half and 15 speakers later, I was asked if I didn't want to say something, and once again the microphone was readjusted – this time on its tallest setting. I took it off its stand.

"I'm almost speechless," I said. This got a big laugh. There have been few times that I haven't had something to say.

I was very nearly overcome with emotion. I was leaving because, as Bob Ruesink pointed out, I had finished the job. How many guys can say that when they retire? If Idaho Fish and Game was feeling generous, maybe they'd hire me and let me just do the fun stuff for a change. No more office, no more pissed-off people on the phone, just me and a truck and my traps and my tent. That's how I wanted it. Like the old days.

I was about to leave things at a simple thank you, but something else came to mind. It was something I'd told everyone separately at one time or another. Seeing all those faces looking back at me brought it to mind again. It's the big picture and – something I'll say until I take my last breath: Having too many wolves isn't the problem, nor is having too few. It's not about the parts, but the whole. We all have to start at what we have in common or nothing can ever get better, I said to the crowd. I saw many heads nodding, but I wondered if they all knew just how much they had in common.

One of the things I learned during the Whitehawk fiasco, apart from the meaning of snafu, was that fladry is a way to buy time for wolves and livestock. On an old, remote and beautiful ranch near Salmon, Idaho, fladry kept the Jureano wolf pack at bay on Eron and Faye Coiner's ranch for 63 days. So far, that's the record. But it took nine miles of it strung around a good chunk of land to be successful. Still, the Coiners were kind enough to let Defenders of Wildlife give it a try. Fladry is labor intensive and takes a dogged effort to maintain. If the wolves get used to it, or worse, if it ends up on the ground because of freak weather or inattention, it no longer works. Rick Williamson went on to invent a type of fladry/portable electric fence combination he calls "turbo fladry." It works nicely, but needs a power source and is only realistic in short sections. Before Idaho Department of Fish and Game yielded to livestock interests and ordered them shot, Williamson used turbo fladry to keep the Buffalo Ridge wolves out of the steelhead pond near Clayton. The best defense against wolves is a combination of things: fladry, guard dogs and vigilant herders. But these things require effort and money and so remain vastly underused.

Sometimes there's no chance to do anything preventative before wolves decide to eat livestock. The Soulen family lost more than 300 sheep in a single year to wolves, many of them in just a couple of nights. The influential Soulens, who own and lease well over 100,000 acres of ranchland near the Oregon/Idaho border, were a good barometer for me when it came to understanding political tides in Idaho. The family has been in the livestock business for many generations, grazing mostly sheep but some cattle in six counties. I can count on one hand the number of reasonable and level headed livestock operators in Idaho and the Soulens are at the top of the list.

I can predict, or at least expect, that people in the livestock business will do certain things. And I can predict the behavior of a wolf or its prey. As a wolf manager, there was a certain comfort in being familiar with both, and it helped me make tentative decisions before the fur started flying. But when it comes down to it, if wolves are really guilty of killing livestock – and that's a big if – there is little anyone can do to stop them, short of killing them.

A lot went in to trying to save the Whitehawk wolves, but they refused to cooperate. I think about this often – the times I did all I could to save wolves only to have them keep misbehaving so that, eventually, the rules said I must kill them. I've been accused of killing a lot of wolves, and perhaps indirectly, I have. I've ordered the deaths of many, but while I've trapped more than 300 and released them, I've only pulled the trigger on 14. That was enough.

Nobody much remembers the Whitehawks anymore, except those who were involved in some way. Our attention span for such things is, unfortunately, quite short. I'm equally unsure how so many people have made the transition from outrage to ambivalence when entire packs are wiped out, including pups in dens. Maybe it's because it's so routine now. There are a lot of wolves in the Northern Rockies these days, so what should it really matter if we kill a dozen here and a dozen there? As an Idaho Fish and Game manager once said, "Wolves are like grass. You have to keep mowing them down." But do we really? What I wonder is, are we mowing for the right reasons? Wolves, for whatever great strides they've made in the modern mind as well as the modern West, continue to be persecuted, and there's truly no basis for it.

The problem, ultimately, is not with wolves, but with those who believe that the only good wolf is a dead one. Inept government investigations and outright lies about the nature of these animals result in bogus statistics and ultimately, more dead wolves. After all the time I've spent dealing with them in my career, I've come to the same kind of thinking that Betty Baker expressed: Why did we bring wolves back if all we're going to do is kill them?

Only time may answer this question. A fresh generation of people may be needed as well. We in the West are fortunate enough to have places that big predators like wolves and lions and bears can roam. We haven't yet given in to carving up every bit of land for our own benefit. In the end, people will determine which animals are allowed to persist. All we need are people who are brave enough to think for themselves, and cherish those things that are still truly wild.

ACKNOWLEDGMENTS

There are many people I wish to acknowledge who are not mentioned specifically (or nearly enough) in Wolfer. I want to use some ink here to thank them, and beg forgiveness from those I've inadvertantly left out:

Jim Holyan, Dean Cataldo, Dr. Doug Smith, Dr. Ralph Maughan, Marlys Rawson, Dr. Richard E. Dierks, Arnold O. Haugen, Vanessa Renwick, John Oakleaf, Kim Holt, John Yoswick, Paul Regan, Dr. Terry Kreeger, Ronald Castellano (manager of Charco's Kentucky Fried Chicken), Dennis Arp, Russell Scott, Tom Monroe, Mark Thompson, Lester and Steve Shickle, Jack Merten (my main pigeon pal), Mrs. Lora Mae Schoneman, Greg Greiman, Gary Thorson, Wayne Allen, Brian Kelly, Dave Parsons, Wendy Brown, Amaroq Weiss, Kent Laudon, Marcie Carter, Cindi Hillemeyer, Adam Gall, Jason Husseman, Jon Trapp, Cheri Beno, Salle Englehart, Eron and Faye Coiner, Ted and Lauri Koch, Rich Howard, Gary Power, Sherm Blom, Steve Nadeau, Jon Rachael, Nate Borg, Craig White, Hilary and Skye Cooley, Wayne Brewster, Janet O'Crowley, Scott Kabasa, Craig Tabor, Roger Olson, Lava Lakes Land and Livestock, Dr. Mark Drew, Marina Smith, the Soulen family, Carol Williamson, Ed Jahn, Rocky Barker, Hal Herring, John Spinks, Todd Wilkinson, Marcia Franklin, Bruce Reichert, James O. Long, Jamie Rappaport Clark, Craig and Dana O'Gorman, Joel Sartore, Renee Askins, Gabrielle Tenenbaum, the U.K. Wolf Conservation Trust, Jon Robison and the Idaho Conservation League, Doug Goetz, Tim Graff, Steve Prescott, Arlyn Miller, Dave Hoerner, Bob Twist, Roger Stradley, Leroy Brown, Bob Hawkins, and the supreme Gary Brennan. And to everyone who has ever gone out of their way to appreciate wolves (or at least tolerate them,) bless you.

Contributing editor Dee Lane made the final manuscript shine, and graphic designer Beth Fischer took all the ideas my editorial team threw at her and turned them into something beautiful. My heartfelt thanks to both of you.

Nicholas Evans took time for me and my story during extraordinarily challenging circumstances. Thank you, Nick.

Finally, a nod and a belt of tequila to those who have passed on: Tom Beno, Charlie Brcka, Bob Danner, Monte Ballou, Rick Bunkofske, Skip Score, Ludy Sheda, Bob Neal, Rick Sanford, Bob Schellinger, Big Dave Nelson, Peter Jennings, Dr. Patricia Gough, Mollie Beattie, and Roy Carpenter.

SUGGESTED READING
AND WORKS REFERENCED

Andrews, R. 1981. *The Red Fox in Iowa*. Iowa Conservation Commission.

Niemeyer, C. *A serological study of rabies in some North Iowa mammals*. M.S. Thesis. 1973. Iowa State University, Ames.

Emergency Rabid Skunk Control in Montana (1974) Proceedings 6th Vertebrate Pest Conference.

Bishop, R. A. *The Mearns quail (Cyrtonyx montezumae mearnsi) in southern Arizona*. M.S. Thesis. 1964. Univ. Arizona, Tucson.

Bishop, R. A. and Hungerford, C. R. *Seasonal food selection of Arizona Mearns Quail*. Journal of Wildlife Management. 1969. 29:813–819.

Endangered Species Act of 1973, as amended (16 USC 1531-1543).

Federal Animal Damage Control Act of 1931, as amended (7 USC 426-426d).

Fischer, Hank. *Wolf Wars*. Falcon Press, 1995. (ISBN-10 1560443529).

Gough, P. M. and Niemeyer, C. *A Rabies Epidemic in Recently Captured Skunks. Journal of Wildlife Diseases*. 1975. 11:170-176.

Hayes, Bob. *Wolves of the Yukon*. Bob Hayes, 2010. (ISBN 9780986737602).

Mech, L. David. *The Wolf*. The Natural History Press, 1970.

Miner, N. R. *Montana golden eagle removal and translocation project*. Proceedings Great Plains Wildlife Damage Control Workshop. 1975. 8:155-161.

Robinson, Michael J. *Predatory Bureaucracy: The Extermination of Wolves and the Transformation of the West.* University Press of Colorado, 2005.

Storm G. L., Andrews, R. D., Phillips, R. L., Bishop, R. A., Siniff, D. B., and Tester, J. R. Wildlife Monograph No. 49. *Morphology, reproduction, dispersal, and mortality of Midwestern red fox populations.* April 1976. 82 pages.

United States Department of the Interior, U.S. Fish and Wildlife Service. *Final Environmental Impact Statement, The Reintroduction of Gray Wolves to Yellowstone National Park and Central Idaho.* 1994. USFWS, Helena, Montana. Available online at www.fws.gov/mountain-prairie/species/mammals/wolf/

Young, Stanley P. *The Last of the Loners.* MacMillan, 1970.

Young, Stanley P. and Goldman, Edward A. *The Wolves of North America* (2 volumes). Dover Publications Inc., 1944.

Professional papers regarding wolves and other wildlife may be found online at the excellent Digital Commons, University of Nebraska Lincoln, http://digitalcommons.unl.edu

Made in the USA
San Bernardino, CA
29 November 2014